D1736565

# The "New Man" in Cuba

Contemporary Cuba

UNIVERSITY PRESS OF FLORIDA

Florida A&M University, Tallahassee
Florida Atlantic University, Boca Raton
Florida Gulf Coast University, Ft. Myers
Florida International University, Miami
Florida State University, Tallahassee
University of Central Florida, Orlando
University of Florida, Gainesville
University of North Florida, Jacksonville
University of South Florida, Tampa
University of West Florida, Pensacola

Contemporary Cuba
Edited by John M. Kirk

# The "New Man" in Cuba

## Culture and Identity in the Revolution

Ana Serra

University Press of Florida
Gainesville/Tallahassee/Tampa/Boca Raton
Pensacola/Orlando/Miami/Jacksonville/Ft. Myers

Copyright 2007 by Ana Serra

Front jacket illustration by Ramón Menocal: "Identidad" (#1), 2005, acrylic/canvas.

Printed in the United States of America on recycled, acid-free paper
All rights reserved

12  11  10  09  08  07  6  5  4  3  2  1

A record of cataloging-in-publication data is available from the
Library of Congress.
ISBN 978-0-8130-3072-2

The University Press of Florida is the scholarly publishing agency
for the State University System of Florida, comprising Florida A&M
University, Florida Atlantic University, Florida Gulf Coast University,
Florida International University, Florida State University, University
of Central Florida, University of Florida, University of North Florida,
University of South Florida, and University of West Florida.

University Press of Florida
15 Northwest 15th Street
Gainesville, FL 32611-2079
http://www.upf.com

To Karl, Lukas, and Lucía, siempre

# Contents

# Preface

This project began as a dissertation in an interdisciplinary program in the Humanities, at The George Washington University. As I remember, at the very beginning of my research I was urged to come up with *one question* that summarized what I attempted to accomplish. Given my background, finding *the question* proved to be very difficult, and over the years my inquiry has departed substantially from my initial objectives. When I started this project I was in my late twenties, having lived the effervescence of the transition to democracy in southern Spain in the mid-1970s, the resurgence of Socialism and Communism after long years of repression, and the romanticization of the "dream realized" in Cuba. I emphasize *southern* Spain because Andalusia, as one of the most depressed areas in Spain, together with Extremadura, is a fertile ground for radical movements from the Left. Toward the end of the Franco era the songs of the Nueva Trova Cubana, the *cantautores*, became extremely popular, with their beautiful messages of love in struggle and the promise of social justice.

The Nueva Trova and stylized images of revolutionary heroes constructed the version of Cuban history that my generation inherited, an ideal of utopia that remains persuasive to this day, in Spain and abroad, and that authors such as Iván de la Nuez are beginning to debunk. Ironically, I started my research in an attempt to find representations of the utopia that *my* revolution had created. Instead, in the novels I read I found sacrifice, pain, restraint, nostalgia, and a compulsion to repeat representations of the past. While I told myself that social justice does not come without costs, I kept running into the fact that Cuba suffered from many of the problems that make a society dystopic: the repression of what I understood as a women's movement, the willful ignorance of certain expressions of ethnicity, race, and gender, the forced homogeneity in society, censorship, manipulation, and a new economic dependence. After more than forty years of revolution, these flaws have become commonplace for a great many people, but as our academic conferences reveal, Cuba still is "the embodiment of a redeeming dream, or the suitable therapy to project one's own discontent with Western culture on a picturesque and faraway place" (de la Nuez 10).

The fact that my quest for utopia put dystopia before my eyes radically changed this project over the years. My research brought me closer to Cuba and to a better grasp of what the Revolution failed to do, owing to its limited resources and perhaps a flawed understanding of the transforming power of culture. The New Man, no matter how elusive, encapsulates the theory of human behavior with which revolutionary leaders operated, and reveals the gap between this theory and an emancipatory society. By looking at representations of the New Man in political speeches I discovered a way to tease out what was lacking in the new Cuban identity, and I found that the most committed revolutionary literature written in the island, what most readers would consider straight political pamphlets, harbored a wish to represent and perhaps covertly denounce that lack. The shadows of the New Man, that is, those Other appearances of official revolutionary identity, are the ones that speak of a society in constant flux and a firmly critical attitude against any form of identity that implies repression. My epilogue on Leonardo Padura Fuentes's novels published during the Special Period shows that the critique of the New Man has become increasingly overt and that his shadows are in fact walking with him. But this image I am trying to re-create is not like an old Socialist realist poster, with a chain of muscular men arm in arm, marching toward a better future. It is an aggregate of men and women, young and old, some of whom have only recently become visible and audible. They too are speaking and writing, looking for questions and answers, and *formas de resolver.*

# Acknowledgments

My sincere thanks go to all of the institutions and individuals who made this project possible:

To Ocean Press and Grupo Nuevo Milenio Press in Havana, for granting me permission to reprint photographs and illustrations. To the editors of *Journal of Latin American Cultural Studies*, *Revista de Estudios Hispánicos*, and *Journal of Gender Studies* for granting permission to reprint earlier versions of chapters 1, 3, and 4. To Ramón Menocal, for granting permission to print his painting "Indentidad" (#1), 2005, on the jacket of this book.

To my colleagues and friends, who have stimulated me with their scholarship and their conversation: Hernán Abeledo, Julie M. Bunck, José Buscaglia, Isabel Fortuño, Myrna García-Calderón, Bill and Esther Gentile, Jane Lewis, Lourdes Martínez-Echazábal, Ramón Menocal, Eyda Merediz, Francisco Morán, Juan Carlos Quintero Herencia, José Quiroga, Ivette Rodríguez-Santana, Serafín Valverde, and Isabel Vergara.

To Yoandra Ramírez and Boris, who exposed me to different Havanas, and gave me a great deal to think about. My utmost gratitude to Sara Más, for opening the archives of the magazine *Mujeres* for me to peruse freely, and for tracking down the most reluctant people.

To the dear colleagues of my department, Jack Child, Nadia Harris, Consuelo Hernández, and Amy Oliver, who have always given me great support and made it possible for me to finish the manuscript. To my students at American University, who have been a continuous source of learning and inspiration.

To my assistant Elizabeth Auciello, for her good mood and invaluable help throughout the process.

To Amy Gorelick, my acquisitions editor at the University Press of Florida, for her professionalism, patience, and understanding.

To Susan Albury, my project editor at the University Press of Florida, for her flexibility and support.

To Christing L. Sweeney, my copyeditor at the University Press of Florida, for her careful and thorough editing.

To John Kirk, the editor of the Contemporary Cuba series, for believing in the project, supporting me cheerfully, and helping me out of every crisis.

To Marilyn Miller, who has been a mentor, a relentless editor, and an excellent reader and critic throughout the process.

To Karl, Lukas, and Lucía, for their love, and for providing opportunities to think about something far beyond these pages.

# Acronyms

AD     Acción Democrática (Democratic Action)

APRA     Alianza Popular Revolucionaria Americana (American Popular Revolutionary Alliance)

CDR     Commité de Defensa de la Revolución (Neighborhood Committees in Defense of the Revolution)

FAR     Fuerzas Armadas Revolucionarias (Revolutionary Armed Forces)

FMC     Federación de Mujeres Cubanas (Federation of Cuban Women)

GNTES     Grupo Nacional de Trabajadores en la Educación Sexual (National Group of Workers in Sex Education)

ICAIC     Instituto Cubano de Arte e Industria Cinematográficas (Cuban Institute of Film Arts and Industry or Cuban Film Institute)

INRA     Instituto Nacional de la Reforma Agraria (National Institute of Agrarian Reform)

MININT     Ministerio del Interior (Interior Ministry)

ORI     Organizaciones Revolucionarias Integradas (Integrated Revolutionary Organizations)

QTATA[2]     Que Todo Alfabetizador Tenga Alfabetizado y Viceversa (Each Literacy Teacher Has a Student and Viceversa)

UJC     Unión de Jóvenes Comunistas (Union of Communist Youth)

UMAP     Unidades Militares de Ayuda a la Producción (Military Units to Aid Production)

UNEAC     Unión Nacional de Escritores y Artistas Cubanos (National Union of Cuban Writers and Artists)

# Introduction

# The Culture That the Revolution Created

Before the 1959 Cuban Revolution, other Latin American movements that had attempted to empower the disenfranchised were only partially successful. After land reform under Lázaro Cárdenas (1934–40) the protracted Mexican Revolution swung to the right with institutionalization during Miguel Alemán's presidency, installing a repressive regime that promoted a strong alliance between Mexican and U.S. businessmen. Radical leaders such as Augusto César Sandino in Nicaragua and Jorge Eliécer Gaitán in Colombia were assassinated, and the Somoza dynasty in Nicaragua and the decades of the period called "the Violence" in Colombia unleashed strong repression of the popular masses in both countries. In Argentina, Perón's doctrine of economic justice for the poor did not produce long-term effects. Mass movements such as Venezuela's Acción Democrática (Democratic Action) and Peru's APRA (Alianza Popular Revolucionaria Americana or American Popular Revolutionary Alliance) were eventually clamped down. Bolivia's 1952 social revolution, when the government supported peasant uprisings in the countryside by nationalizing the tin mining industry, did not prosper. The power of Latin American elites, U.S. opposition to change, and a wave of totalitarian regimes all represented obstacles in the path of movements that favored the masses.

With these antecedents, the new Cuban regime of 1959 became a prime example of a truly radical and nationalist revolution, and as such it turned out to be highly significant in finally realizing the presence of the popular and the local, rather than the elite and the foreign, in constructions of Latin American identity. In addition to a strong emphasis on "the people" and a communitarian attitude, the institutional discourse of the Revolution had to appeal to the radical transformation of every individual to conform to the demands of a Marxist revolution, that is, it had to articulate individual responsibilities vis-à-vis the state. Che Guevara's "Socialism and Man in Cuba" (1965) aptly discussed the tension between the individual and the collective; when he coined the expression "the new man" to refer to the new person embodying the radical change that the Cuban regime was invested in promoting, Che Guevara created a model that quickly became influential in the politics, culture, and identity struggles of Cuba and Latin America.

At the same time, Cuba emerged as a very powerful center for the promotion of culture across Latin America during the early years of the Revolution, as it hosted numerous forums to discuss the role of literature in society, founded cultural organizations that instituted awards and started journals, and published numerous literary classics. The reaction of the United States to such effervescence in Latin American culture cannot be overlooked, since it resulted in large-scale investment in literary journals promoting the new Latin American literature, the creation of scholarships for Latin American writers, and the foundation of Latin American Studies centers across the country (González Echevarría, "Criticism" 2). The Cuban Revolution is credited with the beginning of the Boom in Latin American letters, and many critics agree with the idea that the post-1959 period in Cuba is "the most important political revolution in the cultural history of Spanish America" (Rodríguez Monegal, quoted in Fornet, "*Casa*" 424). This connection between culture and politics that Rodríguez Monegal signaled manifests itself at several levels in the Cuban Revolution, as the state actively promoted a political culture and writers responded with enthusiasm and commitment to the atmosphere of radical change that surrounded them.

In a broader perspective, the Cuban Revolution nourished itself from the liberatory atmosphere of the 1960s in much of the world. It was in that decade that "the Third World began" as a consequence of decolonization and independence in Africa, and the "natives" as well as the "inner colonized" in the First World—ethnic, gender, and class "minorities"—began to be considered as historical subjects (Jameson 180). China's own revolution within the revolution, the Proletarian Cultural Revolution, advanced a radical redefinition of culture from the "people." Nevertheless, during that decade the Cuban regime cultivated a nationalistic discourse that defended the "radical experiment" of the Revolution as something entirely unprecedented, especially in Latin America (Pérez-Stable, *Origins* 99). By presenting itself as instrumental for the liberation of the oppressed, Cuba claimed a leading role in the movement of non-aligned countries and applied itself to the mission of exporting revolution. The presumed uniqueness of the Revolution, the international prestige it enjoyed in that era, and the fact that Fidel Castro's regime was presented as the first regime to defeat the United States, at the invasion at the Bay of Pigs, strengthened Cuba's exemplary role in Latin America.

Whether because of the protagonism that the Cuban regime claimed for itself or because of the confluence of events during those years, the Cuban Revolution marks a turning point in definitions of Latin American culture and identity, and this book focuses on Che Guevara's concept of the New

Man as a theoretical construct that articulates the heart of such a change. In my examination of the New Man, I consider the Revolution as a discursive event, that is, as a social, political, and cultural movement that was represented and reflected upon in a vast amount of textual production, and that strongly influenced subsequent representations and reflections on Cuba and Latin America. Given that the Cuban state invested a great deal of its power on defining discursive limits and providing models of identity, one can consider revolutionary leaders and policymakers as leading emissaries of the discourse on the New Man, while the often invoked "masses" were its recipients. Thus, it is worth looking at the construction of the New Man through the political speeches of the era, since such speeches are textual repositories of the institutional discourse on identity and culture.

The 1960s in Cuba was a momentous time to examine a Cultural Revolution that has set the tone for emancipating practices at the same time that it has laid the ground for the betrayal of the Revolution's promises of liberation. The New Man was shaped in the discursive output of some crucial political campaigns of that decade, and his different appearances proposed radical changes while they also revealed assumptions regarding race, gender, class, history, culture, and nation that had prevailed in previous eras. In my analysis I underscore the importance of discourse, more than actual policy, in creating social change as well as hindering its progress. Ultimately, I hope to broaden the understanding of the New Man through some texts that were instrumental in the attempt to shape this new identity, in order to recognize later appearances of this figure and its specific influence in definitions of Cuban and Latin American identity.

Many of the Revolution's epic campaigns took place in the 1960s, an era of radical changes and mobilization politics, and such campaigns were represented in novels that are in need of close examination. Thus Daura Olema García's *Maestra voluntaria* (1962) (Volunteer teacher; no English translation has been published) features the encounter between literacy teachers and peasants during the 1961 Literacy Campaign; Edmundo Desnoes's *Memorias del subdesarrollo* (1965) (*Inconsolable Memories* 1967) depicts the conflicted writer in the face of new historical events and the call for the integration of all intellectuals to the ideological task of educating the masses; Miguel Cossío Woodward's *Sacchario* (1970) (Of sugar; no English translation has been published) presents the heroic cane cutter as the archetype of the Cuban nation during the historical Sugar Campaign of 1970; and Manuel Cofiño's *La última mujer y el próximo combate* (1971) (The last woman and the next combat; no English translation has been published) showcases the ideal gender models for the revolutionary woman at a time of intense campaigning

for the integration of women into the labor force.[1] While the speeches of
Fidel Castro and other state representatives can be taken as blueprints for
the institutional articulations of identity elaborated during these campaigns,
the novels highlight the different guises that the New Man and occasionally
the New Woman took according to the needs of the time. The Cuban leader
is purposely referred to here as "Fidel," rather than "Castro," to allude to the
discursive position of this political figure within the Cuban regime, which
has been appropriated and transformed by Cubans over the ensuing years.
As Ambrosio Fornet explains, "'Fidel' is a mirror in which millions of Cubans
see themselves reflected; 'Castro,' on the contrary, is a wall behind which
eleven million Cubans are hidden from view" (Fornet, *Bridging* 9). Though
I would qualify Fornet's claims to the extent that "Castro" is Fidel Castro's
international name rather than his name in the United States alone, I use
"Fidel" to refer to Fidel's position in the island, as Fornet describes.

My use of novels in addition to political speeches of the period demonstrates my interest in looking at the Cuban Revolution as a discursive event
and in cultural products, particularly literature, as central to the reflection
on culture and identity in the Revolution. The choice of the novel as opposed
to other literary genres can be explained by the idea that, since it lacks a
specific form, the novel arguably lends itself to ideological reflection more
than other literary genres, and novels have "often assumed . . . [the form]
of a given kind of document endowed with truth-bearing power by society
at specific moments in time" (González Echevarría, *Myth and Archive* 8).
In the context of the Cuban Revolution, the task of the novelist, according to Alejo Carpentier, was to define the *epos* of Latin Americans, evalu-
ate the struggle of forces in the revolutionary present, and point to "truths"
that would be helpful in the future ("Papel" 162–69). The association of the
novel with a pedagogical intent and the forging of a national consciousness
is not exclusive to Carpentier, but it definitely summarizes a belief that characterized the early years of the Revolution. In addition to the novels just
mentioned, this study examines Pablo Armando Fernández's *Los niños se
despiden* (1968) (The children say good-bye; no English translation has been
published), a novel that did not directly respond to a government campaign
but centrally reflected on the issue of revolutionary identity.

It is significant that with the exception of *Memorias del subdesarrollo*
(1965), all of the novels I examine were awarded the Casa de las Américas
prize. As the renowned writer and critic Ambrosio Fornet acknowledges,
since its institution in October 1959, the award had been "under the sway
of the political discussions of those years" (Casañas and Fornet 8). In other

words, the literary prize was of necessity awarded to works that were supportive of the Revolution's mission. No less than seventy-four novels were published in Cuba during the 1960s and early 1970s (Menton 277–79), but the five novels just cited are particularly representative of key points in the construction of the New Man in institutional discourse. Not only were these novels sanctioned as revolutionary, they are among the few that specifically represented the Revolution in its then present time and tackled campaigns and issues that were very influential in the process of forming revolutionary identity.[2] As customary with texts receiving the literary award, Casa de las Américas published twenty thousand copies of each of these five novels, and Ediciones Huracán issued one hundred thousand copies, as the back flaps of each of these editions confirm. By the account of the author Miguel Cossío Woodward, the copies were sold quickly, and they were extremely popular among Cubans in the island (e-mail interview with the author, January 2006). The only novel that did not receive the Casa de las Américas literary award was turned into the film *Memorias del subdesarrollo* (Memories of underdevelopment) by Tomás Gutiérrez Alea (1968); it was one of the most popular and influential films in Cuban cinema. By the account of many Cubans nowadays, the novels were widely read.

In looking at the intersection between state discourse and literature in the construction of the New Man, speeches and novels are taken as rhetorical constructions with the objective of persuading an audience. However, at this point in history, one cannot ascertain whether the masses to whom these speeches and novels were addressed were in fact persuaded to embody the new revolutionary identity. Instead, my interest lies in using this body of texts as a showcase of the institutional revolutionary rhetoric of the 1960s in Cuba. If Guevara emphasized the importance of direct and indirect education of all Cubans (Guevara, "Socialism" 7), I consider political speeches and popular novels as textual conduits of the pedagogical mission of the Revolution.

Each of the novels examined here is a narrative of identity, in that each aims at enacting how a character becomes a revolutionary, a "new man," or in one case "a new woman," as the text unfolds. As such, each novel represents a "dominant encoding" of identity, in Stuart Hall's formulation, or an official version of identity with which the reader is enticed to identify. The dominant encoding is defined as "the mental horizon . . . of possible meanings" that is in turn directly related to power relations in a cultural environment. This encoding within the dominant discourse "carries with it the stamp of legitimacy" and is identified with what is "natural," and "inevitable" about the social order (Hall, "Encoding" 102). In other words, there is no room for questioning revolutionary identity within the dominant encoding, and discourse at this level seemingly presents no gaps.

My initial overview of the discourse of leaders and policymakers of the Revolution provides the background for understanding the elements of this "dominant encoding" of identity, where the New Man appears in his different guises. At this level, it is possible to pose the following questions: In what ways do four instances of highly representative and widely popular novels reproduce official discourse concerning the New Man? How did revolutionary identity evolve in its different textual appearances over the first decade of the Revolution? How do the novels differ from the political speeches in the rhetorical strategies used to create the New Man?

 However complicit with state discourse, each novel also contains the inadvertent transgression or subversion of its prescriptions in the form of an Other—that is, "different" and "alien"—identity or identities in the text. These are the "shadows" of the New Man: the blind spots of this identity or the surplus in the text that accounts for "Other" identities. Hence, I also approach these novels as an "oppositional reader," in Hall's terminology, or as someone reading outside the dominant definitions of identity (Hall 103). From an oppositional reading it becomes clear that one cannot consider the novel either as intrinsically liberating or as wholly complicit with state power; rather, it is *language* that lends itself to different and often opposed readings. When attempting to answer the question "how do the literary texts wittingly or unwittingly subvert the same political agenda they set out to support?" I use various theoretical frameworks—such as gender, psychoanalysis, postcolonialism, film theory, or deconstruction—to articulate a number of possible oppositional readings that these texts can yield. Larger questions of how the New Man evolved in that first decade, whether this identity delivered its promise of liberation, and what specific contribution literature lent to forging the ideal of the New Man are also central to my inquiry.

The reading of the body of political speeches and novels surrounding four state campaigns yields an undercurrent of criticism or deconstruction of the idea of the New Man as represented in the literary texts, and this attitude is also represented in the fifth novel I examine, Pablo Armando Fernández's *Los niños se despiden* (1968), which coincided with the celebration of the "Hundred Years of Struggle" since the inception of the Cuban independence movement from Spain (1868). My analysis of this text offers some conclusions on the ways in which literature contested the New Man by pointing at the many aspects of Cuban identities that were repressed or at least underrepresented in the official identity. Many ideas in this chapter are tied with the epilogue, where I examine the deconstruction of the New Man in recent literature.

The look at the 1990s in the epilogue allows me to emphasize the prevailing relevance of the New Man in contemporary Cuban culture. Beyond the radical differences between the two periods, present day Cuba resembles the first decade of the Revolution in its awareness that important changes are occurring, and in the coexistence of certain master narratives, as José Quiroga's recent book has noted. After the sovietization of the 1970s, the complacent Boom of the 1980s, and the terrible scarcity of the 1990s, the regime is relaxing its hold with a cultural policy that some characterize as "intelligent" or adaptable to the circumstances (Padura, "Epilogue" 183). The Cuban regime is allowing writers and artists to participate in discussion forums and publish abroad, displaying considerably more tolerance toward difference in areas such as gender, race, and religion, and widening acceptance of certain topics and forms of creative expression that were hitherto considered counterrevolutionary. At the same time, the degree of skepticism and fear felt toward the new changes in recent Cuba is comparable to the resistance experienced in the context of the 1960s, during the formative years of the Revolution. Most of the control mechanisms of cultural institutions still hold significant power, as the state manages publication and literary prizes. But in the new millennium, as in the 1960s, there are multiple voices that make themselves heard despite the "conditional freedom" with which writers aspiring to some recognition may need to live (Padura, "Epilogue" 185).

The critic revisiting the 1960s confronts the fact that Cuban writers who have long enjoyed a reputation as loyal revolutionaries are reluctant to have that reputation tarnished by certain details of their past. This is the case of Pablo Armando Fernández (National Literature Award 1996), who has maintained fervent support of the Revolution to this day, and who has consistently rejected a reading of the novel *Los niños se despiden* as a negative critique of the state of the Revolution in its early years. Writers in Cuba have always lived under the shadow of Che Guevara's famous *dictum*: "The fault of many of our artists and intellectuals lies in their original sin: they are not truly revolutionaries" (Guevara, "Socialism" 13). However, many novels published in that first era consciously or unconsciously pose serious critical questions and debunk many of the myths of those early years, even as they remain within the limits of what could be safely stated and published. In this respect, once again, the past reflects itself in the present, as writers such as Leonardo Padura Fuentes walk the tightrope as recognized writers in Cuba, and to some extent supporters of the regime, while managing to be extremely critical of the current state of affairs.[3]

## Cultural Policy and Socialist Realism before 1971

As E. J. Hobsbawm's classic work has established, determining the phases of a revolution is usually cause for countless debates. The first four years of the Cuban Revolution can be said to be the most event intensive from a strictly historical point of view: the triumph of the Revolution in January 1959 was followed by the cancellation of elections and the concentration of power in the person of Fidel in July 1959. Widespread land reform was instituted in May 1959, concurrent with the break from the United States due to the nationalization of private companies and an economic alliance with the Soviet Union (1959–60). The same period saw the creation of Comités de Defensa de la Revolución (Committees in Defense of the Revolution or CDRs) (1960), the Literacy Campaign (1961), the invasion of Playa Girón (April 1961), the proclamation of the Socialist character of the Revolution (April 1961), the missile crisis (October 1962), and the re-establishment of cane sugar as a monoculture (1963), among other crucial events in the development of the Revolution. The death of Ernesto Che Guevara (1967) and its aftermath, as well as the Ten-Million-Ton Sugar Harvest and its failure (1969–70) were also extremely significant in this period. In terms of cultural policymaking, some analysts claim consistency on the part of the Cuban intelligentsia from the beginning (Portuondo *Itinerario*), while others allege increasingly stricter control on the kind of literature that could be produced (Casal, "Literature"; Menton).

Nevertheless, the first few years of the Revolution mark the time when writers generally displayed more enthusiasm and the ability to express themselves with relative freedom. In the first five years, most novelists—a good exception to the rule is Daura Olema García with *Maestra voluntaria* (1962)—turned to the prerevolutionary era in an effort to come to terms with and explain the causes of the many changes that were taking place at the time.[4] After five years of intense political turmoil and power struggles, many writers seemed to feel more ready to represent the revolutionary epoch, as is shown in novels written in the second half of the decade. For that reason, most of the novels studied here were written after 1965, once the process of identity constitution initiated at the start of the Revolution had begun to coalesce.

My focus on roughly the first decade of the Cuban Revolution is determined, above all, by the history of cultural policy in Cuba, particularly from

1961 to 1971. In 1961, Fidel gave two speeches that significantly influenced the definition of the role of culture during the Revolution. The first was his "Words to the Intellectuals," in which he pronounced the famous dictum "Dentro de la revolución todo, contra la revolución nada" ("Within the Revolution everything, against the Revolution, nothing"). The second was his speech at the closing of the First Conference of Writers and Artists in Cuba, in which he referred to writers and artists' duty to teach and cultivate the Revolution among future generations: "All of us without exception have the role of teachers: . . . our most important task is to prepare the future; we are, in this hour of the Fatherland, the handful of seeds that is sown in the furrow of the Revolution in order to build the future (Fidel Castro, "Clausura," Nuiry Sánchez 53). In this instance, Fidel recalls the biblical parable of the farmer who sows seeds in several places, with the seeds that fell in good soil producing a very large crop. The farmer is God's elect, who is to spread the message, symbolized in the seed. Writers—as good, honest citizens of God's kingdom—are charged with spreading the message so that they and others can *believe*. The writer's calling is associated with the idea of conversion of self and others, which in my view explains the identity transformations that writers would try to foster in their fiction.

As these brief citations show, political authorities exercised control over culture from the beginning of the Revolution, and they recognized the need to create a discourse that would usher in a new era in Cubans' conception of themselves. After Fidel's speech at the First Conference of Writers and Artists, the government made several controversial decisions condemning certain forms of art. The banning of the movie *PM* by Sabá Cabrera Infante and Orlando Jiménez Leal and the closing of *Lunes de Revolución* (both in 1961) prompted tighter surveillance of the press and inaugurated a time of unrest for writers and artists. During his speech, Fidel confirmed that different revolutionary groups had come together under the ORI (Organizaciones Revolucionarias Integradas or Integrated Revolutionary Organizations), which was controlled by prominent Communist leaders such as the hardliner Edith García Buchaca in the field of culture (Luis, "Exhuming" 8). The harassment of homosexuals, culminating in the creation of the UMAP labor camps (1965), and the incarceration of so-called antisocial elements, among them Virgilio Piñera, José Mario, and Ana María Simó, together with the dissolution of the group El Puente and the first closing of *El caimán barbudo* in 1968, demonstrated the power that the state wielded in the cultural arena.[5]

El Puente was a group of writers associated with an independent publisher of the same name, which published mostly poetry and occasionally short stories. Since it was privately funded, the El Puente publisher constituted a major literary outlet not controlled by governmental policy or by a writer's union. The group was characterized by its rejection of committed literature and its openness to all kinds of experimentation, which caused an inevitable clash with the regime (Casal, "Literature" 450). Writers affiliated with the group were strongly influenced by the former Orígenes group, headed by José Lezama Lima, which produced poetry that the regime considered escapist and esoteric. The group turned out to be controversial because many of its members were homosexual, and as such they were accused of "deviant sexual behavior" (Howe 38).

*El caimán barbudo* was the literary supplement of the militant newspaper *Juventud rebelde*, and its commitment was demonstrated in "Nos pronunciamos" (We declare) a manifesto against El Puente published in 1966, in which writers advocated a literature that was new and audacious but had no experimental aspirations, unlike the "decadent" literature of El Puente (Howe 39). But *El caimán barbudo* suffered a fallout with the cultural intelligentsia as a result of the dispute between the writers Heberto Padilla and Lisandro Otero, during which the stance of the magazine was deemed too critical of the Revolution. The editorial board resigned and the supplement reopened a few months later with a more militant agenda (Menton 135).

The banning of *PM* and the turmoil experienced at various publishing venues might also be associated with the 1965 publication of Che Guevara's "Socialism and Man in Cuba." While Guevara's influence had made itself felt since the very beginning of the Revolution, this landmark essay provided the first attempt at defining that revolutionary identity explicitly. Of the many points that should be underscored in Che Guevara's programmatic text, his comments on education and Socialist realism are extremely useful to explain the cultural policy of this first decade.

In "Socialism and Man in Cuba," Guevara stated that in the first years of the Revolution the identity of the Cuban individual must be created anew in order to build a Communist society. In his words: "To build communism it is necessary, simultaneous with the new material foundations, to build *the new man*. That is why it is very important to choose the right instrument for mobilizing the masses. Basically, this mechanism must be moral in character. . . . In moments of great peril it is easy to muster a powerful response to incentives. Retaining their effect, however, requires the development of a consciousness in which there is a new scale of values. Society as a whole must be converted into a gigantic school" (Guevara, "Socialism" 6, emphasis mine). The link between the building of Communism and the creation of a new consciousness inevitably brings in the element of language, as language structures consciousness and is the main vehicle for teaching. The metaphor of the gigantic school embodies the tight environment that would be needed to sustain the Revolution mainly on moral rather than on material incentives. It is clear in Guevara's pedagogical model that the leaders are the ones responsible for constituting and teaching this new identity, and that every possible means of expression needs to serve this purpose. It is thus fitting that in order to examine the construct of revolutionary identity one should focus on the language of political leaders and how such language was reproduced in the cultural arena in highly committed novels.

With his call to political commitment in the arts, Che Guevara would seemingly support Socialist realism, according to which literature needs to support "the task of ideologically reshaping and educating the toilers in the spirit of Socialism" (Zhadanov, quoted in Hosking 3). Nevertheless, Guevara explicitly decried Socialist realism as the heritage of a frozen past and a kind of art that languished in sterile representations of a utopian society. Instead, Guevara indicated that the new art required a new kind of expression likely to be enunciated by a new generation of revolutionary writers. Such a new generation would be free of the "original sin" that writers in the Revolution had allegedly committed before, the sin of not being true revolutionaries ("Socialism" 13). The task of the new revolutionaries, according to Guevara, would then be to sing "the song of the 'new man' in the true voice of the people" (ibid.).

From the early years of the Revolution, the ghost of Socialist realism had hung over Cuban letters as a model to avoid. Guevara's essay reaffirmed this warning and prompted a proliferation of articles and pronouncements by authors decrying the dangers of this form of writing. Indeed, many writers succeeded in escaping its influence for many years, especially before the 1970s. Nevertheless, the institutional discourse of the Revolution promoted a kind of artistic expression that featured many of the characteristics of Socialist realism as it had been practiced in the Soviet Union, even in the act of denouncing this style as inadequate.

An examination of the history and practice of Socialist realism in the Soviet Union provides an interesting comparison with the theory and practice of culture in the early years of the Cuban Revolution. According to Geoffrey Hosking, the Soviet bloc started to promote Socialist realism in 1932 with the formation of the Union of Soviet Writers, and it was finally adopted as an official format after the first congress of the same union, in 1934. According to Andrei A. Zhadanov, the secretary of the Central Committee of the Soviet Communist Party at the time, "Socialist Realism . . . demands from the writer an authentic, historically specific depiction of reality in its revolutionary development" even as this genre attempts to safeguard the writer's "creative initiative" and the choice of "various styles and genres" (Hosking 3).[6] In his speech at this congress, Zhadanov stressed the alliance of Socialist realism with the doctrines of Marx, Engels, Lenin, and Stalin. Socialist realism continued to be practiced and enforced by the Soviet cultural intelligentsia well after the death of Stalin in 1953, an event that brought about a period of soul searching and revision in Soviet politics, resulting in a wide variety of Socialist literature. The Soviet cultural context falls outside the scope of this project, but the impact of the doctrine of Socialist realism on Cuban cultural policy is undeniably relevant.

Despite Guevara's seeming antipathy to Socialist realism, revolutionary leaders often reproduced Zhadanov's encouragement to create an art that represented the reality of the Revolution. In "Words to the Intellectuals" (1961), for instance, Fidel had exhorted Cuban intellectuals and artists to make the Revolution their central concern and ensure the success of the revolutionary endeavor. Zhadanov's idea of a didactic art that "combined the task of ideologically reshaping and educating the toilers in the spirit of socialism" was echoed not only by Guevara himself, but by Fidel when he claimed that "the education and the ideological development of the people" should be the main goals of a revolutionary art (Castro, "Words," Baxandall 282). Fidel, like Zhadanov in the speech quoted above, tried to calm writers and artists' fears concerning the degree of creativity that would be allowed within the Revolution: he stated that there would be no limits as far as "form" was concerned, but he added—as Zhadanov had also asserted—that the "content" of creative work must remain within the limits of what was considered revolutionary.

In "Words to the Intellectuals," Fidel announced the imminent creation of a writers' union. Against the advice of numerous intellectuals, among them Jean-Paul Sartre, who warned that such a union would stifle Cuban cultural production as it had Soviet culture, the UNEAC (Unión Nacional de Escritores y Artistas de Cuba or National Union of Cuban Writers and Artists) was formed in 1961. At the closing session of the first congress, Fidel praised writers and artists for having formed this union and committing to work for the Revolution.

Increasingly, it seems, much of the literary creation of the first decade was enlisted in the revolutionary effort, and further demands were made for a literary criticism that supported state ideology. During those years, *Casa de las Américas*, among other journals, published numerous articles on Marxist aesthetics, many of which defended the ideas of Marx and Lenin as the only possible foundation for Cuban letters. Such was the case of Ambrosio Fornet's "Las ideas estéticas de Marx" (Marx's aesthetic ideas) (1966). More explicitly, Leopoldo Ávila—possibly a pseudonym for José Antonio Portuondo—wrote in *Verde Olivo*, the journal of the armed forces in Cuba: "Let us look at things from the point of view of the Revolution, from the point of view of a nation at war, which is a realistic point of view. A criticism that analyzes from a political standpoint, which goes to the heart of literary works, would help and give guidance to the new creators" (Ávila 16). Leopoldo Ávila's "Sobre algunas corrientes de la crítica y la literatura en Cuba" (On some trends of criticism and literature in Cuba) was published in 1968: his description of Cuba as a state at war reflects the tense climate that was established in institutional discourse in the early years.

The ambiguity and equivocation of official discourse on Socialist realism is also manifested in the way that some authors of the first decade courted the topoi and style of this genre while at the same time avoiding many of its presuppositions. For instance, according to Geoffrey Hosking, a recurrent characteristic of Socialist realist novels is that their heroes—who are usually male—rise among "the people," are guided by the party, gain revolutionary conscience, and become able to lead their people in some revolutionary endeavor. Contrary to the Soviet novels, in Cuban novels "the people," or idealized representations of the lower economic classes, are always present in the background, but the heroes of these Cuban narratives of identity do not rise among "the people" but among the bourgeois class. In order to purge their own "sin of not being true revolutionaries," the authors of these literary works were compelled to represent bourgeois characters as heroes who become proletarian revolutionaries, thereby betraying a fundamental principle of classic Socialist realist novels.

In terms of writing styles the five novels under scrutiny would be approved by Socialist realist standards as being destined to a wide readership, since the authors strive to be faithful to the reality of the Revolution, and they try to "depict" it as closely and simply as possible. Once again, some qualifications may need to be made, since *Los niños se despiden* is what some would characterize as a postmodern novel, and *Memorias del subdesarrollo* is didactic only in an oblique way.[8] The fact that the protagonists are middle class would seem to point to a different readership, if one considers that these narratives try to elicit identification with the New Man. Ultimately, these narratives point to the need for a vanguard—not necessarily of "the people"—that has formed itself through strenuous instruction and effort and is meant to guide others.

As for the effect of these works on audiences who can see themselves represented in them, Hosking explains that Socialist realist works are written as hagiographies or lives of saints, with protagonists who serve as examples and provide worthy subjects for everyday meditation and self-improvement (Hosking 14). Thus, as is the case with *Maestra voluntaria*, a present-tense narration in the first person may be read as some form of individual recitation that persuades the reader to undergo the same thought processes and the gradual identity transformation that the novel's protagonist experiences. Darío's musings on his youth in *Sacchario* are aimed at engaging the reader by representing many of the experiences of the average person growing up in Havana. The skepticism of Malabre in *Memorias del Subdesarrollo* is meant as a sort of exorcism of the negative thoughts cropping up in some educated people's minds in the early years. The fact that these novels allegedly represented shared personal experiences of Cubans in the island made them popular in the years in which the testimonial as a genre had reached its height; as Elzbieta Sklodowska reminds us, in 1969 Casa de las Américas instituted a literary prize specifically for the testimonial, and many took this chance to brand this genre as quintessentially Latin American (Sklodowska, "Testimonio" 56–60).

The five revolutionary narratives examined here follow, to different degrees, the basic schema of a *bildungsroman*, or novel of apprenticeship, where a character undergoes a series of trials until he or she achieves greater harmony within him or herself and society. This would seem to align them with Socialist realist works, where, according to Katerina Clark, the transformation of the main character is highly ritualized, punctuated by a series of rites of passage toward enlightenment. The "master plot" of these works, according to Clark, is the resolution of a conflict between "consciousness" and "spontaneity," where consciousness is taken to mean actions or political activities that are controlled, disciplined, and guided by politically aware bodies. In contrast, "Spontaneity . . . means actions that are not guided by complete political awareness and are either sporadic, uncoordinated, even anarchic, or can be attributed to the workings of vast impersonal historical forces rather than deliberate actions" (Clark 15). In the case of *Maestra* and *La última mujer*, for instance, the identities described in these works also vacillate between stages of spontaneity and consciousness until they reach a stage where full revolutionary consciousness prevails.

Lastly, according to Clark, Socialist realist works contain a double plot, in that they represent the transformation of a character and always present the success of a government campaign as a background to the story. As I have noted, each of the novels—with the exception of *Los niños*—is situated in a revolutionary campaign, or it illustrates issues of vital interest to the Revolution, such as the role of the revolutionary writers or the importance of

national unity. In that sense, political speeches are an indispensable comple-
ment to these literary works, because it is in those speeches that the different
appearances of the New Man are constituted with a government campaign
as background. It must be noted, however, that in its first decade Casa de
las Américas published other novels that did not dwell on government campaigns—Lisandro Otero's *La situación* (1965), Jaime Sarusky's *Rebelión en la
octava casa* (1967), Manuel Granados's *Adire y el tiempo roto* (1967), among
many—and they also received literary prizes.

Thus, though Socialist realism had a strong presence during the early
years of the Revolution, as writers tried to find their own means of committed expression, it was only half-heartedly adopted in the narratives of
identity of that era. Cuban writers took some of the characteristics of this
genre, such as political commitment, direct expression, linear character development, and engagement with the reader, but they did not thoroughly
subject themselves to the boilerplate formulae of Soviet-style novels. What
is more, unlike what occurred in the Soviet Union, in Cuba Socialist realism
was not enforced to the exclusion of other literary styles or genres, though
it may have been more prominent in the years after 1971 with the increased
sovietization of culture.

The so-called Padilla case deserves special attention, as it displays the
contrast between Che Guevara's strong call for commitment on the part of
all Cubans and the artists' wish to retain their individual freedoms. Heberto
Padilla, a poet and essayist, had been affiliated with the Revolution from the
beginning, holding important posts in the establishment until he became
disenchanted and increasingly more critical. In 1967, he published an essay
criticizing Lisandro Otero's *Pasión de Urbino* (1967) and praising Guillermo
Cabrera Infante's *Tres tristes tigres* (1967) (*Three Trapped Tigers*, 1971) both
finalists for the Seix Barral literary prize. Given that Lisandro Otero had
achieved recognition from the regime while Cabrera Infante's novel was
considered counterrevolutionary, Padilla lost his position in the newspaper
*Granma* as a result of his criticisms, and his relations with the intelligentsia
became strained. In 1968, the UNEAC agreed to publish Padilla's book of
poems, *Fuera de juego*, which had won the UNEAC poetry prize that year,
but insisted on prefacing it with a cautionary note that chastised Padilla for
expressing counterrevolutionary sentiments in the book. Padilla's ordeal cul-
minated in his arrest on March 20, 1971 but soon after he was released and
forced to issue a confession. From the beginning, the Padilla proceedings
attracted considerable negative publicity on the international front, resulting in stricter controls in the overall cultural policy of the Revolution (Casal,
"Literature" 462). This explains the irate tone of Fidel's speech on April 30,

1971, at the closing of the First National Congress of Education and Culture: "In order to win a prize in a national or an international competition, one must be a true revolutionary, a true writer, a real poet, . . . and the journals and awards are not open to phonies. There will only be room here—without any kind of hesitation . . . for the revolutionaries. . . . For us, a revolutionary people in a revolutionary process, there is value in cultural and artistic creations inasmuch as they are useful for the people. . . . Our evaluation is political" (Nuiry Sánchez, "Clausura" 118).

Fidel's allusion to literary prizes and magazines was especially significant in a country where literary production was managed by state institutions. The fact that prizes and publications in journals were henceforth reserved for true revolutionaries prefigured the control that would be exerted at all levels of literary production and its forms of public recognition. Fidel's proclamation that there would be room only for "true revolutionaries" and that evaluation of literary works would be political in the new society, amounted to announcing the imposition of censorship at all levels. Thus, if in the earliest years of the Revolution there was room for many voices contrary to the regime, 1971 ushered in what was called "el quinquenio gris," or the "five gray years" when freedom in literary production would be severely restricted. The gray years may in fact be said to have lasted far longer, "approximately from 1968 to 1983," as certain writers encountered varying degrees of control or censorship depending on their relationship to the regime and its institutions (D. Navarro 703).

This book focuses on the years before 1971 because, in comparison with later years, the relatively more lenient attitude of the government toward the arts in the first decade enabled writers to use a wider variety of forms than would be possible after 1971. The 1960s in Cuba saw a proliferation of voices addressing the uses and forms of art, some of them favorable to Socialist realism, but many of them expressing concerns or at least a degree of skepticism toward the Revolution. Certain texts such as Pablo Armando Fernández's *Los niños se despiden* (1968) could not have been published in Cuba after 1971, though in fact they could have been published after the Special Period (1992 and beyond). While in terms of freedom of form and themes the current era might seem more interesting than the early years, my interest lies in the revolutionary discourse that was foundational to the Cuban Revolution as it was originally conceived, not as it has evolved after the fall of the Soviet bloc. Thus, though the epilogue refers to the Special Period, it is aimed at connecting this phase of the Revolution with the discourse of the early years.

From "Words to the Intellectuals" (1961) to the speech at the closing of the

First National Congress of Education and Culture, these landmark speeches delineate the development of cultural policy in the first years of the Revolution, which proved to be defining for the following two decades. In addition, one should bear in mind the heated debates on the subjects of culture and politics that took place in Latin American countries in the 1960s, in which Cuba played a protagonist role. The Boom in Latin American letters and the projection of Latin American literature into the international market originated amid much discussion on the role of literature and other creative expressions in society, at the same time that censorship—whether external of self-imposed—was enforced. Simultaneous with the repudiation of Socialist realism or the adoption of some of its tenets, a multivocal dialogue on the role of literature and cultural institutions in society was taking place. Most of these discussions were featured in the many journals published in those years in Cuba: *Unión*; *Revolución*, with its short-lived supplement *Lunes de Revolución*; *Mundo Nuevo*; *La Gaceta de Cuba*; *Bohemia*; and of course *Casa de las Américas*. A thorough study involving the discourse of these journals remains to be done. The disputes among writers in those years influenced cultural policy and shaped the understanding of revolutionary culture, but to a certain extent, "one finds that at the heart of this and that debate . . . there was a struggle to secure a place, impose one's criteria or specific politics; that is, in the end, in the middle of a bigger battle, the battle to reach and capture utopia, there were quite earthly interests at play" (Jaime Sarusky's intervention in "Literatura en los 60").[9] Those disputes were also the product of the enthusiasm, fear, and confusion of the years immediately following 1959. With the exception of the story of the poet Heberto Padilla, which had a decisive impact on culture and identity politics, this study dwells on these discussions only tangentially, as it examines the identity that was constituted in institutional revolutionary discourse, regardless of the many personal conflicts that served as a background to that era.

## Criticism on Cuban Revolutionary Discourse: Heated Debates, Area Maps, and Omissions

The field of Cuban studies displays a surprising lack of careful examination of revolutionary discourse in political speeches, and this book has no parallel in its study of the ways literature represents political discourse. Several critical studies dwell upon Che Guevara's testimonial discourse, particularly *Pasajes de la guerra revolucionaria* (1963) (*Episodes of the Revolutionary War*, 1968), with analyses of his style and the impact of his doctrine on culture and politics worldwide.[10] However, despite numerous references to revolutionary identity, or the New Man, no studies to date zero in on the intersection between literature and official discourse in their mutual task of building this identity in the Cuban Revolution.

Juan Carlos Quintero Herencia's analysis of the journal *Casa de las Américas* (*Fulguración*) represents a significant contribution to the study of official discourse in the Revolution. While both Quintero Herencia and I engage in interpretations of institutional discourse using theoretical tools, his study does not focus on the reproduction or subversion of this discourse in fiction. Nevertheless, his review of *Casa de las Américas* is extremely comprehensive and suggestive, and it adds depth and critical interest to the earlier studies of the journal by Luisa Campuzano, Judith Weiss, and Nadia Lie.

The work of political scientists and historians on the culture of the Cuban Revolution has been foundational to this study. In particular, Julie Marie Bunck's *Fidel Castro and the Quest for a Revolutionary Culture in Cuba* (1994) reveals the Cuban regime's concerted effort to create a new culture by targeting youth, women, labor, and sports. Tzvi Medin's *Cuba: The Shaping of the Revolutionary Consciousness* (1990) also touches on the concept of a new identity in the Literacy Campaign and in detective fiction. In terms of careful readings, John Kirk's *José Martí: Mentor of the Cuban Revolution* (1983) has been very influential in providing a comprehensive model for the analysis of an author's life work and the development of his ideas. Donald Hodges's *Intellectual Foundations of the Nicaraguan Revolution* (1986) also supplies an extremely rich model of political and cultural analysis in a different context. However, while Cuban revolutionary culture is historically situated and deeply political, it goes far beyond historical facts. Discourse analysis and cultural critique provide crucial points of entry into cultural issues that transcend literal or historicized readings. Further, critical theory offers insights into the ways that political language has been articulated and views on how this language may have been received and rearticulated in turn by its target audience.

For the purpose of this book, "the literature written in the Cuban Revolution" refers to those texts written in Cuba roughly between 1959 and 1971, with a brief visit in the epilogue to the 1990s; among these, "revolutionary literature" refers to the texts that cite or to a great extent reproduce the official discourse of the Revolution. This differs from previous definitions of revolutionary literature, according to which any literary work written after 1959 qualified for the rubric.[11] The radical changes following 1989, with the fall of the Soviet bloc, the proclamation of the Special Period, and its aftermath, make it difficult to speak about the Cuban Revolution in the strict sense, even if the regime continues to use the word and many writers persist in invoking it. From the 1990s on, many literary texts have maintained direct or indirect thematic connection with the Revolution, but cultural policy and people's attitudes have changed to the point that new standards, and new rubrics, need to be applied. Additionally, the critical work on Cuban literature has changed dramatically since the 1990s: the field has experienced a boom in primary and critical works. Despite such interest, the study of what I have called "revolutionary literature" has continued to suffer neglect or attacks on its ideological content.

During the early years of the Revolution there were heated debates in Cuba concerning the place of *littérature engageé*, or literature committed to denouncing social injustice and cultural and economic imperialism. Soviet Socialist realism acted as a looming threat to this commitment, as most writers deemed it impoverishing and threatening to their creative freedom. Yet, as shown in the previous section, shortly after 1959 many writers chose a style that could be compared to the Soviet genre. The main forums for the debate on literature of social engagement were the periodicals *Unión* and *Casa de las Américas* on the one hand, and the literary magazine *Mundo Nuevo* on the other hand, with both sides taking the idea of "revolutionary literature" to mean "consistent with the official discourse of the Revolution." *Unión* was published by the UNEAC, created in 1961, and *Casa* was founded in Cuba in 1960, operating initially under the direction of Antón Arrufat and becoming increasingly more militant when Roberto Fernández Retamar assumed leadership of the periodical. *Mundo Nuevo*, created in 1966 with a base in Paris and then Buenos Aires, was guided by the Uruguayan Emir Rodríguez Monegal. *Mundo Nuevo* was often signaled as antagonistic to *Casa*, and Fernández Retamar charged that it was being financed by the CIA (*Calibán* 75). Some of the articles published in the two Cuban periodicals were excerpts of resolutions adopted in conferences and congresses of artists and writers, presided over by Fidel and members of the cultural intelligentsia such as Osvaldo Dorticós or Fernández Retamar himself.[12]

Though this study focuses on institutional discourse—the "teque" or revolutionary propaganda, as Cubans in the island call it—it must be noted that *Unión* and *Casa de las Américas* also published poems and short stories that were contrary or indifferent to the political commitment of the journals. Alongside writings by Mario Benedetti, Pierre Macherey, or René Depestre—fervent proponents of Marxist art outside Cuba—and issues devoted to the literature of Vietnam, South Africa, China, Hungary, or countries of the Soviet bloc, these journals published works by Calvert Casey, Antonio Benítez Rojo, José Lezama Lima, Virgilio Piñera, Eliseo Diego, José

Triana, and Onelio Jorge Cardoso, to mention a few. Even the 1968 issue of *Unión*, which was devoted to the death of Che Guevara, published Piñera's "El que vino a salvarme" and Lezama Lima's "Fronesis," neither of which had anything to do with the memorialized political icon. Despite the dominating influence of the official discourse of the Revolution, a vibrant literary discourse emerged in those early years of the new government.

At the end of the 1960s and the beginning of the 1970s, attention was galvanized on the case of Heberto Padilla, which divided writers into two main camps: those who accused Cuban cultural policy of being Stalinist, such as Guillermo Cabrera Infante, and those who defended it on revolutionary grounds, such as Lisandro Otero. From the end of the 1970s to the present, criticism of the literature produced in the Cuban Revolution has been scarce in comparison with other periods of Latin American literary history, such as the so-called Boom, even though the literature of the Boom and the Cuban Revolution are often defined in relation to each other. Already in 1969 the Mexican author Carlos Fuentes referred to the Boom literature as the "new literature," and claimed that it attempted to subvert traditional literature and reified notions of reality, thus achieving its own form of artistic and political revolution (Fuentes 94–95). Following that, in 1971 Roberto Fernández Retamar lashed out against Fuentes's claims in his essay "Calibán" (1971), stating that Cuba offered the only kind of revolution capable of ending social injustice, and that the Cuban Revolution was *the* historical event that lent significance to Latin America in the world. For Fernández Retamar, only the Cuban Revolution could explain the increasing interest in Latin American literature during the 1960s (Fernández Retamar 65–69). In his seminal book on the Boom, Emir Rodríguez Monegal claimed that the Cuban Revolution was one of its determining factors (18), particularly because it prompted the foundation of the journal *Casa de las Américas* (1960). Indeed, during the first years of the Cuban Revolution, *Casa* was open to Cuban and international experimental literature, and it organized conferences and prizes that soon situated Cuba as one of the main cultural centers of Latin America. According to Rodríguez Monegal, the Boom writers were first promoted and made known in Cuba, and it was from there that they aroused interest in the rest of the world. Rodríguez Monegal admitted that after 1965 the editorial board of *Casa* enforced political commitment more strongly, but he insisted that the real Boom of Latin American letters took place in Cuba at the height of the proliferation of the arts in the first years of the Revolution (22). While I do not intend to settle the discussion on whether the Cuban Revolution was directly responsible for the Boom in Latin American letters, it seems clear that both phenomena influenced each other and gave Cuba a powerful presence in a key debate in Latin American studies.

When it comes to delimiting the field of the literature of the Cuban Revolution, Seymour Menton's *Prose Fiction of the Cuban Revolution* (1975) is a foundational text, as it catalogues the entire literary production of novels and short stories in Cuba from 1959 to 1974. Aware that this was new critical territory, except for certain bibliographies published previously, Menton devoted himself to being exhaustive and precise, assigning every published work to a specific period with an explanatory title.[13] His comprehensive study reviewed these texts against the characteristics of canonical literature and provided judgments on their literary quality, but it did not attempt to interpret them in depth or to suggest a canon of "Cuban revolutionary literature." The heirs of Menton's critical tradition regarding this literature chose the works that best illustrated their political allegiances or grouped the texts according to thematic affinity. Other books on the literature of the Cuban Revolution have continued to be large in scope but lacking in depth, such as those of I. Álvarez, Méndez y Soto, and Fernández-Vázquez, the latter of whom writes on literature produced outside Cuba since 1959.

As Roberto González Echevarría has noted, the "remarkable achievements" of academic criticism in Cuba in the 1960s and 1970s concern mainly prerevolutionary literature ("Criticism" 7). The closeness of events to the time of writing and the need for critics as well as writers to demonstrate political commitment hamstrung the analysis of literature produced in the first thirty years of the Revolution. For instance, Rogelio Rodríguez Coronel claimed that an essential characteristic of any criticism of literature written during the Revolution should be its *partidismo* or commitment to the Marxist ideology that in his view inspired the literature of the Cuban Revolution (17). Ineke Phaf's *Novelando La Habana* demonstrated the influence of sociological approaches to literature in an attempt to make literary criticism more "objective": her book reads the corpus of novels written during the Revolution as a survey of life in Havana, providing a scrupulous compilation of the details of daily existence in the city but disregarding theoretical and textual concerns of these novels.

There are some exceptions to the trends of political dogmatism and scientism in commentary on literature written in the first thirty years of Revolution, but those in-depth studies often leave out the more politically committed texts. For instance, Roberto González Echevarría included in his study of "the novel of the Cuban Revolution" (*Biografía* 110–23) Edmundo Desnoes's *Memorias del Subdesarrollo* (1965) and Miguel Barnet's *Biografía de un cimarrón* (1966) (*Biography of a Runaway Slave*, 1994), a testimonial novel, but dismissed the "literature that indulges in the ephemeral language of current politics or that is satisfied with the vapid jargon of the social sciences" (123). Miguel Barnet's ethnographic work is often hailed as a "good product" of the Revolution because it manages to be politically committed while avoiding direct engagement with its contemporary situation. There are other books on Cuban revolutionary literature, such as that of Julio Ortega, that manage to completely fail to mention all novels on the Revolution, as well as testimonial novels; Ortega dwells on the impact of the Revolution in canonical works of the period written inside and outside Cuba. His view of the literature of the Revolution is quite detached from the historical and political context in which these texts were produced, and it offers interpretations of texts where the subject of political revolution, understood in literal terms, is avoided.

A good exception to the general biases and oversights in the book-length studies is the more recent book by Armando Pereira, ambitious in its thirty-year scope of revolutionary literature in Cuba, but providing by far the most interesting readings of revolutionary texts. This study is the only one on the subject that works within a poststructuralist theoretical framework. Pereira illustrates the fact that, while revolutionary literature is historically situated and therefore calls for a contextualized reading, a theoretical framework allows the critic to articulate several possible readings of the texts that transcend the original ideological purpose for which they were conceived.

Most in-depth readings of the literature of the Cuban Revolution can be found in articles, and most on individual works and authors, particularly on Edmundo Desnoes's *Memorias del subdesarrollo* (*Inconsolable Memories*), which became widely popular thanks to a film version by Tomás Gutiérrez Alea (1968).[14] The rest of the novels studied in this book have escaped critical attention almost entirely, except for a few reviews and fresh responses written at the time of the novels' publication, or general comments included in books on the period. The author of the novel considered in my fifth chapter, Pablo Armando Fernández, has been called "the poet laureate of the Cuban Revolution," after Nicolás Guillén, and was awarded the Cuban National Poetry Award in 1996, yet there is to date no extensive critical work on any of his prose fiction. There are some interesting studies, however, on the discourse of the Revolution as represented in the literature of the last part of what I have called the revolutionary period, such as the readings on the novels of Jesús Díaz by Manuel Cachán and Antonio Vera-León.

The map of the era has been charted, the passionate debates on which texts were worthy of the title "literature of the Cuban Revolution" have been indefinitely suspended, and some scholars seem to have lost interest in discussing the new concept of literature that the Revolution instituted—even though this discussion radically changed the history of Latin American letters. What still needs to be done is to actually read revolutionary works as literary texts and to focus not just on the stories they tell, but on how they are told and what discourses they enunciate. There seems to be an assumption that militant texts—those that actively promote institutional discourse at any given moment—only offer a literal reading, and yet many of these novels are profoundly multilayered and display the same rhetorical devices celebrated in works of literature respected on aesthetic grounds. Regardless of the aesthetic achievements of these novels, they offer invaluable insights if examined as ideological discourse. I urge that these texts be appreciated as part of Cuba's literary production, and that discussions of the difference between the literary and the nonliterary in post-1959 Cuba be rendered unnecessary.

## Itinerary

The first chapter of this book focuses on the figure of the volunteer teacher as constituted in the 1961 Literacy Campaign, the cornerstone of Cubans' cultural revolution. An analysis of speeches, images, and testimonials of the campaign reveals the complex process of identification between literacy workers and students that the campaign fostered. Further, the volunteer teacher's desire to embody the alleged values of the peasant students, such as simplicity, honesty, and strength, coupled with a certain ambivalence toward them—because of their perceived brutishness and ignorance—can be traced to the relationship between the guerrilla fighter and the peasantry showcased in foundational texts of the Revolution, such as Che Guevara's *Pasajes de la guerra revolucionaria* (*Episodes of the Revolutionary War*). Daura Olema García's novel *Maestra voluntaria* (Volunteer teacher) the winner of the 1962 Casa de las Américas prize, represents the identity politics of the campaign as it seeks to construct the New Man in the form of a Literacy Campaign worker who aspires both to teach revolutionary values to peasants and to learn from their genuinely revolutionary potential. However, the students—in this case, the peasants—hardly appear as subjects in official discourse or in the novel: they are the object of the literacy worker's gaze or an emblem of what needs to be *changed* in the interest of the Revolution. With the theories of Paulo Freire, Slavoj Zizek, and Carlos Rangel in mind, the reader can reconstruct the identity of the peasant students, explain the reasons for the lack of agency of students in the campaign, and describe the rhetorical strategies used to constitute the centrality of the volunteer teacher.

The second chapter studies the relationship between Cuban intellectuals and the revolutionary regime as a backdrop to the representation of the fledgling writer in Edmundo Desnoes's *Memorias del subdesarrollo* (1965) (*Inconsolable Memories*, 1967). The nationalization of most printing presses, the increasing regulation of publishing by the state, the changes introduced in publishing policies, the creation of cultural state institutions, and the resulting development of a more stringent cultural policy all contributed to the profound crisis of intellectuals in that era. Desnoes's *Memorias del subdesarrollo* rewrites and "rectifies" previous works by the same author, and even attempts to illustrate in literary form the theories explained in the author's essays. Such an obsession with revisions illustrates the anxiety many writers experienced as they attempted to measure up to the ideal of the new intellectual during the first decade of the Revolution. Malabre, the protagonist of *Memorias,* is a very ambiguous persona of the author, who on the one hand possesses all of the characteristics of the stereotypical bourgeois intellectual, and on the other hand expresses many of the legitimate complaints and doubts of writers and other intellectuals at that time. Although the author described the novel as some sort of an "exorcism" of his darker self, one wonders whether this text is not in fact an opportunity to release the pressure that institutional measures were creating for intellectuals at the time.

A Sartrean reading of the body politics of this novel, or the numerous references to the body as a way of being and *getting to know* the world, explores how the character's perception of his own body and the way it is perceived by others contribute to his profound sense of anxiety. Such reflection on the body and perception compels the reader to go beyond the stereotypical image of Malabre as a self-centered bourgeois writer toward an understanding of the intellectual task in a world in turmoil. Finally, three stories appended to the original Spanish edition dwell on issues of underdevelopment and ventriloquism that invite us to reread the novel while carefully considering its metafictional and multivocal elements.

The third chapter examines the 1970 Ten-Million-Ton Sugar Campaign and how this collective effort contributed to the creation of a new revolutionary nation. In the speeches of this campaign and the novel (*Sacchario,* 1970) by Miguel Cossío Woodward, the figure of the New Man emerges as the "average" Cuban with a history of independence struggle. The institutional discourse that accompanied the Sugar Campaign is represented in the novel in its three constants: the metaphorization of the nation as a homogeneous whole, with a history that is intimately tied to Revolution and sugar production; the plotting of Cuban history as both "continuity and rupture" (in Benítez Rojo's expression, "La cultura"); and the representation of the *people* as raceless. In spite of the historical background it offers, the novel does not represent the protagonism of Afro-Cubans in the history of cane cutting in Cuba. On the contrary, the main character of the novel is a white man, and the lack of treatment of race in the novel confirms the fact that during this campaign the revolutionary regime focused on the unity of the nation at the expense of racial difference. Indeed, the exclusion of Afro-Cubans in public discourse has been a recurrent critique of the Revolution to this day, and this novel typifies the absence of Afro-Cuban protagonists in identitary representations of the early revolutionary period.

However, the idea of the nation as a collective identity in *Sacchario* is contested by the pleasure of the text, in Roland Barthes's term, displayed in the narrative techniques and self-referentiality of the novel. In other words, the narrator defies the notion of revolutionary literature as a "straight narrative" and refuses to forsake his role as an individual craftsman in favor of the collective idea of a nation. In addition, the narrator's nostalgia for the places of memory, in Pierre Nora's terminology, of prerevolutionary Havana also calls into question the official idea of Cuban history as a linear progression toward liberation, in which the prerevolutionary period was a time of scarcity and depravity in Havana. To sum up, the persona of the narrator as creator subverts the concept of the nation as described in official discourse.

The fourth chapter is devoted to the analysis of the New Woman as constituted by the Federation of Cuban Women, a governmental women's organization, Fidel Castro's speeches on the role of women in the Revolution and the Family Code, and feminine role models popularized by magazines such as *Mujeres*. Negative figures, such as the housewife, the prerevolutionary woman, and the prostitute, and positive ones, such as the female worker, emerge in these texts as role models prescribing codes of behavior and drawing women either to reject or identify with such models. The role of the mother is simultaneously presented as the core of women's identity and an obstacle to their liberation. While Manuel Cofiño López's *La última mujer y el próximo combate* (The last woman and the next combat) (1971), which won the 1971 Casa de las Américas Prize, exhibits the masculinist biases of institutional discourse, it also inadvertently points at positions from which these identity figures can be questioned. In an intensely cinematic text in which women characters are constructed through the gaze of the narrator, the reader, and other characters, one figure in particular produces her sexuality as a masquerade or spectacle, as defined by Mary Ann Doane, thereby unsettling all of the classifications of women in institutional discourse.

The fifth chapter takes up the subversion of the idea of the New Man in *Los niños se despiden* (1968) (The children say good-bye) by Pablo Armando Fernández. This text does away with the idea of determinate, prescriptive identities through the use of a child narrator and characters who fuse with one another in a fragmented plot. The novel attempts to validate Afro-Cuban tradition in a way that runs counter to the official rhetoric of the regime. The child narrator's playful attitude toward gender identities confronts the masculine definitions of the New Man. In fact, this novel embodies the idea of Cuban identity and Revolution as evolving processes, thus undermining the monolithic concept of the New Man and questioning institutional discourse in a general sense.

The epilogue serves to reassess the impact of the idea of the New Man from the perspective of recent literature, such as Leonardo Padura's tetralogy. While other writers in this and more recent decades have been critical of this identity figure, Padura is especially significant because he rewrites and parodies the detective novel, a genre that had been thoroughly pro-institutional since its creation in the 1970s. Additionally, the popularity of his novels rivals the diffusion of revolutionary novels during the early years, and to a great extent they voice popular critical sentiment just as earlier revolutionary novels radiated enthusiasm but also criticism "from within." Although he appears as a pathetic antihero, the protagonist of Padura's novels, the detective Mario Conde, is the most complete picture of what remains of the New Man as he has emerged following the Special Period.

Much has been written on the history, politics, and culture of the Cuban Revolution, but this study represents a fresh attempt to look into all three of these subjects as they intertwine in the discourse on identity that this era produced. In probing into the ambiguous relationship between politics and literature, I underscore how literature can reproduce a dominant political discourse and at the same time expose its blind spots, as demonstrated in the critique of revolutionary novels and other texts that subvert this discourse. My interpretation of the novels outlines the strategies literature uses to construct identity and the forms of discourse that intervene in this process in literary works, as opposed to political discourse understood in literal terms. Most importantly, to analyze the Revolution as a discursive event cutting across these disciplines is an urgent task if one considers that much of the criticism leveled at the Revolution cites the fact that the regime did not accompany the implementation of its policies affecting gender, race, and class with real change in people's long-standing prejudices. By focusing on four political campaigns of the period before 1971 as foundational to the discourse on identity, this book delves into the characteristics of the alleged new revolutionary and the extent to which its flaws predetermined the failure of the attempt to create a new revolutionary consciousness. While controversial for many readers, the literary texts I examine need to be recovered and reassessed, as they showcase the rhetorical means by which a country's official myths are forged, promoted, diffused, and ultimately subverted. Further, the speeches and literary texts under scrutiny flesh out a construct of identity that continues to be influential in Cuba and beyond, many decades later.

# Speaking at Cross Purposes

## The Failed Identification between Teachers and Students
in the Literacy Campaign

The 1961 Literacy Campaign was a cornerstone of the Cuban cultural revolution. To a large extent, it fulfilled what Fidel had announced the previous year, in a speech at the General Assembly of the United Nations: "Next year our people propose to launch an all-out offensive against illiteracy, with the ambitious goal of teaching every illiterate person to read and write. Organizations of teachers, students and workers—the entire people—are preparing themselves for an intensive campaign and within a few months Cuba will be the first country in the Americas to be able to claim that it has not a single illiterate inhabitant" (quoted in Fagen 9). As Richard Fagen has noted, this first declaration of the campaign already foreshadowed certain motifs that would become constants not only in the Literacy Campaign itself but in the revolutionary discourse of later years. Borrowing from military rhetoric, Fidel cast the offensives and mobilizations of the campaign as collective efforts coming from "the people," thereby strengthening the sense of national pride and defiance not just against other Latin American countries, but especially the United States, a perennial enemy of the Revolution. Beyond the highly positive results the campaign produced, it is worth examining its significance in the process of articulating a new identity in Cuba.[1]

The campaign proved to be pedagogical in many senses, since its underlying principles, its implementation, and the incidents that accompanied it created a climate for the creation of a new language that was first taught in the campaign's primers and then adapted and slowly transformed as the Revolution progressed. A New Man emerged in the campaign in the person of the literacy teacher, and the speeches created a fantasy image of the peasant with whom the volunteer teacher would interact and eventually fuse identities, assuming the ideal qualities of the peasant uncontaminated by urban materialism.

The symbolic identity fusion between volunteer teachers of the city and student peasants was aided by the mythical status that the Sierra achieved during the guerrilla warfare. During the development of the Literacy Cam-

paign in rural areas, the countryside became the repository of revolutionary values and a liminal space or contact zone between people of different
classes and levels of awareness of revolutionary doctrine. As Fidel put it in
his address to the Varadero Literacy Brigades: "You are going to teach, but at
the same time you will learn. . . . They [the peasants] will teach you what they
have learned from the hard life they have led up to now. They will show you
what rural life in Cuba was. . . . They will teach you the why of the Revolution better than any book. . . . They will teach you, at the same time, what is
a healthy, sound, clean life; what is upright morality, duty, generosity, sharing
the little they have with visitors" (19610514).[2] The literacy workers were to
emulate the peasant as a sort of "natural man" and incarnate what seemed
his "true revolutionary spirit." For their part, after learning revolutionary
theory, the peasant students were supposed to become teachers and transmit their knowledge to others. As Regis Debray explained, "The mountain
proletarianizes the bourgeois and peasant elements" (quoted in Lacqueur
334): the Literacy Campaign in rural areas revived the spirit of the guerrilla
and called for a new encounter promoting the fusion of contraries in the
revolutionary commitment.

However, the texts that describe the Literacy Campaign as it was taking place do not bear witness to the identity fusion between teacher and
peasant. These texts focus instead on the figure of the volunteer teacher
to the exclusion of the student. As literacy workers were the bearers of the
revolutionary message, the campaign aimed at instilling their principles and
generalizing their form of identity—that of literate revolutionaries—as the
"true Cuban identity." Rather than a fusion of identities there was an impulse
in both groups to take the characteristics of the other, and yet both groups
remained the same in spite of the radical change that the campaign operated
in their minds. In other words, the teachers did not abandon their elite status
for that of the peasants, and the peasants, as objects rather than subjects,
never enjoyed the same degree of agency as the teachers.

Daura Olema García's novel *Maestra voluntaria* (1962, henceforth *Maestra*), one of the first winners of the Casa de las Américas Prize established in
1961, staged the emergence of the New Man as literacy worker. Among a wide
field of fictional and testimonial texts that addressed the Literacy Campaign,
it provided an exceptional example of how fiction can reveal the contradictions at the heart of the symbolic articulation of the campaign while simultaneously enjoying the broad support at the official level. In contrast to the
protagonists in other fictional texts of the revolutionary period, the narrator
of *Maestra* fully embodies the ideology that the text promotes: the shadows
or darker selves of the New Man in the narrative do not represent the sub-

version of this identity figure as it appears in official discourse. Rather, the novel confirms the absence of the peasants as subjects with an agency in the symbolic articulation of the campaign. The peasant students appear only as a fantasy image of the "natural man" prevalent in official discourse, and the teacher protagonist chooses her own models for her self-transformation.

*Maestra* was written at a time of great change in the Revolution. As mentioned in the introduction, in June 1961, Fidel met with writers to discuss the events following the closing of *Lunes de Revolución*—a cultural weekly supplement to the journal *Revolución* characterized by its heterodoxy—and the banning of *PM*, a short film made by Sabá Cabrera Infante and Orlando Jiménez Leal showcasing prerevolutionary night life in Havana. Fidel's speech following the meeting, "Words to the Intellectuals," demanded commitment from writers and artists in the Revolution and inaugurated an era in which culture would be regulated through the UNEAC, constituted in August 1961. The year of the Literacy Campaign was also a time of great political and ideological changes highlighted by the official proclamation of the Socialist character of the Revolution in April 1961, after the CIA bombings that preceded the Playa Girón, or Bay of Pigs, invasion.

The protagonist of Olema García's novel represents the ideological confusion of certain sectors of the Cuban population during those years. Vilma, a volunteer teacher, enters a training camp in Minas del Frío as a total cynic, but by the time the training is finished she has experienced a kind of conversion to become a convinced revolutionary. The stages of her conversion are made plausible by a series of trials in the process of adaptation to the dynamics of the camp. Because the narrative focuses on the teacher training aspect of the campaign, rather than on the actual instruction of the peasants, Vilma's identity transformation takes the *teachers* as a model, not the peasants. In fact, the peasants learning to read and write hardly appear in the novel; they are only represented insofar as they have already become literate.

In the following sections I look into the pedagogical uses of the Literacy Campaign and analyze the reasons for and implications of the conspicuous absence of the peasants as subjects in political speeches. One can say that the articulation of the Literacy Campaign in political speeches bears strongly on the peculiar representations of peasants in the novel. Or perhaps both political and literary representations rely on age-old stereotypes of peasants as Janus-faced emblems of exemplary behavior on the one hand, and savageness on the other.

Beyond Literacy: The New Language of Cuban Primers

The Literacy Campaign began at the end of 1960, with the training of teachers and the writing of campaign primers, and officially ended on December 22, 1961. It took barely a year to teach 700,000 people to read and write, with a total of 100,000 students and 15,000 workers mobilized as volunteer teachers (Medin 72).[3] The efforts of the Year of Education continued in the following years to give the already literate primary and secondary education, with 530,000 adults graduating at those levels by the academic year 1971–72. During that first decade, a law nationalizing education was passed, instituting free education and closing all private schools. The practical consequences of such a wide-ranging campaign to end illiteracy in Cuba are obvious, since it gave people a new sense of dignity and increased the possibility of social mobility and integration. Additionally, the campaign had the objective of spreading a revolutionary message that was articulated in the first words that the literate peasants would read and write.

As J. Elspeth Stuckey's *The Violence of Literacy* (1991) shows, literacy campaigns often are characterized by the problematic aspects of modernization projects and are frequently felt as impositions on a population that does not necessarily desire or value literacy. Further, such campaigns fail to address the tension between the learning of useful skills (reading and writing) and the fact that literacy is defined from the point of view of the cultural or intellectual elite. Indeed, being literate entails embracing a system of dominant values carried with the written and "articulate" spoken word, and the literate person seldom questions the "naturalness" of those values. Literacy serves to contain and to integrate "marginal" sectors of society into an ideal notion of the modern nation. In the case of Cuba, the Literacy Campaign served to rally certain sectors of the skeptical upper middle class—many of those who acted as volunteer teachers—and the peasants of remote rural areas as champions of the Revolution.

The rationale behind the pedagogical dynamics of the campaign was later enunciated by Che Guevara in his essay "Socialism and Man in Cuba," written four years after the Literacy Campaign. In this text, Guevara insists on the need to develop a revolutionary consciousness by turning "society as a whole . . . into a gigantic school" (6). For Guevara, the word *school* refers both to a learning experience that does not need to take place in a classroom and to an institution of learning that teaches not just concepts but a certain worldview. This form of massive instruction that Guevara advocated had already been implemented in the Literacy Campaign, in the forms of what he called "indirect" learning from the example of others and "direct" education or straight instruction. The volunteer teachers and workers who were taken to the countryside to teach peasants often stayed with their students and experienced a kind of life they had never before come into contact with. Years after the campaign, in the many texts paying tribute to it, the tales of the literacy workers always include the moment of shock they experienced when they first arrived at the place of instruction assigned to them. For instance, Nieves Vidal, a teacher who was sent to La Magdalena, stated that even though some of the teacher brigades sent to the Sierra were made up of factory workers from Havana, such as the brigade called Patria o Muerte, "the poorest person in the city is not comparable to the one who has lived in the Sierra" (Séjourné 241).

Indirect education, or emulation, was supposed to take place between teachers and peasants, but also among the teachers themselves. As the main character in *Maestra* demonstrates, volunteers who had some misgivings about the Revolution met others whose model behavior impressed them to such an extent that they allowed themselves to be recruited unconditionally. Among those models, the teachers who perished in armed confrontations with rebels in the area achieved the status of heroes for all volunteers.

In the more conventional meaning of "school," the Literacy Campaign was aimed at teaching students the mechanics of reading and writing as well as the ideological principles of the Revolution. As Tzvi Medin puts it, "Illiterates were taught not just a language, but the language of the Revolution" (69). Two primers were written especially for the purpose of this Literacy Campaign, one called "¡Venceremos!" (We will win!) and the other "Alfabeticemos" (Let us teach). The titles of the lessons were in themselves revealing, such as "La tierra es nuestra" "(The land is ours), "La Revolución gana todas las batallas" (The Revolution wins all battles), and "Fidel es Nuestro Líder" (Fidel is our leader) (Ministerio de Cultura, *Alfabeticemos* 8). Grammar, vocabulary, and arithmetic concepts were illustrated using texts on the positive values of the Revolution. The final test consisted of the dictation of a paragraph synthesizing the objectives of the revolutionary government, and the final requirement was to write a letter to Fidel (Medin 73–74). A UNESCO report on the campaign stated that despite the wide reach of radio and television in Cuba, media was not used in the Literacy Campaign, unlike in other countries such as the Soviet Union. It was the people-to-people contact that made the campaign a success, not just in terms of providing access to literacy but also in creating a revolutionary consciousness (UNESCO 73).

From the preparation for the campaign to its successful implementation in 1961, the regime used strategies such as bureaucratization, massive mobilizations, volunteer work, and the elaboration of ideological motifs, all of which would become recurrent in later years. The organizational aspects of the campaign resulted in the deployment of newly founded departments, a total of eighteen, which continued to exist afterward. As early as 1959, the government was calling for volunteers to teach in the remotest areas of the country; at the time nine thousand teachers were unemployed, but many were older and not amenable to going to these areas (UNESCO 16). Since the administration could not pay these teachers enough for them to do the job, it recruited students from secondary schools to go to the Sierra. The latter were more willing to work without pay, and their youthfulness embodied the atmosphere of the time: a new Cuba was replacing the old in the same way that the youngsters were meant to eradicate the old ways of the countryside.[4]

As part of the larger project of modernization of the Revolution, the Literacy Campaign followed the 1960 Land Reform, which caused discontent in peasants who had to share their land, and which aimed at incorporating pockets of indifference or rebellion in the countryside into the revolutionary project. Significantly, the first areas the volunteers were sent to included Ciénaga de Zapata, the site of the Girón invasion, and the Escambray Sierra, where resistance continued well into the 1970s. To a large extent, the *brigadistas*, or volunteers grouped in "brigades" or teams, completed a process that even the anti-Batista forces had not been able to fully accomplish in the countryside.

The initial idea that the literacy workers were going to rescue a form of "natural man" was combined with a desire to *civilize* that man and turn him into someone resembling a citizen of an ideal modern revolutionary city. According to the testimonial of Orquídea Canel Pendás, the first teacher brigades sent to the Sierra included medical workers as well as barbers and hairdressers, and their curriculum comprised cultural and recreational activities as well as courses on personal hygiene. As Pendás put it, "It was a beautiful effort in the interest of *humanizing* those who had been marginalized by previous regimes" (Ares 31, emphasis in the original).

The icons of the campaign contributed to this effect, as the oil lamp brought by the teachers replaced the less efficient *chismosilla* of the peasants, thus becoming a symbol of the campaign. As Fidel expressed it in one of his speeches that characteristically mixed the rhetoric of modernization with that of a religious mission, the teachers were "missionaries of culture, as champions of literacy, like torches lit to bring light, to carry out the most beautiful of tasks" (Ares 53). The idea that the peasants were "coming out of the dark" was confirmed by the fact that the local authorities struggled to get the peasants to come forward as illiterate, as many were reluctant to admit that they could not read and write. It is significant that in the final report on the success of the campaign, the minister of culture, Armando Hart, mentioned that the only illiterate people remaining had some impairment or handicap: "25,000 Haitians living in the areas of Oriente and Camagüey who, due to the fact that they do not have a good command of Spanish, have turned out to be impossible to teach in the Literacy Campaign. . . . The mentally and physically disabled, and the people that due to their old age or poor health have been declared incapable of learning to read and write" (quoted in Séjourné 291). Clearly, those who remained illiterate were considered impossible to incorporate into the Revolution.

The campaign relied on certain ideological motifs that later became commonplaces of revolutionary ideology, such as the idea of existence as a struggle, the revolutionary fervor of students and workers, and Cuba's heroic resistance to the imperialist siege of the United States. In a revolutionary rhetoric that would increasingly speak of every undertaking as a confrontation, the Literacy Campaign was alluded to as "a battle against ignorance" (19610817). The fact that it mobilized vast numbers of Cubans showed the leaders that it was possible to count on people from every social group to make sacrifices in order to fulfill their revolutionary duties. The enthusiastic participation of workers and student volunteers served to redefine their roles in the Revolution, for though they had been contentious during the dictatorships of Machado and Batista, they supported the Revolution unconditionally during the campaign. The conversion of the barracks of the former Escambray counterrevolutionaries into a new school symbolized this new level of cooperation. From then on, the task of the literacy instructors was not only to teach reading and writing but to suppress the possibility of counterrevolutionary attacks.[5] The main motto of the campaign, "Estudio, trabajo, fusil" ("Study, Work, Rifle") further illustrated its message by portraying the literacy workers carrying big pencils on their shoulders as if they were guns. The songs that the *brigadistas* sang always paired instruction with defense, such as the chant "volunteer teachers are soldiers that arm themselves with weapons, primers, and Fidel's ideas" (Séjourné 241).

The fact that the campaign continued undaunted through the Playa Girón, or Bay of Pigs, invasion, set the tone for the heroic dimension that revolutionary leaders attributed to Cuba in the face of the imperialist attacks of the United States. As José Ramón Bermúdez puts it, "Girón marked the before and after of the Cuban Revolution. . . . The Year of Education . . . ended up being the year of the defense and victory of the first Socialist revolution of the Western Hemisphere . . ." (Bermúdez 78). The critic refers to the fact that the Socialist character of the Revolution was proclaimed after the bombardments that preceded the invasion of Playa Girón in April 1961. In the timing and discursive articulation of that proclamation, Fidel unmistakably tied the ideology of the Revolution to a siege mentality.[6] Later, when the Literacy Campaign concluded, its achievements were used as score points in the long-standing rivalry between the United States and Cuba; the Cuban leaders claimed that the United States had vowed to do in ten years what Cuba as a revolutionary nation was able to do in one year. The success of the Revolution despite U.S. intervention gave Cuba a much needed international projection, especially among the least powerful countries of the world.[7] Finally, with its military intervention during the Literacy Campaign, the United States provided Cuba with a necessary adversary. In the words of Fidel: "Any revolution which is not attacked is not a true revolution . . . . Revolutions need to fight, to struggle; they need an enemy before them" (19610128).

At the level of the nation, the communications of the Literacy Campaign prepared Cubans for a highly bureaucratized country, reliant on massive mobilizations and volunteer work. The Revolution, as a communal endeavor, was to be as youthful and enthusiastic as the volunteers of the campaign. The emphasis in integrating all areas of the country in the "civilizing mission" of the campaign revealed from the beginning that the regime was not going to tolerate dissent or indifference, and that it was going to favor urban, educated individuals over those considered ignorant peasantry. On the one hand, the peasant was idealized as possessing the characteristics of the inherently good person; on the other hand, he or she was considered to be in need of learning basic academic skills and proper behavior. The New Man that emerged from the campaign was a person enlightened by the learning of revolutionary principles who at the same time retained all of the characteristics of an idealized image of the peasant.

## The Encounter between Teacher and Student

In agreement with its pedagogical objectives, the Literacy Campaign used an assortment of catchy emblems and images. One that synthesized the main goal of the campaign was the acronym "QTATA[2]" (qtata squared), or "que todo analfabeto tenga alfabetizador, y que todo alfabetizador tenga analfabeto" (For every illiterate person a teacher, and for every teacher an illiterate person). This expression became so popular that people started saying "cutatear" or "cutatizar" (a word made from the acronym *qtata*) when referring to the goal of the campaign to create a complete symbiosis between

Fig. 1. A campaign poster of the Literacy Campaign, which appeared in the book *Cuba: Territorio libre de analfabetismo*, by Equipo de Ediciones Especiales de la Editorial Ciencias Sociales, 1981. Reprinted by permission of Grupo Nuevo Milenio, Havana, Cuba.

literacy teacher and peasant student. The poster that proclaimed this formula illustrated an additional aspect of this relationship, as it depicted two hands locked in a handshake: the white hand was labeled "literate" and the black one "illiterate" (see Fig. 1). Following the racial motif that the poster portrayed, Che Guevara revealed his idea of education at the University of Havana in these terms: "I have to ask it [the university] to paint itself black, to paint itself *mulatto*, not only among students but also among professors; let it paint itself the color of workers and peasants, let it paint itself the color of the people, because the university is not the property of anybody, it belongs to the people of Cuba" ("Que la Universidad," Nuiry Sánchez 11).

Both in the poster and in Guevara's comment, blackness is associated with some ideal of "the people." The racial content of this equation complicates a relationship that was already very ambiguous. The Literacy Campaign was addressed to "the people," represented as "the colored," and was supposed to utilize some of the people's intrinsically revolutionary characteristics: unity, attitude of combat, courage, intelligence, and sense of history.[8]

Two pictures of campaign propaganda reveal the symbolic focus of the Literacy Campaign. In the first one there is a volunteer teacher sitting on a chair, with two adult students sitting on either side of her (Fig. 2). Though the figures in the picture appear relaxed, the setting seems contrived. In

Fig. 2. A photograph of a volunteer teacher and students in the Literacy Campaign, which appeared in *In the Spirit of Wandering Teachers: Cuban Literacy Campaign, 1961/Con el espíritu de los maestros ambulantes: La campaña de alfabetización cubana, 1961*, ed. Alexandra Keeble, p. 30. Reprinted by permission of Ocean Press.

the foreground of the picture there is a fence of barbed wire. In the background there is a hut with a straw roof. The picture looks staged: the barbed wire establishes a barrier between viewer and subject and forces the viewer to see the subjects as three objects to be viewed. Rather than looking at the camera, which would highlight their agency, the people in the picture are looking down at their notebooks. The military uniform of the volunteer teacher contrasts with the simple garb of the peasants. Every element of the picture is loaded with meaning, as it was in the campaign. The picture is meant to stress the contrast between country and city, and how this difference was resolved with literacy. But as happened in the campaign, the value of spreading literacy is superseded in this picture by the strategic symbolic use of the campaign as a spectacle promoting the modernizing effect of the Revolution. This photograph also happens to show that there was no such racial divide between teachers and students.

A second picture frequently included in books, pamphlets, and memoirs from that period is that of a volunteer teacher sitting in a wooden hut with a student (Fig. 3). The student has his back to the camera, while the teacher faces it, though she is looking at the piece of paper on the table and speaking as if caught in the act of teaching. Behind the teacher there is a blackboard filled with basic reading vocabulary, and in one corner behind the volunteer there is a small child looking at the camera. The door is open to a field, and next to the door there is a peasant woman with a child on her lap, listening intently. The focus of the picture is placed on the teacher and her activities. The student is denied a specific identity, as he is faceless for the viewer. The portable lamp next to him signifies the enlightening effect of literacy in this hut and the hope for the mother and baby who stand by the table, as if waiting their turn.

Both images illustrate certain faults with the Literacy Campaign, concerning issues that have been explored by the pedagogy theorist and literacy champion Paulo Freire in his *Pedagogy of the Oppressed* (1970). Reasoning within a Marxist conception of social change, Freire claims that in order for the oppressed to be liberated, one must first create the material circumstances that make this liberation possible. As applied to the Cuban Revolution, Fidel enabled the peasants to achieve a higher economic status with the Agrarian Reform (May 1959), which provided them with land to cultivate. Freire adds that after establishing the material basis for liberation from oppression, the oppressed need to become aware of the possibility of their liberation. This awareness or *conscientização* is achieved through literacy understood in the broad sense of the term, that is, not just the mechanics of reading and writing but the transmission of a certain emancipating worldview.

Fig. 3. A photograph of a volunteer teacher and students in the Literacy Campaign, which appeared in *In the Spirit of Wandering Teachers: Cuban Literacy Campaign, 1961/Con el espíritu de los maestros ambulantes: La campaña de alfabetización cubana, 1961*, ed. Alexandra Keeble, p. 35. Reprinted by permission of Ocean Press.

According to Freire, the pedagogy that creates in the oppressed the consciousness of liberation is not made *for* the oppressed, but *with* the oppressed, and such a pedagogy is based on the oppressed becoming aware of their agency: "The correct method for the revolutionary leadership to employ in the task of liberation is, therefore, not 'libertarian propaganda.' Nor can the leadership merely 'implant' in the oppressed a belief in freedom, thus thinking to win their trust. The correct method lies in dialogue. The conviction of the oppressed that they must fight for their liberation is not a gift bestowed by the revolutionary leadership, but the result of their own *conscientização*. . . . The oppressed . . . must reach this conviction as *subjects*, not as *objects*. They also must intervene critically in the situation which surrounds them and whose mark they bear; propaganda cannot achieve this" (49).

If we analyze the Literacy Campaign on the grounds set forth by Freire, its failures become clear. By representing peasants as passive objects in need of instruction, by including revolutionary propaganda through their primers, by employing a unidirectional method of teaching—the literacy workers appearing as the only agents of the campaign—instead of creating a *dialogue* with the oppressed, the Literacy Campaign emphasized the objective of spreading literacy in a wide sense, instead of its stated aim of emancipation of the peasants.[9]

In spite of its material basis, Freire articulates his views on literacy in a language showing affinity with a psychoanalytical interpretation, which the Literacy Campaign, with its attempt at mirror identification between teacher and student, also lends itself to. The Subject, as Lacan defines it, is constituted by a lack that needs to be filled with the desire of the Other (Lacan chapters 5, 6). According to Slavoj Zizek, an ideological fetish conceals the lack around which one's subject is constituted, which in fact can never be filled. Ideology provides a symbolic expression to the fact that only by projecting one's desire on the Other, by identifying with the Other, by wanting to be the Other, is one's lack partially satisfied (Zizek 45). In terms of the Cuban Revolution's Literacy Campaign, "the people" are the ideological fetish, the symbolic expression of the desire of the Other, a construct that eludes representation because it signifies a lack: "the people" are the Other of the bourgeois, whose desire for identification with a hypothetical working class can never be fully satisfied. As represented in the campaign, the volunteer teacher is the only subject, but in claiming that the volunteer teacher's efforts are devoted to teach "the people," it is understood that the teacher's principles will be instilled at the same time that "the people" become literate. By suggesting that ultimately the volunteer teacher's identity will be transformed by identifying with "the people," the leaders of the Revolution are expressing their own lack, their desire of the Other and finally their failed attempt to *be* the Other. The peasant student as an identity figure is the repository of the establishment's ideas, and as such it embodies the leaders' ambition to *become* "the people."

Returning to Che Guevara's speech quoted above ("Que la Universidad," Nuiry Sanchez): "in order to reach the people one needs to feel like the people" (12), and "one needs to paint oneself black, *mulatto*, the color of workers and peasants, one needs to go down to the people, one needs to vibrate with the people" ("Que la Universidad" 13). Guevara struggles to become the Other, but in the process of identifying with the Other the desire of the Other reverts to the desire of Guevara's own self, and of his own transformation. For Guevara, the process of total identity transformation seems to be easy enough, as the metaphor of painting oneself one color or the other reveals. With this image, Guevara reduces class differences to *color*, assuming that "the people," "the workers," are black. Such a reduction reveals that it is as impossible for a volunteer teacher to become a peasant as it is for a white person to "turn black" by simply painting his or her face black.

Following Zizek's theory, ideology is a field that is constituted by "floating signifiers" whose literal meaning is determined in relation to a chain of other signifiers that are all connected through what seems to be an all-encompassing signifier: "the multitude of 'floating signifiers,' of proto-ideological elements, is structured into a unified field through the intervention of a certain 'nodal point' (the Lacanian *point de capiton*) which 'quilts' them, stops their sliding and fixes their meaning" (87). Thus, in the Literacy Campaign, "the people" become a nodal point: the campaign is structured around the idea of "the people" as the objective of mobilizations and the ones whose living conditions provided material for the articulation of the campaign. At the level of the unconscious, "the people" also embody the object of desire sought by the campaign. As will be shown in the reading of *Maestra*, the chain of signifiers that is quilted by the nodal point of "the people" links the volunteer teacher and the peasant student, and this pair, as all other pairs that are quilted, bears an adversarial relationship as well as identification. The other pairs implied are "the people" versus the intellectual, country versus city, instruction versus ignorance, and revolutionary versus counterrevolutionary.

In practice, these dichotomies became blurred, as the attraction and rejection volunteer teachers felt toward peasant students came to be reflected in the identity of the New Man. This figure encapsulated the idealized characteristics of the peasants while it simultaneously implied their inferiority or lack, apparent in the need to improve their level of political commitment and "civilization." The Revolution promoted the transformation, in the words of Carlos Rangel, from "the noble savage to the good revolutionary." In my reading, the Literacy Campaign played a crucial role in this transformation. On the one hand, the peasants embodied the image of purity, simplicity, and selflessness of the "noble savage," before they became literate. On the other hand, the teachers represented the willingness to fight, commitment, and civilization. The "good revolutionary" emerged at the point when the encounter with the teacher "improved" the "noble savage" so that he or she would now resemble the guerrilla fighter. As Rangel puts it, "The guerrilla fighter must be like a saint of the revolution, somebody who is superior to the other men not only in personal worth and revolutionary conscience, but also in virtue and in compassion toward the oppressed. And those pure, ascetic revolutionaries would be supposedly capable, once they took power, to exercise it with equal virtue and devotion, and also to transmit their sense of altruism to the masses, until they succeeded in bringing about the 'new man'" (122).

In the process of building the new identity, both the volunteer teacher and the peasant student became pawns of the regime, as they were both urged to reconstitute their identities. However, one can presume that Literacy Campaign instructors as identity figures enjoyed more agency than pupils, for many of them truly believed in the value of revolutionary principles. This is not to say that peasant students were not happy to be taught, but they were not as liberated as they could have been, had their role in the Literacy Campaign been articulated differently, and the emphasis shifted away from forced indoctrination in favor of empowering the illiterate. My reading of *Maestra* illustrates the absence of the peasant students as subjects in the discourse of the campaign and analyzes the appearance of the new revolutionary.

## *Maestra* and the Journey to the Revolutionary Self

*Maestra* commences with the protagonist Vilma riding on a bus en route to the teacher training camp of Minas del Frío. The bus trip is the first of many trials Vilma endures, at the end of which she is transformed from a critical skeptic to a convinced revolutionary. The style of the first part of the book illustrates what Mikhail Bakhtin characterized as "hidden polemic," a dialogic style that integrates at least two voices: the voice representing the author's point of view, which is given prominence, and the voice of the Other, which is antagonized. In Bakhtin's words, "In a hidden polemic the author's discourse is directed toward its own referential object, as in any other discourse, but at the same time every statement about the object is constructed in such a way that, apart from its referential meaning, a polemical blow is struck at the other's discourse on the same theme, at the other's statement about the same object" (Bakhtin and Medvedev 107).

In the case of *Maestra*, this double voicing is created as Vilma internally debates opposing views of the revolutionary project. In an interesting twist, the voice that takes prominence in Vilma's interior monologue is the voice of the Other (the skeptical, the nonrevolutionary). But her voice is juxtaposed with that of fervent revolutionaries, presumably representing the author's point of view. In the dialogue with her fellow travelers Vilma's thoughts are systematically contradicted. For instance, if she reacts with shock to the thought of being transported in the back of a truck with other people, the person next to her remarks: "'Well, you'll have to go no matter how, little comrade. The Revolution does not count on luxury cars to take us places. The money that we invest belongs to the people and one has to avoid spending what is the product of their daily toil.' [To which Vilma responds internally by thinking] 'We'll have to put up with his preaching. This guy bothers me. I see no need for having to go in a truck like a log of wood if I can pay for a rental car'" (D. García 17).

At the beginning of the novel, Vilma's constant complaints about the hardships of the trip, her resistance to other people's opinions, and her self-centered behavior reveal what by revolutionary standards would be a bourgeois personality. This will change as the novel progresses. The character expresses a great deal of the concern and ideological confusion that must have been common in the early years of the Revolution, when the political climate was changing very rapidly. For instance, Vilma distrusts her traveling companions as supporters of Socialism, an ideology she vehemently resists. Her final coming to terms with the idea of Socialism pays literary tribute to the efforts of the Cuban regime in making people accept the recently proclaimed Socialist character of the Revolution.[10]

The journey to the Sierra represents a time of exposure to new ideas and identity transformation for Vilma. By the time she gets to the camp, many of her initial doubts and fears have been left behind, though some skepticism remains. After Vilma has been in the camp for a while, the narrative voice of the novel shifts, changing from the singular "I" ("yo") to the plural "we" ("nosotros"), thus indicating that Vilma is more integrated in the group and increasingly more accepting of the collective spirit of the Revolution. For instance, she muses: "When I remember my old confusion, I feel ridiculous. . . . When I am back and tell all my friends about this, they will say I have been brainwashed and that I am proselytizing. . . . However, *we* believe in the equality between men [*sic*] and in the strength of a people, because *we* have experienced it and have proven it day by day" (139, emphasis mine). From that moment, the two points of view of the narrative are reduced to the one that expresses Vilma's newfound identity. The traces of the Other—the counterrevolutionary, the skeptic—still operate in the text as an element of contrast, but Vilma progressively distances herself from it.

In contrast to the representation of revolutionary transformation as the product of the interchange between teacher and student so common to the official discourse of the campaign, Vilma's transformation in the novel is attributed to the influence of her colleagues, all of them convinced revolutionaries, and to the example provided by certain peasants. The peasants appear briefly in the novel and their role is reduced to emblems of either "backwardness," "purity," or "simplicity," always lacking in agency. For instance in the following image: "I will still keep in my mind, for a long time, the memory of those little shacks badly covered by a few branches of palm trees, of those faces with sad smiles, of those children in whose eyes one can see hunger as if looking through glass. . . . [It is] as if I saw again those hammocks full of patches, where five children slept. And I see that girl running in front of me. . . . She has lived five sad years, and she is rocking a bottle full of mud in her arms, and calling it 'my baby'. . . . I remember everything . . . . even that one bed in the house. That relic of a bed where, as the owner says with pride, Fidel slept once" (99).

As in this fragment, neither Vilma nor the other volunteers are seen interacting with the poor peasants in the course of the novel. Instead, Vilma describes her gaze on them: she literally sees through them. The description of the children appeals to the emotions of the reader: the poor children smile in spite of their misery, and their look is clear and honest, reflecting only hunger. The girl holds a bottle that is now filled with mud and that may have contained alcohol, stressing the dangers she is exposed to. This mud mirrors her life's misery, but the girl shows her innocence by rocking the bottle like a doll. The children's place of rest is a simple hammock, and the only bed the family had in the house was the one they offered to Fidel. The vision of the "backward" poor justifies the modernizing impact of the Literacy Campaign, and at the same time, in the midst of these shacks, the poor reveal their essentially well-disposed spirit. These images of frugality, generosity, and purity represent the figure of the peasant as a natural man who holds great potential for the Revolution. The peasants are but an emblem to illustrate that the New Man has his roots deep in the Cuban soil.

Two peasants in the novel deserve further scrutiny, as they appear as supporting characters. These are Asunción and her husband, Fermín, who have a little store in the camp where Vilma goes regularly to have coffee. The contrast between these two characters illustrates the importance of instruction in order for somebody to be considered not just literate, but a "good person" in official discourse. Asunción is the only one who is really given a voice, and she is agreeable to Vilma because she has begun to "understand" the truths of the revolutionary message, first through her simplicity and later through instruction. By contrast, her husband, Fermín, hardly appears on the scene. As the plot unfolds, one understands the reasons for such neglect: Fermín has betrayed the Revolution by having another store in town where he is making a profit on the cost of the merchandise. Though she is friends with Asunción, Vilma comes to understand why the Camp Service Corps expropriates Fermín's store. At that point, Fermín is virtually transformed into a despicable miser in Vilma's eyes, while Asunción gains in the wisdom of the Revolution. Vilma thinks to herself: "I have watched Fermín's face many times, while his shaky hands, full of greed, were counting the money. And I have noted how—while Asunción was doing her 'homework,' rummaging among her books with interest—Fermín's eyes were full of a contemptuous jealousy. Those eyes seemed to crush Asunción's young hands, which were writing at a slow pace, carefully, as if wanting to caress the white paper in admiration" (92). While Fermín represents the capitalist ills that the Revolution is eliminating, Asunción epitomizes purity and conscientiousness, an example of the noble peasant redeemed by revolutionary instruction.

In other instances in the novel, the idea of "the people" takes the abstract form of the symbols of the revolutionary nation. For instance, from its opening lines, the text of *Maestra* places the reader in a context that is full of references to various mythological sites of Cuban revolutionary history. The training camp for volunteer teachers is in Minas del Frío, the location of the first camp for instructors in the Literacy Campaign. On her way to Minas del Frío, Vilma passes by Yara, a landmark of revolutionary activity. The famous Grito de Yara, after the Demajagua rebellion (1868) marked the beginning of the independence movement against Spain. Oriente, the area that Vilma visits, had been hailed as the most revolutionary region in Cuba since those early independence struggles. By extension, the people who lived in Sierra Maestra were considered inherently revolutionary. It is thus paradoxical that the 1959 Revolution first claimed the Sierra Maestra as the most loyal area to the regime and then crushed any attempt at rebellion in the area. As the first contingent of the Literacy Campaign sought to eradicate pockets of rebellion left in the Sierra, the Sierra Maestra (*maestra* means "master," in the sense of "teacher") was then asked to honor its name, since the mountains that had once formed revolutionaries had become the site of instruction of illiterate people as well as the place where skeptics such as Vilma realized their mission as true revolutionaries.

Similarly, the peasants' tendency toward good revolutionary behavior is represented in the abundant references to natural elements associated with the values of the Revolution. A complex metaphor is thus created, involving the Cuban nation, its nature, and the ideological motifs of the Revolution, where the Revolution appears as "natural" in the historical progression and current state of the Cuban nation. For instance, Vilma describes the sunset in highly emotional terms: "The strong sun of Cuba makes up its mind to fight. It is a long agony of dawn in our fields. The sun bleeds itself to death over leaves, stones, rivers. . . . Its already dry blood twists itself into the tree trunks, and into the roots that take their gnarled fingers out of the soil. Somebody taps on my shoulder. . . . 'It is Cuba' an elderly voice says at my back, a voice cracked by age. . . . The same old Cuba . . . but this time truly ours, for the first time in history" (16). The sunset becomes loaded with meaning, when the sun, its intensity symbolizing the nation of Cuba, shows its determination to fight until the end: the sunset is a metaphor for a process that has been repeated throughout the history of Cuba, the struggle for independence. Nature in Cuba is represented as a long-suffering fighter, oblivious to the amount of blood he has shed. Cuba, or the Cuban soil, has suffered so much that the gnarled roots of her trees are red with blood. By metonymic association with this nature, "the people," and especially the peasants who are in contact with this nature, are represented as fighters. The entire history of Cuba is metaphorized in the natural phenomenon of the sunset, with a sun that struggles to continue to shine, just as Cuba had fought to free itself of foreign powers. Thus Cuba is represented as revolutionary *by nature.*[11]

At the same time, in the fragment just quoted, the voice of history—an elderly man—makes it clear that although Cuba is still inherently revolutionary, it is now in the possession of "the people," which means that "the people's" rebellious attitude is to be channeled through the struggles defined as legitimate by the Revolution. As the reader learns later in the text, the sun *is* vanquished in the sunset, and the essence of Cuba as a rebellious spirit is subdued. Once the Revolution has been established, paradoxically, rebellious Cuba is laid to rest. This is shown in the text when the light of the sun, conventionally associated with the masculine, strength, or a combative temperament, is substituted by the light of the moon, traditionally associated with the feminine, the mild, or the conciliatory; the moon's light softens the contours of the objects it illuminates. When the sun goes down, the teachers are not left in the dark: the moon emerges, big, round, and yellow, to guide the teachers in their long walk toward the camp (24).

The paradox that the Sierra Maestra teaches, that Cuban nature can represent the proverbial Cuban rebelliousness and at the same time the discipline and commitment necessary to the Revolution, is something that Vilma comes to understand after she has been fully immersed in camp life. In that sense, the trip seems to be a journey toward the depths of the self, since a revolutionary is understood as someone who has come to terms with what she or he already is *in essence.* The idea of nature being the scenario of revelation and instruction through hardship is recurrent in other texts on the experiences of revolutionaries. Juan Duchesne, writing on Che Guevara's *Pasajes de la guerra revolucionaria* (*Episodes of the Revolutionary War*), and Omar Cabezas's *La montaña es algo más que una inmensa estepa verde* (1982) (*Fire from the Mountain: The Making of a Sandinista*) (1985) refers to this principle of self-improvement through sacrifice as *askesis*; the mountain forms the New Man through a spiritual and physical struggle that forces him to strengthen his moral basis. One can argue that in the case of Cuba, the idea can be traced to José Martí, often hailed as the father of Cuban patriotism: Martí also promoted sacrifice, in a very physical sense, as an essential element of the patriotic spirit. What is more, he insisted on the renunciation of all material comfort culminating in total disembodiment, or the forsaking of one's physical needs and pleasures, as the only way to fight for the land: "One goes to serve the Fatherland naked, for the wind to take one's flesh, and the fierce animals to drink from [the marrow of] one's bone, so that there will be no remnant of the sacrifice, [a sacrifice] more willingly [made] than the light that guides and encourages its assassins [is carried]" (Martí, quoted in Le Riverend 46).

Given the historic prominence of this symbolism, it should not be surprising that Vilma's identity transformation culminates in the climbing of El Turquino, the highest mountain peak in the Sierra Maestra. During the guerrilla war, Fidel and the guerrillas climbed it, claimed it as part of their territory, and considered it their headquarters. According to legend, the climb took only one day—an unbelievably short time—and when they got to the top Fidel shouted, "We have won the war!" (Quirk 127). A plaque and a bust of Martí commemorating the feat of the guerrillas were placed at the top of the mountain, and an ascent of the peak was used as a test of endurance and degree of revolutionary commitment. The novel represents three different ascents, as they were common in teacher training camps. Vilma emerges "victorious" after these ascents, for she has fought tiredness and the excruciating pain of a strained ankle. The exhausting walk is repeatedly presented in the text as an allegory for revolutionary effort, besides literally being the proof of the instructors' endurance: "The path is long, very long. The hill is difficult to climb. Don't try to rush too much. The important thing is to get there. In the steepest stretches you will find roots you will be able to hold on to, in order to climb more safely. When you do that, you must check that the root is firmly attached, so firmly that it will support the weight of the body. . . . The Turquino is our mission because our Socialist Revolution needs us, because the future of our country depends on us, on our resistance and our morale" (122). The metaphor of a long walk as the revolutionary path to a better future recalls Che Guevara's words in "Socialism and Man in Cuba" (1965), where his cautions about time and the amount of effort needed in the Revolution were reiterated, although there was hope of a new era at the end of the path: "The Revolution is made by men [*sic*], but men must forge their revolutionary spirit day by day. Thus we march on. . . . The road is long and in part unknown. We know our limitations. We will create the man of the twenty-first century—we, ourselves" (Guevara, "Socialism" 16–17).

In the novel's passage, the ascending road of the Revolution is also long and arduous, and—as in Guevara's speech—the climbers are warned that they should not go too fast; they can hold on to certain roots that may help them on the way, but they have to make sure that these roots are strong, that is, revolutionaries should not hold on to false hopes. The success of the Revolution relies on their endurance, a military principle based on the notion of existence as struggle. Climbing the Turquino is a test of the teachers' ability to fight: it is no wonder that, once they reach the peak, they shout "¡Vencimos el Turquino!" ("We vanquished the Turquino!") (134).

The ritual ascent to the peak brings out an element that does not seem important in the narrative, the fact that Vilma is a woman. Official discourse did not explicitly acknowledge the overwhelmingly feminine participation in the campaign, perhaps because of the need to de-emphasize difference in favor of unity. As Luisa Campuzano well documents, the rhetorical construction of the campaign was based on class consciousness, and it took traditional gender roles for granted (Campuzano, "Cuba 1961" 55). But by getting used to the hard conditions of the countryside and the ritual ascension to the peak, Vilma illustrates "the physical transformation, the adaptation to the environment, . . . the triumph, in a word, of that female body that had always been considered weak . . . and now it is making itself strong, resilient, powerful" (Campuzano, "Cuba 1961" 55). In other words, Vilma embodies to the full extent of the word the regime's inherent contradiction between silence with respect to gender and the fact that women, especially their bodies, were defined by the masculine norm of the Revolution that expected women to comply with the demands of hard physical work.

Vilma returns from her trip in the same third-class train that she took on her way to the training camp. The timeline of the novel is thus circular, but at the end the protagonist has gained wisdom and maturity. In her last words in the novel, "Now . . . I already know my path" (148), Vilma asserts her newfound revolutionary identity, which she has acquired from reflecting on revolutionary principles and from the trials and tribulations in the literacy camp. The fact that Vilma shared the usually male-dominated public space for a few months is mitigated by her going back to where she came from at the end of the novel. As Campuzano notes, it is also significant that Daura Olema García, an unusual female presence among mostly male writers, never wrote another novel, despite having received the Casa de las Américas Prize. In fact, the novel was coolly received, and one critic commented that this prize was "un reportaje de escasa calidad literaria" ("an account of scarce literary quality") among the texts considered for the prize (López Valdizón 55).

In this chapter I have sought to show the contradictions between the stated goals of the Literacy Campaign, that is, to restore dignity to "the people" through the teaching of reading and writing, and one of the implicit aims of the same campaign, namely to transform them into docile citizens. Although the Literacy Campaign did succeed in radically reducing illiteracy in Cuba, it did so at the cost of providing a space for its citizenry at the margins of the gigantic pedagogic machine of the state. Through the inclusion of revolutionary ideology in basic primers, the Literacy Campaign attempted to assimilate the identity of the new readers into that of the new revolutionaries. In this process, "the people" were objectified, to the point that they are almost completely absent from the speeches in the campaign.

The objectification of the peasants also occurs in the novel studied here, to the extent that their full development as characters depends exclusively on their degree of revolutionary education. The fact that there is a certain uneasiness in the representation of the peasants is noticeable in that they are displaced by a representation of nature in Cuba, with which they are presumed to have a special connection. It is through these representations of nature that "the people" mutedly speak. When Vilma achieves the final stages of her transformation, the issue of her gender suddenly appears, as *nature that has been trained.* Thus, despite her weak female body and a leg injury, Vilma succeeds in climbing the Turquino peak.

It is useful to look at other representations of the campaign to find a genuine exchange between the literacy worker and the peasant, and perhaps also to encounter peasants who play a more active role. In the next section I compare and contrast *Maestra* to other accounts of the Literacy Campaign.

## Toward a Fair Hearing of the Peasant Students' Voice

Given the degree of enthusiasm that this campaign inspired and the fact that it became one of the major successes of the Revolution, it is not surprising that fictional and nonfictional texts on the period proliferated in the following years. Those testimonial and fictional texts written soon after the events of the campaign generally offered a representation of the peasant students and the literacy workers that was as skewed as the idealized version found in the official discourse. It was only years later that the contradictions between the stated liberatory goals of the campaign and the rhetoric in which it was coached were seemingly resolved.

Two short stories published shortly after the campaign exhibit features that are notably similar to *Maestra*: José Rodríguez Feo's "Impresiones de un alfabetizador" (Impressions of a literacy teacher) and Matilde Manzano's "Apuntes de una alfabetizadora" (Notes from a literacy teacher). The former consists mainly of a monologic account of the literacy teacher's impressions of the peasants, in which the peasant students appear as characters, or rather, examples to prove points about the Revolution. In "Impresiones de un alfabetizador," the peasants supposedly are living proof of the injustice of the pre-Revolution, but also of country people's natural inclination to accept the revolutionary message. The literacy worker actually expresses more concern about what the peasants need to learn in terms of hygiene and general improvements in lifestyle than about their lack of education, and he sees his role more as "civilizing" than teaching the ABCs. As the protagonist often expresses incomprehension of or resistance to their behavior, his monologue contributes only to distance the narrator from the peasants. There is thus no symbolic exchange of identity between the literacy worker and the student, despite the observations that the volunteer teacher makes: "They were all Cuban, those who still suffered the abandonment and ignominy in which their ancestors lived for centuries, the ancestors who were like them victims of the exploitation and cruelty of landowners. Whoever went to teach literacy to the Cuban countryside was able to encounter the monster that our countryside had turned into. We, the volunteers of the urban brigades, would now suffer the scarcity and the sadness of the exploited. . . . We were going to see the horror and the poverty that justify once, a thousand times, all the laws of our glorious Socialist Revolution. . . . I understood then for the first time what Marx said, that ideas that are not proven in practice are false" (Rodríguez Feo 54). The impression that the peasants make on the literacy worker remains at the *conceptual* level. It is in a sense a self-serving situation, for the peasant provides proof to the literacy worker of what he wanted to believe. Steeped in the rhetoric of modernization, the protagonist has no regard for the peasants' contributions to the Revolution *on their own terms*. He sees them only as remnants of the past that need to be transformed. In fact, the narrator gives advice on how best to convince the peasants to change their ways and underscores that the peasants' almost total lack of exposure to any ideologies makes them the most suitable recipients of a revolutionary consciousness (Rodríguez Feo 57).

The autobiographical account of Matilde Manzano offers the perspective of the Literacy Campaign's work in urban areas. Still, the narrator experiences quite a shock when she witnesses the humble houses of the peasants and their lack of knowledge. The objectification of the peasants is constant in the text, with detailed descriptions of their appearance and specific comments on the effects of living in the country. For instance, "That lady must have been very pretty, I think, while she writes her uneven lines. Now she is all burnt by the sun, her hair looks as if it had been scorched, her teeth are full of cavities" (93). As the peasant students are learning to read, the qualities underscored are their enthusiasm, innocence, and "backwardness." Along with all the qualities of the "noble savage," the peasant students are depicted as children.

The final metaphor that the narrator in Manzano's text proposes to describe the campaign illustrates the one-sidedness of the process: " . . . I feel like we have all made a coal oven together. We started preparing the tinder. . . . We carefully set the tinder on fire. We had to arm ourselves with patience, blow at times to rekindle the flames, endure the smoke, the itchiness and even the tears in our eyes, but finally [the flame] burned strongly and accomplished its objective, leaving behind the warm embers of the Follow-up Plan" (Manzano 17). In agreement with the pedagogical character of the campaign, the passage uses a metaphor that peasants can understand. However, in the description of the energy expended and the privations that they suffered, there is only one group with agency: the volunteer teachers. The peasant students are the object, the tinder that is being kindled, and the force of the revolutionary rhetoric is underscored by the fire lit in the peasants. But the initial objectives of liberating the peasants through literacy, in order to make them subjects, are lost in the metaphor, as they were lost in the campaign.

Later accounts of the campaign have featured more balanced testimonials of the role of the peasant students and their experiences. For instance, the very popular movie *El brigadista* (1977) (the title refers to the member of a brigade or group of volunteer workers, in this case teachers) directed by Octavio Cortázar and Luis Rogelio Nogueras, is set in a small village in the Ciénaga de Zapata, and it narrates the story of the campaign from the peasant's point of view. The movie bears witness to the encounter of different figures and how they learned from each other. The volunteer teacher is a young man who learns a great deal from the peasants through his attachment to a town leader, an older man who does not know how to read. In *El brigadista*, identity transformation takes place both in the case of the volunteer teacher and the peasant student as each helps the other: the young city man overcomes his fear of natural elements and the older man is able to sign public documents. Considering that the movie dates from 1977, sixteen years after the campaign, one can speculate that memory bridges many of the gaps that seem unbridgeable when events are close to the time of telling them.

Araceli Aguililla's *Por llanos y montañas* (1978) (Through valleys and mountains) is also noteworthy. It features a female protagonist who, in comparison to the volunteer teacher in *Maestra,* has the attributes of her gender, even if these are defined in a conventional way. In this novel, Raquel, a volunteer teacher, falls in love with Ambrosio, a rough peasant, who is learning to read. Ambrosio is somehow not gentrified by instruction but constantly characterized as a brute, with an animalistic demeanor. Nevertheless, the meeting between the world of the country and the city is symbolized by the happy consummation of their love at the end. The conventional femininity of the protagonist is used to signify the refinement that volunteer teachers brought to the countryside, and the stereotypical masculinity of the student embodies the strength and "primitiveness" of the peasants. This novel turns out to be an interesting use of gender discourse serving the symbolic articulation of the Campaign.

In this chapter I have pointed out some discrepancies between one of the stated goals of the Literacy Campaign, that is, to promote a symbolic exchange between teachers and students, and what actually happened or how the objectives of the campaign were actually articulated. Rather than acknowledging the influence of the peasants and allowing their contributions to the discourse of the nascent revolutionary nation, the campaign relied on preconceived notions of ignorant but innocent *guajiros,* a derogatory way of referring to the peasants, and interpreted those preconceptions as evidence of the need to submit to the modernizing influence of the Revolution. Though conditions in the Cuban countryside were ripe for improvement, these negative representations of the peasants and the silencing of their voices in the earliest years of the Revolution caused Cuban culture after 1959 to be distinctively urban based, with only idealistic or mythical representations of the Sierra as the site of historical Cuban rebelliousness. It was only years later, with the valorization of folklore, that new conceptions of Cuban peasant culture would enter official discourse.

# Body versus Mind

## An Intellectual's Memoirs Expose His Negative Image

From the exhilaration of the early years through the international condemnation in response to the Padilla case, up to the most recent statements about jailed dissidents, the debate concerning conditions for Cuban intellectuals has polarized international support of the Cuban Revolution. Further, the status of intellectuals in Cuba has had a profound impact on the development of Latin American literature, as the Revolution has provoked numerous discussions concerning escapist versus committed literature, literature of the Boom versus *testimonio*, and the role of intellectuals as elites or as activists. Edmundo Desnoes's *Memorias del subdesarrollo* (1965) (literally, Memories of underdevelopment but published in English as *Inconsolable Memories*, and henceforth referred to as *Memorias*)[1] is a crucial text when revisiting these debates, as it tackles many of the issues that were central to these discussions and it was published at the time that the intellectual policy of the Revolution was being defined. The protagonist of this novel displays a degree of ambivalence toward revolutionary discourse that many Cuban writers struggled to overcome, and to a large extent his critical attitude is an antecedent of the events of the Padilla case and its aftermath. After the post-1971 crackdown on culture, the ambivalence and criticism of *Memorias* would be far more difficult to find in Cuban letters in the island.

In the years immediately preceding the publication of *Memorias* the regime took some steps that would change the field of Cuban culture dramatically. To begin, the revolutionary leaders strived to revive a long dormant political conscience among intellectuals. According to Rafael Rojas, a renowned Cuban writer currently living in Mexico, a kind of "nihilistic attitude" regarding politics had prevailed among Cuban intellectuals since the colonial period. In the prerevolutionary era, from the Orígenes project (1944–56) to the poetry of Eliseo Diego and Fina García Marruz, writers focused on creating a sense of national time through intimate memories, instead of through history (Rojas 83). In particular, the generation of the 1950s, with the protagonist roles played by Virgilio Piñera and José Rodríguez Feo, who together headed the journal *Ciclón*, displayed near contempt

for politics. Piñera himself explained the apoliticism of this generation, calling the literature they produced "abstracted" and arguing that in the midst of
frustrations with the politics of the time, writers took refuge in "Literature,
the Beautiful, [and] the Noble" (Piñera, "Notas" 2).[2]

Many of the writers who came of age with the Revolution, and of those
who had been in the cultural scene long before, shared the same spirit that
nurtured *Ciclón*, for which "politics itself and even Cuban history were vul-
gar and dirty territories that should not contaminate 'the acts of the high
spirit'" (Rojas 85). In addition, post–Second World War European avant-
garde aesthetics would direct artists' focus toward formal experimentation,
rather than political content in the strict sense. Writers and intellectuals
such as Guillermo Cabrera Infante, Severo Sarduy, Heberto Padilla, Roberto
Fernández Retamar, Pablo Armando Fernández, Lisandro Otero, Edmundo
Desnoes, Ambrosio Fornet, and César López, to concur with Rojas's list, received both the influences of apoliticism and experimentation and struggled
in the face of the demands that the new regime would gradually impose. The
Revolution called writers to forge a "new conscience" and a "new expression" that would use some of the elements of Cuban tradition but would
constitute, as José Antonio Portuondo called it, "a negation of the previous
negativity" (Portuondo, *Itinerario* 12). The writer had to offer constructive
criticism and positive reinforcement of the Revolution rather than being a
critical conscience of his time and providing alternative models of reality.

After the ebullience and enthusiasm of the first months of the Revolution
came the founding of the various institutions that harnessed its creative potential. The Instituto Cubano de Artes e Industria Cinematográficos (ICAIC,
Cuban Institute of Film Arts and Industry or Cuban Film Institute) was the
first, in 1959, followed by Casa de las Américas in 1960, and in 1961 the Unión
Nacional de Escritores y Artistas Cubanos (UNEAC, the National Union
of Cuban Writers and Artists). March 1959 also saw the creation of the Imprenta Nacional, or the National Press, which aimed to stimulate the production of literature and science among Cubans. According to Luis Suardíaz, the
little private publishing houses that coexisted with the Imprenta Nacional
gradually became reduced to producing private greeting cards and "Sweet
Fifteen announcements" (Suardíaz, in an interview quoted by Smorkaloff
122); they eventually closed down, with the exception of La Tertulia and El
Puente, two of the small publishing houses that managed to survive until
1965 and published many of the young writers (Casal, "Literature" 450). In
1968, all private industry in publishing became nationalized under the institution of the Imprenta Nacional, whose goal was to make the book reach
as wide a readership as possible, and to give priority to texts that directed

readers in the right direction, that is, books on Socialist theory, or classics of international and Latin American literature by writers who directly or indirectly supported the Revolution.

From the time of the Literacy Campaign in 1961, "education and culture, literacy and literary production went hand in hand" (Smorkaloff 124). The first massive job of the Imprenta Nacional was the production of primers for the Literacy Campaign. In the hands of the Imprenta Nacional, the task of publishing infused literature and culture with a functionality that was unseen before in Cuba: everything that was published needed to "make readers think" and possibly lead them to write, thus broadening the reach of cultural products and the scope of the producers of culture. Such a strong emphasis on pedagogy yielded the many books for children edited by the Imprenta Nacional in its earliest years. According to Smorkaloff, between 1959 and 1962 there were hardly any new publications, with the exception of a few writers who concentrated on publishing "what they had inside their desk drawers" (Suardíaz, quoted by Smorkaloff 139). Shortly after the literacy primers came the famous edition of one hundred thousand copies of Cervantes's *Don Quijote* followed by the publishing of Latin American classics by Neruda, Vallejo, and Rubén Darío.

In 1962, the Imprenta Nacional gave way to the Editora Nacional, which decentralized the production process of books, if not the decision on which books would be published. The Editora Nacional emphasized youth and children's literature. Additionally, Edición Revolucionaria was founded in 1965 and focused on textbooks, of which there had been a severe shortage since the beginning of the Revolution, introducing the cost-saving technique of publishing what were essentially photocopies of books. UNEAC, which founded a publishing house called Unión, and Casa de las Américas worked within the Editora Nacional as relatively independent publishers until the creation of the Instituto Cubano del Libro, in 1967, which recentralized all processes related to book production. In that same year Fidel declared that, since it would not be possible for Cuba to publish books copyrighted in foreign countries, international copyright laws would not be observed, and the same would have to apply to Cuban books.

Because *Memorias* was published in 1965, it did not bear witness to abolition of copyright, or to other significant moments such as the extension of the publishing process to rural venues such as the massive Combinado Poligráfico Juan Marinello in Guantánamo, which was created in 1977 (Smorkaloff 181). But the text certainly cannot have escaped the influence of the new concept of culture and literature that the regime had introduced. *Memorias* is the fictional diary of Malabre, a character who embarks on a search for his own identity about three years after the beginning of the 1959 Cuban Revolution. At a moment of great social and economic changes, when the institutional discourse of the Revolution advocated a new Cuba and a "new man," this novel depicts a man who turns inward to determine whether he can identify with revolutionary ideals. *Memorias* is written in the style of the confessional novel, in which the protagonist strives to get in touch with his "true" self by putting together the fragments of his present life and reconstructing his past through memory. As the structures of prerevolutionary Cuba crumble and his family and friends have left, Malabre attempts to recover a sense of order in the illusion of a unified self. However, the character only becomes more isolated and confused, and the imminent Missile Crisis provokes a sense of fear and hopelessness that make him feel paralyzed. In his inability to incarnate the intellectual who can engage in combat, Malabre and his diary are a controversial counterpart to Che Guevara's model in *Episodes of the Revolutionary War* (1968), and if the latter author is the epitome of the "new man," Malabre provides the negative of that image.

Michel Foucault's concept of the author as the persona of the writer constructed by his writings and the reception of his texts is useful for a reading of *Memorias*. According to Foucault, "The author's name manifests the appearance of a certain discursive set and indicates the status of this discourse within a society and a culture" ("Author" 107). This discursive set and its status, which Foucault generically calls "the author function," is "only a projection . . . of the operations that we force texts to undergo, the connections we make, the traits that we establish as pertinent, the continuities that we recognize, or the exclusions that we practice" (110). In the case of the Cuban Revolution, the context of the events that were happening played a crucial role in producing a certain image of Desnoes as an author, mainly because, as Román de la Campa has claimed, the criticism of the literature of this period is tied to a sense of referentiality, or a strong connection to the contemporary reality of the text ("Novela/Texto" 1041). In addition, Desnoes has fed the impulse of critics to read his works in the context of his life by declaring that he writes about himself and that he essentially has written the same novel over and over (Desnoes, "America Revisited" 18). In synthesis, Desnoes is the paradigmatic case of an author who has actively worked on "the author function of Desnoes," or tried to have a hand in the way he is interpreted, and for this he can be taken as an example of the anxiety and confusion that writers in the Revolution have undergone as they seek validation for their work. Before examining Desnoes's authorial function, one needs to remember the circumstances and the debates that shaped his persona.

The Young Revolution in Its Most Active Years

The centralization of publishing in the early years of the Revolution tried unsuccessfully to resolve a tension between the belief in the excellence of canonical works of literature and the conviction that the Revolution had to make literature available, quite literally, to the masses, thus making pedagogical texts a priority. Not surprisingly, publishers focused mostly on textbooks and youth literature rather than on more "complex" literary classics. It was thought that the rules of publishing had changed in favor of writers, as they were no longer at the mercy of a few isolated publishing houses that made authors carry most of the costly weight of book production. But this freedom of access came at the cost of considerably limiting what authors published and what people got to read. To some extent, until 1967, editions by Unión and Casa de las Américas compensated for the lack of original and contemporary Cuban texts published in other venues, but the scarce variety in printed materials had a deep impact in the writing scene.

Writers' dependency on the state was compounded by uncertainty about unwritten rules on the limits of expression. As Roberto Fernández Retamar put it, "How could we survive if counterrevolutionaries destroyed the revolution?" (quoted in Dopico 137). Since the Revolution was believed to be under siege in its early years, self-censorship became a necessity. What is more, long-standing preconceptions of writers as effeminate and unproductive remained strong after 1959, culminating with the UMAP (Unidades Militares de Ayuda a la Producción, Military Units to Aid Production). Aimed at rehabilitating "antisocial elements" (that is, people who did not work, and homosexuals), the UMAP affected writers and artists deeply, as many were sent to these camps (Casal, "Literature" 459).

The much regretted closing of the literary supplement of *Revolución*, *Lunes de Revolución*, has been chronicled often, and the relevance of this journal to the Cuban and Latin American contexts is unquestionable.[3] The journal was edited by Carlos Franqui, Guillermo Cabrera Infante, and Pablo Armando Fernández, and included many prominent young writers as collaborators. Its thirteen issues became a forum for publication and discussion of writers, intellectuals, artists, and essayists from Cuba, Latin America, and many other countries of the world. Each edition of the supplement sold more than two hundred thousand copies and enjoyed the privilege of accompanying one of the official periodicals of the former June 26 Movement. According to Pío Serrano, who has recounted the events of the first years of the Revolution, the closing of *Lunes* was due to the confrontation of two groups of writers: the *Lunes* team and the writers of the establishment (Serrano 263–64). The *Lunes* team supported the Revolution but absorbed the apolitical members of the contributors to the former *Orígenes* and *Ciclón* (Virgilio Piñera and José Rodríguez Feo among them) and espoused a vision of the intellectual as a *provocateur* and a critic. Although they did not declare a specific political allegiance, the writers of *Lunes* did show revolutionary commitment by dedicating numerous issues to the literature and art of third world countries, publishing writings from the Left hitherto unknown in Cuba, and frontally opposing cultural colonization by the United States.

Before describing the confrontation between the two groups of intellectuals, it would be helpful to examine another piece of the conflict that exploded in 1961: the banning of the twenty-three-minute documentary *PM*, by Sabá Cabrera Infante and Orlando Jiménez Leal, which showed people dancing and drinking in what seemed to be the Playa de Marianao area of Havana. The film was declared "libertine" and obscene by the Head of the Revising Commission of the ICAIC, Alfredo Guevara, and other leaders, on the grounds that it portrayed negative images of the people partying at night rather than working for the Revolution.[4] A long debate followed in Casa de las Américas where Mirta Aguirre, another hard-line member of the administration and a movie critic of the journal *Hoy*, accused the intellectuals supporting the short movie of "Budapestismo," in reference to the counterrevolution in Hungary. At issue, as has been mentioned repeatedly, was not just the content of the documentary, but the fact that it had been made with a low budget and that as an independent movie it challenged the authority of the ICAIC (Antón Arrufat's intervention in "Literatura en los 60"). The controversy represented, once again, a struggle to find a place in the framework of what had been officially defined as legitimate and revolutionary.

The protests caused by the banning of *PM* motivated the convocation of a series of meetings between cultural leaders, writers, and intellectuals in the National Library in June 1961. The *Lunes* team, which had opposed the banning of the documentary, was accused of being divisive and not sufficiently committed to the revolutionary mission (Serrano 263). Alfredo Guevara, a long-time president of the ICAIC, and Edith García Buchaca, a high-ranking functionary of the Consejo Nacional de Cultura, advocated a form of politicized art, while the *Lunes* team was trying to ward off the threat of Socialist realism. The meetings yielded the definitive banning of *PM* and the closing of *Lunes*, which would be substituted by *Unión* and *La Gaceta de Cuba* as journals published by the soon-to-be-created Unión Nacional de Escritores y Artistas de Cuba. Fidel's speeches at these June meetings and later at the first congress of the UNEAC deserve close scrutiny.

In his "Words to the Intellectuals" speech, Fidel began with a gesture that set him apart from his audience: he asserted that he was not an intellectual and then referred to himself during the speech as "we the revolutionaries," thus establishing a chasm between those who did the work of the Revolution and those historically considered "dilettante," as was the case with intellectuals. He then declared his intention to extend to the field of culture the Revolution that had already occurred in Cuban society and economy. He aimed at creating a strong feeling that Cuban culture was experiencing a new beginning, in a Revolution that had been brought about in record time, and with leaders who were still learning and improvising. At the same time, the newness of the Revolution imposed on writers and artists a sense of urgency to ready themselves for the new tasks: as Roberto Fernández Retamar wrote in 1967, "It is true that we intellectuals had to make up for lost time . . . and become intellectuals *of* the Revolution *in* the Revolution" (Fernández Retamar, "Hacia" 10) (emphasis in the original). But rather than looking at the past and lamenting their lack of contribution as guerrilla fighters, intellectuals needed to learn mechanisms to come to terms with their being *behind*, as a way of "relieving the backwardness of their education as intellectuals and revolutionaries" (Fernández Retamar 10). Fidel's famous speech constituted intellectuals as revolutionaries and highlighted the gap between their enthusiasm and the long path toward becoming genuinely committed.

The beginning of "Words to the Intellectuals" displays a conciliatory tone designed to put its very agitated audience at ease. Fidel declared that it was possible that some honest people were not revolutionary, and that some excellent writers were not revolutionary. But as he invoked constructs such as "the people" and "the Revolution," groups in which he included himself but whose source of agency was diffuse, it became clear that "good" writers and "honest" people were synonymous with revolutionaries, as Fidel stated that "it is from this point of view [the Revolution] that we analyze the good, the useful and the beautiful of every action" (Castro, Baxandall 274). Good "values," good morals, thus became associated with what was approved by the Revolution, something that writers were part of and at the same time judged by. If the Revolution had the right to incorporate all honest people and writers in its mission, it was implied that those who remained "outside," those who were not what Fidel described as "us" or part of "this Revolution," were banished as somehow morally objectionable and therefore unworthy of the Revolution's benefits. As Juan Carlos Quintero Herencia has expressed it, this speech draws a sort of "topography of the Revolution," with its inside and outside, and feeds authors' anxieties to "position themselves" within this topography (Fulguración 348–49). At the same time, questions remained about how writers would show their allegiance, whether through explicit declaration, their writing, or their collaboration with revolutionary tasks.

Fidel's "Words to the Intellectuals" also fomented a sense of bad conscience in those who had doubts about how the Revolution was going to establish its authority in the realm of culture. For the revolutionary leader, those who doubted were the ones who wavered in their revolutionary convictions, thus also causing suspicion as to whether they were genuinely "inside" the Revolution. The idea of doubt as lack of faith, and Fidel's liberal use of Christian rhetoric throughout this discourse invited self-justification, an obligation to repent, a wish to commit; these attitudes were common during the controversies of those years, and the literature of the period bore witness to those same anxieties. As Roberto González Echevarría ("Biografía") and others have noted, confessional narratives held a privileged place in the literary production of the Revolution, creating a need to exorcise one's past as an "unbeliever" and responding to the famous dictum by Che Guevara in 1965: "The fault of many of our artists and intellectuals lies in their original sin: they are not truly revolutionaries" (Guevara, "Socialism" 3).

As Fidel emphasized that the duty of the writers and intellectuals was to "educate and ideologically instruct the people," or "provide for their cultural needs," the Cuban leader unveiled the master plan of the cultural revolution in Cuba: the proletarianization of culture. As noted above, the Imprenta Nacional, followed by the different ventures of the Editora Nacional, and later the Instituto del Libro had all aimed at producing a type of literature that would be understandable and educational for the great majority of Cubans, thus enabling the masses to become writers themselves. Fidel hypostasized "the Cuban people" to mean the most deprived sectors of society, "the oppressed and exploited," and declared that the goal of cultural institutions should be to educate the marginal sectors. To some extent, the urban culture of the journals and periodicals of that era, the books edited by Casa de las Américas, Unión, and others, represented but a small fraction of the cultural products of the Revolution, some of which were created on the sidelines of the leaders' grand project. While the literary journal *Unión* would publish educational articles such as Desnoes's "La educación del gusto popular" (The education of the people's taste) on how to teach "the people" to appreciate painting, for instance, a great deal of material published in the above-mentioned periodicals during the period did not respond to educational demands. This brings one to the issue of the gap between the ways that the cultural intelligentsia was defining culture in essays published in those years and the actual cultural production at the time. The first decade of the Revolution witnessed the manifestation of a double discourse between public commitment in essayistic texts and individual positions in literature.

Whether or not writers and artists heeded the call of institutional discourse to submit to the standards and needs of "the people," creators could not ignore mounting pressures to radically transform the notion of culture. Not surprisingly, foreign writers exercised that pressure particularly strongly, as they nourished utopian images of the Revolution. As the Salvadorean poet Roque Dalton, a firm supporter of the regime expressed it, "Here the Revolution . . . has suggested 'a social bath' for writers, or the immersion in work and life" (quoted in Pereira 14). Revolutionary leaders established the priority of manual versus intellectual tasks, stressing that writing, art, or philosophy should be connected to "life," and the last was understood as what took place at workshops, factories, or rural workers' cooperatives. The emphasis was placed on "material" products of culture, rather than on "intellectual" reflection on culture. This emphasis was made clear in Ezequiel Martínez Estrada's celebrated metaphor: "We intellectuals should resign ourselves to being practical and build first, together with the rest of the citizens, the foundation and walls of a future temple that starts as a workshop, a farm, a rural cooperative, and a school today. For now, we should not think of putting a dome on it or embellishing it with paintings and sculptures, with music and dance. And we should offer to give not just the books but the sacred substance with which they are written, so that in case of an emergency somebody may make spice sacks with their pages and rifle handles with their covers" (Martínez Estrada, "Por una alta cultura" [In Praise of High Culture] 73).

As the last line of the quotation indicates, the dire needs of food and defense assumed such a central role in the Revolution that "culture" had to be literally sacrificed in their favor, and intellectuals had to be divested of their status as members of a lettered class group. It was suggested that the intellectual should not resist having the same social status as "un *machetero*" (Pereira 15). The threat of these directives against intellectuals' conceptions of themselves and their desire to preserve their due recognition may have motivated the bitter disputes of those years, as well as the struggle to secure a place among those who were considered *inside* the Revolution. This idea of losing one's status as an intellectual is also what Malabre, the protagonist in *Memorias,* resists, because he finds the average person repulsive and thus wishes to maintain his difference from "the people."

In "Words to the Intellectuals," Fidel emphasized artists' responsibility to create works that represented their current reality. He thus eschewed the idea of writing for posterity and instead established the duty to address the contemporary problems of the reader of literary works. At the same time, the regime promoted historical investigation in order to find out "the roots" of the Revolution. As Roberto González Echevarría has noted, poetry tends to represent the present time more than narrative, which "appears to be bound to a feeling of belatedness" (González Echevarría, *Biografía* 113). Thus, many of the novels of the first decade of the Revolution and after were situated in the Batista era, that is, they focused on the investigation of historical roots. *Maestra voluntaria* and *Memorias del subdesarrollo* are exceptions, as they are two novels that chronicle the present, they are written in the form of a diary, and they feature first-person narration in the present tense. But of these two texts, only *Memorias* displays the challenge an author faces when narrating the present.

In "Words to the Intellectuals," Fidel amply explained the need to have an institution that regulated culture, "a highly qualified organization that can be relied upon to stimulate, develop and guide, yes, guide, that creative spirit" (Baxandall, "Words" 279) and announced the creation of the UNEAC, a union of writers and artists whose activities and production would be protected and regulated by the state. Sartre, among other renowned intellectuals who visited Cuba in the early 1960s, had warned against the harmful effects that the writers' union had had in the Soviet Union, and as late as 1964, long after the UNEAC was constituted, Sartre stated in an interview published by the journal *Unión* that the "peaceful competition of ideas" was essential in Cuba and such free flow was hindered by a writers' union (Rinascita 152). In fact, through pressure by the union the regime put into place a form of censorship in 1968, which was strengthened in 1971 and further implemented following those years. As Antonio Vera-León expressed it referring to Jesús Díaz, writers in Cuba were writing "on the state's stationery," which caused them to comply with the requests of the state (69). Already in "Words to the Intellectuals" (1961), Fidel had promised to designate an area of Isla de Pinos for writers and artists to rest and create (289), signaling the coming of an era in which writers would receive multiple benefits from the state in exchange for their allegiance.

After the mention of the union, Fidel announced that then contemporary writers were preparing the future for the younger writers, and that the advancement of culture in Cuba would show its best results a few years later. This passing comment on the idea of future generations of revolutionary writers provoked discussions published mostly in *La Gaceta de Cuba,* where writers disputed the generation they belonged to and who was on their team

(Portuondo 23, n. 10). As Portuondo has recognized, however, the debate did not yield significant insights, but it did reveal the urgency that writers and artists felt to situate themselves in the revolutionary sphere and define their influences.

Barely two months after "Words to the Intellectuals," the newly created UNEAC celebrated its first congress. In the opening speech, Osvaldo Dorticós, the president at the time, emphasized the calling to historical situatedness and archival exploration that has become constant in the Revolution to this day. For Dorticós, a country's transformation could not take place without first accounting for the cultural production of the past. He claimed that revolutionary culture must save Cuban tradition and recover it for the new generations, interpret the past with good revolutionary judgment, and show the link between the Revolution and the nation's past. The historian Louis Pérez has amply illustrated that history has many uses in Cuban institutional discourse, which has motivated a virtual explosion of historiography and historical exploration in government organizations. As Pérez has noted, the exploration of the past was intended to delineate a logical historical progression from the colony to the Republic, all the way to the advent of the Revolution. According to Pérez, "Cuban historiography is possessed of an experiential dimension, one in which post-Moncada generations can experience and relive, if only vicariously, the dismal days of capitalism and, by implication, acquire a heightened appreciation for the accomplishments of socialism" ("Toward" 6).

Within the historical exploration of the past, Dorticós explained, there existed a need to "rediscover, purify, and promote the wealth of our folklore" (45), as it could enrich Cuban literature and art and help writers and artists reach out to the people. As Dorticós put it, writers and artists had to strive to "understand"—or speak the "language of the people"—but also "comprehend" or be aware of the social and economic problems that "the people" had been a part of (Dorticós 48). He advocated a political art, in which every author or creator would engage with contemporary issues. Dorticós's speech placed a strong emphasis on the need to regulate culture and have every writer and artist lend his or her contribution to the Revolution. He made clear that obscurity and overly complex works should be avoided and abstract artists should find new means of expression, thereby hindering the possibility of freedom of form that Fidel had outlined. In other words, in 1961 institutional discourse was already establishing the boundaries of revolutionary culture very clearly: although these limitations were not technically enforced until 1968, and more clearly in 1971 after the Padilla case, the pressure to adhere to the new rules was already in place in 1961.

In the closing speech of this same congress, Fidel picked up where he had left off in his June speech, by decrying the intellectuals and artists who had "abandoned their duty" toward their country by going into exile. Their departure was welcomed, as they would not have served the regime well, but it also increased the sense of urgency for the rest of the writers and artists to apply themselves to the work of the Revolution. Throughout the speech, Fidel revealed that in his mind the proper task of intellectuals and writers was didactic, rather than creative. Put simply: "All of us without exception have the duty to teach. . . . The most important task for all of us is to prepare the future; we are, in this hour of the fatherland, the handful of seeds that is sown in the revolution's furrows to create the future. The future is much more important than the present" (Castro, "Clausura del primer congreso" 53). Since the congress was taking place in the midst of the Literacy Campaign, a choir of youths connected to the campaign was invited to provide entertainment for the evening. Fidel cited the refrain of one of their songs— "We are instructors, hear this well, who are going forward under Fidel's command" ("Clausura" 56)—as an opportunity to digress and speak on the Literacy Campaign, thereby associating intellectuals and artists with literacy instructors. Fidel thus collapsed intellectual tasks with those of teachers' duties, which were far more urgent in the revolutionary context. In the same vein, Fidel referred to the then recent attack in Playa Girón and reinforced the need to be militant in order to serve the Revolution. His final cry underscored some of the constants in this discourse, such as the proletarianization of culture, the primacy of teaching over artistic creation,, and the need to have a militant attitude: "Forward, comrade writers and artists! On with the construction workers! On with the peasants! On with those who defend the land! Fatherland or death! We will win!" (57).

The speech closing the conference for the first time positioned the intellectual in the midst of the real and rhetorical war sustained between Cuba and the United States, a leitmotif in the official discourse of the Revolution to this day. At issue was the need for a fusion between the intellectual and the guerrilla fighter that Che exemplified. It is therefore not unusual that in an article titled "Notas para el estudio de la ideología de la revolución cubana" (Notes for the study of the *ideology* of the Cuban Revolution [1960, emphasis mine]), Che Guevara wrote an analysis of guerrilla strategy and mentioned that the duty of the intellectual would be to "outline the theory [of the guerrilla]" (19). The positioning of the intellectual as someone standing side by side with those who work with their hands and the belligerent tone with which the speech concluded traced a line of continuity between these early speeches and Roberto Fernández Retamar's *Calibán* (1971), as Quintero Herencia has stated (62–65).

A significant milestone in the continuous line of aggressive institutional discourse is surely Fidel's speech titled "Segunda declaración de La Habana" (Second declaration of Havana, February 1962), delivered after a meeting in Punta del Este in which the members of the Organization of American States ceded to U.S. pressure and expelled Cuba from the organization. Rather than acknowledging imminent isolation, Fidel chose to present Cuba in this speech as the leading force for Latin American countries against imperialism. At this point, poverty and oppression seemed to be an element that gave identity to Latin America as a unit: "No Latin American country is weak, because it forms part of a family of two hundred million brothers who suffer the same scarcity, harbor the same feelings, have the same enemy, dream together of a better destiny and count on the solidarity of all honest men and women in the whole world" (Castro, "Segunda" 106). The declaration was enthusiastically endorsed by UNEAC with the argument that Cuba would maximize its creative potential and become an example for Latin American countries.[5]

Further, Fidel linked the idea of Cuba's awareness of its own underdevelopment, the need to overcome it, and the writer's duty, as the end of the "Segunda declaración de La Habana" shows: "Now finally, history will have to count with the poor of [Latin] America . . . who have decided to start writing their story themselves, from now on . . ." (107). In the context of the defiant tone that the speech maintained, writing against the oppressor was presented as the only purpose for writing, which Fidel further established by quoting Martí at the very beginning of the speech: "'I can write now . . . now I am in danger of [having to] give my life for my country and my duty every day . . .'" ("Segunda" 91). A situation of danger in which one may be called to sacrifice his or her life was thus one that truly legitimized the task of writing and provided its subject matter. As we shall see, *Memorias* plays with these ideas and exposes their risks.

Particularly in the earliest years of the Revolution, Casa de las Américas embarked on the mission described in the Second Declaration of Havana: to place Cuba at the heart of the alliance between countries of the so-called third world. As Nadia Lie has stated, the first period of the journal, which she marks as 1960–65, promoted a kind of pan-Americanism wherein America would be redefined as *Latin* America. In this mission, Casa de las Américas would act as the convener of meetings and forums to make sure that the unity that had to some extent failed in the OAS on political grounds would materialize in the cultural arena with Cuba at its center (Lie 60–68). The idea of Cuba succeeding in a mission that independence movements of Latin America had failed to accomplish can be traced back to the writings of Martí. As Quintero Herencia has aptly put it, paraphrasing Lezama Lima: "[This mission implies] the *restoration* of the promise unfulfilled by the warlike *logos* of *cubanidad*" ("Fulguración" 80). The sense of renewal of institutional discourse in the Revolution is thus betrayed by a reproduction of many of the topoi that had been constant in previous public discourse of the Cuban Republic and beyond. Casa de las Américas did act as a cultural center for Latin America, especially in the first decade of the Revolution, but its mission would see itself coopted by the preeminence of long-standing revolutionary values over cultural reconciliation.

There is no doubt that the socioeconomic transformations of Cuba in the first years of the Revolution, together with the changes announced by institutional discourse in matters of culture, forced writers and artists to reckon with their own role in society. As the publishing venues became more accessible, they also became more regulated, in association with the newly created cultural institutions such as UNEAC, ICAIC, Casa de las Américas, Instituto del Libro, and so forth. The early incidents surrounding *PM* and *Lunes de Revolución* stressed the urgency for all writers and artists to follow along the dictates of revolutionary institutions and to secure a place for themselves *inside* the Revolution. The rules were as yet unwritten, but there were expectations that a new form of expression needed to be found, and content had to refer to the here–and–now. The most ardent supporters of the new culture fostered a pedagogic art, useful for the instruction of the masses, and called intellectuals to humble themselves to the level of manual workers. The leaders also delivered a strong message concerning Cuba's central role in the realization of Bolívar's dream of pan-Americanism. Many writers and artists participated in the revolutionary zeal and, as Lisandro Otero has put it, at that moment "it was more important to be a revolutionary than to be an expert, because political trust counted more than one's qualifications" (Otero, *Llover* 16). Those were the years of a "contagious fervor" (14). However, while most writers who remained in the island supported the Revolution in their public pronouncements, many in the first decade continued to cultivate a form of writing that did not follow the institutional dictates or that went so far as to question them. This contradiction, together with the sense of guilt and ambiguity motivated by it, is what Malabre, as the epitome of the intellectual, symbolizes. The next sections are devoted to these and other readings of the protagonist of *Memorias*.

Malabre as the Despicable Alienated Writer

Edmundo Desnoes's *Memorias* has had numerous versions and revisions. The first time it was published—in 1965, by Ediciones Unión, a publisher dependent on the recently created UNEAC—it included three short stories that followed the main text. These stories were supposedly written by the protagonist of the novel, Malabre, and edited by a friend of his called Edmundo Desnoes, who appears briefly in the novel as a paper presenter at a conference. The English translation of the novel, published in the United States in 1967 and in England in 1968 with the title *Inconsolable Memories*, did not include the short stories. With or without the short stories, the novel has been said to be a rewriting of a previous failed novel by Desnoes, *No hay problema* (1961), and this rewriting plus the general ideological point of the novel are explained in a series of essays that, as Enrico Mario Santí has put it, intend to constitute a sort of "companion volume" to the novel ("Edmundo" 52). A movie version of the novel with a script by Desnoes, directed by Tomás Gutiérrez Alea, followed in 1967. This version bears the same title as the novel but it includes several extra scenes.

Critics have turned to Desnoes's biography to find explanations for the self-referentiality between the texts, as well as the long textual genealogy of the novel and the different layers that each version added to it. Through the life of the author, readers have hoped to ascertain whatever has been ambiguous and resistant to interpretation in the text. For my purposes, however, I want to consider the various versions of the text and the background of Desnoes's life and novelistic production as elements in the construction of the author function in a revolutionary situation. To put it succinctly, whether of his own volition or as a result of the will of his readers, Desnoes manages to comply with the expectations that institutional discourse set for writers in the Cuban Revolution, while at the same time remaining critical of that discourse. In the midst of this textual web, Desnoes provides an idea of the predicament of intellectuals in the first decade of the Revolution and the ways they chose to negotiate between their public stance and private views.

In a literal reading of *Memorias* the protagonist represents the bourgeois alienated intellectual as characterized in public discourse. Judging by the story of his past, Malabre is a member of the former "decadent" class: he was the manager of a family-owned furniture store, married an elegant lady, and now lives off the rent of various apartments he owns. Due to the impact of post-1959 changes, Malabre's parents and wife have just left, and he decides to stay because "[he] does not want to evade the hole . . . [he has] inside any more" (26). He ends up writing a diary in the spirit of a confession, which goes along with the style of confessional narratives of the early years of the revolution. Both as diary and confession, however, the text is predictably a failure: though Malabre's musings provide a chance to air all of his flaws, they do not lead to any form of enlightenment, and there is no hint of change or conversion in his words. If anything, the diary serves to keep him more self-centered and to isolate him from the rest of the world, which confirms the stereotypical image of the alienated bourgeois. As Henry Fernández has described it: "*Inconsolable Memories* is a bourgeois novel, and not a very original one. The *éducation sentimentale*, the alienation of the individual, the disintegration of personality, the constant erotic preoccupations, the powerlessness in the face of the historical upheavals, these are all the traditional themes of the bourgeois novel" (59). The many readings the novel lends itself to, however, point at interpretations that diverge from the typical bourgeois novel.

In his dealings with the other characters in the novel, Malabre shows clear resistance to and even disgust with what Fidel would call "the people," represented in Elena—a young lady with whom he has an affair—and the individuals he observes when he walks around Havana. He identifies the average Cuban with the underdeveloped, as a fundamentally negative aesthetic quality that leads him to lament that "Havana looks now like a province of the interior. . . . It does not look like the Paris of the Caribbean, as tourists and whores used to say. Now it looks more like one of those dead, underdeveloped cities, like Tegucigalpa. . . . Now everybody you see in the streets looks humble, dresses badly. . . . All women look like maids, and men look like construction workers" (15). The alleged proximity of all revolutionary intellectuals to "the people" elicits in Malabre his most class-conscious comments.[6]

Malabre aspires to set himself apart from his fellow Cubans by taking the protagonist of the French movie *Hiroshima Mon Amour* (1959) as a model. In this movie, directed by Alain Resnais with a script by Marguerite Yourcenar, the female protagonist goes to Hiroshima to witness the effects of the atomic bomb tragedy and to elaborate what she calls "an inconsolable memory." As the movie progresses, however, one realizes that the protagonist's sympathy has little to do with the Japanese, but with her own lover, a German soldier killed in World War II. The "inconsolable memory" of the Japanese victims turns out to be the objectification of the protagonist's grief for the death of her lover. Malabre declares that he, too, wants to elaborate an "inconsolable memory": he objectifies the bitterness of his wife leaving him in the anger and confusion that the revolutionary process was producing in some around him. He identifies with those whom he sees as victims, as a metaphor for his own individual frustration. This once again confirms his self-centeredness and disinterest in the communal spirit of the Revolution.

With the advent of the Revolution, Malabre states that he does not want to have things, but he clearly transfers his greed to women, whom he aspires to possess and embellish as his own objects. He confesses that he "worked to keep his wife as if she had been born in New York or Paris" (9), and his interest in Elena, a woman he met by chance, is shown by his gift to her of all of his wife's dresses and accessories. As John Mraz has noted, "Sergio's [he refers to the protagonist of the movie version, but in this respect the script does not alter the original] sexual mentality could be described as imperialistic: women are objects of conquest and colonization—underdeveloped colonies to be conquered and transformed" (104). His idea of a "developed aesthetic" in the middle of the Cold War seems to be epitomized by Europe, as he finds both Americans and Russians unrefined.

When it comes to responding to the urgent call of commitment in the arts, *Memorias* is, once again, a resounding failure. If this text was meant to be pedagogical in any way in an institutional sense, it fails to drive home any message other than a negative one: intellectuals are unable to make a contribution to the Revolution. The novel is not creative in the conventional sense: there is hardly any character development, dialogue is scarce, and the plot is thin. The character does not engage with the reality around him or attempt to comprehend "the people," as Dorticós had put it in the opening speech of the First Congress of Writers and Artists (1961), by immersing himself in history, let alone folklore. His allusions to what is going on in Cuba are not informed, but are the result of his very personal, negative views. The only clear allusion to current events is the reproduction of a speech by John F. Kennedy and fragments of the response by Fidel, during the Cuban Missile Crisis. After some reflection, these speeches drive Malabre to a feeling of impending doom and he is paralyzed, unable to write any more. When it comes to taking the role of the fighter, the intellectual protagonist of *Memorias* disregards the examples of Martí and Che cited above: he chooses silence.

The end of the novel delivers poetic justice to a character who may seem despicable to many readers, as he fails to meet any of the requirements of a committed intellectual and proves unable to contribute to the Revolution in any meaningful way.[7] If this were the only reading, Desnoes's novel would be a political pamphlet. Fortunately, the text reproduces not just institutional discourse, but also the voices that question it. In Román de la Campa's words: "Malabre's discourse . . . does not intend to efface a heterogeneous discourse through reified structures, or lead [the reader] to a grand signifier, but to make more transparent the space in which the strength [of the signifier] operates" (de la Campa 1054). In other words, the novel delineates the field of power forces at play in the discourse on culture at the time.[8] Malabre reproduces the contributions of the many participants in this discourse: this is why, as I will illustrate later, the figure of the ventriloquist is apt for describing *Memorias*'s protagonist. The next section offers a reading of this character as steeped in the philosophical tradition of existentialism.

## The Face(-Off) of Intellectual and Author in *Memorias*

An insightful interpretation of Malabre could view him as an anti-hero in the existential sense, akin to the protagonists of Sartre's *La nausée* (1938) or Camus's *L'etranger* (1942). José Miguel Oviedo states that *Memorias* provides the "Havana version" of Camus's text, where the French author's ethical vision of his contemporary situation becomes appropriated by Desnoes to articulate the feeling of emptiness provoked by the disintegration of his pre-revolutionary world (Oviedo 65). As an existential hero, Malabre despises all human beings and states that "a man alone is wondrous, and many men together are depressing" (Desnoes 105). In his role of observer and questioner Malabre emerges as the identity figure of the intellectual in his own right and reclaims for himself the voice that institutional discourse was trying to silence. Malabre's existential angst not only behooves him as an intellectual, but it is a means for him to emerge as an independent thinker in the midst of all the institutional calls to become one with the collective. Beyond an exercise in confession, the diary is the product of individual thought and expression. The writing of the diary provides the character with a chance to sort out his confusion, to be reborn as an intellectual *and* a revolutionary on his own terms. It is worth considering Malabre as the construction of an independent intellectual who "clashes" with the author of the text.

With the text divided into two parts, the body of the text and the short stories, the novel shows some intention of formal innovation resembling Nabokov's *Pale Fire* (1962) as has been pointed out (Rodríguez Monegal, "Literatura Cine" 581). Although the short stories have not been published with later editions of the text, the original project consists of the imaginary biography of a writer, plus some stories that add to the construction of Malabre as an author. In addition, the short stories provide clues to interpret the body of the text and refocus the novel in its textuality, not just its content, thus pointing to the task of the writer as a craftsman who deserves recognition, rather than as someone merely conveying a message.

The fact that *Memorias* is a sequel and to some extent a rewriting of one of Desnoes's previous novels—*No hay problema* (1961)—further refers readers back to the status of the novel as *text*. *No hay problema* is set in the prerevolutionary period, and it traces the evolution of a character from a bourgeois life in New York to a return to Cuba, his political coming-of-age and finally his alliance with the clandestine struggle against Batista. The novel was criticized for its allusions to the so-called generation of writers of the Revolution, as Desnoes's contemporaries could not see themselves represented in the writer protagonist, Sebastián. The critique, published in *La Gaceta de Cuba,* included the response of the following writers: Virgilio Piñera, Antón Arrufat, Heberto Padilla, José Soler Puig, César Leante, and Lisandro Otero. In particular, Padilla and Leante protested against anyone taking Sebastián as representative of the ultimate Cuban writer who demonstrated his patriotism by going back to Cuba and joining the revolutionary struggle: not only was Sebastián North American on his mother's side, but "he was a frivolous guy who could not symbolize the Cuban man" (Piñera et al. 5). Malabre in *Memorias* does not aspire to become a symbol of *cubanía*, unlike the protagonist of Desnoes's first novel, but rather he questions the construct of a Cuban identity. Malabre represents—as Desnoes has put it—a different point of view on the insertion of the intellectual in society. Whereas Sebastián stands for "someone who returns [to Cuba] and solves the problem [of the conflict between the Revolution and one's own experience,] *Memorias* presents another problem, that part of me concerned with the values of being educated in the Western Tradition" (Desnoes, "America Revisited" 13).

In an interview with William Luis in response to the reception of the novel at the time, Desnoes stated that he identified with the protagonist of *No hay problema,* rather than with Malabre, and that the latter was a part of himself that he was trying to "get rid of, to understand, to exorcise, like catharsis" (Desnoes, "American Revisited" 11). What is interesting in these declarations is the gap between how *Memorias* constructs the figure of an intellectual and a writer, and how Desnoes constructs himself through interviews and essays: we witness a gesture of denial and the deferral of accountability from the author to someone other than himself, in the text that he labels "an exorcism."

The distancing of Malabre as a construct of the intellectual and Desnoes as a writer is reemphasized in an encounter between the protagonist and the author himself, who appears as a character attending a literature symposium. The gesture of disavowal is this time from character to author, as Malabre criticizes Desnoes's latest work—clearly, *No hay problema*—and his politics, lamenting that he left his job in New York to join the Revolution. "Look at yourself Eddy! Now, Edmundo Desnoes!" Malabre sneers (Desnoes 70). A former Bohemian and an anarchist, "now he [Desnoes] is sitting on the podium, smoking a cigar and pontificating about literature" (71). This climactic scene has been interpreted as proof that the novel is not autobiographical, and that Malabre does not represent what the author Desnoes would like to see represented as himself. And yet, one wonders whether this scene is not precisely another exorcism, where Desnoes as a character in the novel represents the type of establishment author that Desnoes the real author would not like himself to be seen as. The exorcism can thus go both ways, and it is clear that, without the interviews and essays produced after the novel, Malabre's comments stand by themselves: they can constitute a critical statement of the cultural establishment, rather than an ironic, self-effacing representation of the cynicism that revolutionary intellectuals needed to purge.

Thus, *Memorias* showcases the polysemic nature of revolutionary discourse during that period and after, as the novel can be interpreted in many ways according to the reader's point of view. For instance, when the novel first came out a reviewer noted that "not all this [the bourgeois] world is overcome, rejected in the book. That explains, in part, the splitting, the ambiguity, the equivocation [of the novel]" (F. Álvarez 149). But rather than interpreting the ambiguity in the text as an attempt at questioning institutional discourse in its own right, the reviewer tends to read the novel as Desnoes indicated in his essays, that is, as the author's reckoning with his own past (149).

Aside from his political stance in the literal sense, Malabre is a rather extreme example of a character who is heavily influenced by the written word, and thus he stresses the peculiarity of intellectuals as individuals who express themselves, *live through* texts. What readers get to know of him is through his own writing in the diary, in which Malabre works out his scorn and comes to terms with what his wife represented to him. When asked what he wants his parents to bring him from the United States, he requests only magazines. His infatuation with Noemí, his maid, starts after he spins a story about a picture he sees of her. Malabre is more of a contemplating and observing man than a figure of action. The little that happens in his life is material for reflection, rather than for the development of his personality. Further, in redefining underdevelopment as a "state of mind," Malabre directs the focus away from Cuba's economic situation and introduces the specific effect of underdevelopment on intellectuals. As Méndez Ródenas has aptly put it, "underdevelopment" for Malabre is another way of saying "barbarie," as in the classic dichotomy of "civilización y barbarie" ("civilization and barbarism") established by Domingo Faustino Sarmiento ("Escritura" 333). For Malabre, "civilization consists of . . . knowing how to associate things, not forgetting anything. That is why there is no civilization possible here: the Cuban man forgets his past easily: he lives in the present too much" (Desnoes 30–31). For Malabre, as for Sarmiento, an underdeveloped environment is deterministic of the intellectual who lives in it, marking him with a lack of sophistication he cannot overcome. Before the Revolution, Malabre complains, he was able to stay in touch with the cultural production of Europe and the United States through magazines and travel, but since the Revolution, he no longer has access to these sources. He feels his isolation more than ever and complains that "newspapers only have political slogans" (66).

Except for one essay, Desnoes's declarations on underdevelopment and Malabre's words in the novel present substantial differences. In general, Desnoes presented underdevelopment as a direct consequence of twenty-eight years of the Republic, during which poverty and dependency on foreign powers became generalized in Cuba. Only in his essay "El mundo sobre sus pies" (The world on its feet) does Desnoes introduce the notion of the effect of underdevelopment on people's conscience (*Punto* 86). For Malabre, underdevelopment is a sort of colonized mind that material wealth cannot repair and that the Revolution aggravated considerably. While institutional discourse also recognized this form of negative baggage from before the Revolution, it placed emphasis on the economic consequences of poverty and dependency. Malabre's reflections concerning the effects of underdevelopment on a would-be intellectual are thus unique when contrasted to the institutional discourse he partially reproduces. In addition, his complaints as to how the intellectuals' isolation from the rest of the world increased in the Revolution showed him in radical disagreement with the promise that the institutional Revolution offered, according to which Cuba would have a leading cultural role in Latin America.[9]

The concept of "mental underdevelopment" is central to the novel and its powerful ending. When Malabre is finally in bed with Noemí, the maid, he listens to a radio speech by President Kennedy, who announces the intention to launch missiles in Cuba if any Russian missile were fired from Cuba to the United States. Once again the Cuban Missile Crisis (1962) is cast in terms of the dilemma developed versus underdeveloped, as the narrator selects the following segment of Kennedy's speech, which he quotes in English: "Now your leaders are no longer Cuban leaders . . . they are puppets and agents of an international conspiracy. . . . Yours [*sic*] lives and lands are being used as pawns by those who deny you freedom" (*Memorias* 120). It is clear by this speech that Cuba is caught between the two superpowers at the time, and that the danger she faces is due to the unequal nature of an encounter in which Cuba is marked by her past and present dependency on the United States and the Soviet Union respectively.

With Kennedy's speech as a background, Malabre's seemingly unconnected musings take on a broader meaning. In the context of Cuba's situation of dual dependency, he states, "I feel that everything is disproportionate. We and the rest of the world. Nuclear energy and my small apartment" (123). With disbelief, he quotes Fidel saying that "we are at the same level as the [first] world, not as the underdeveloped world" (123). Finding himself in the midst of a struggle between two superpowers and Fidel's desire to challenge both, Malabre responds, "This island is a trap and the Revolution is tragic, tragic because we are too small to survive, to triumph. Too poor and too few. Our dignity is very expensive. I do not want to think" (124–25). Clearly, the conflict is articulated as evidencing the inequality between developed and underdeveloped, not so much in terms of military resources, as Cuba had the Russian missiles at the time, but in terms of attitude, or mental predisposition. For Malabre, it is the Cuban mind that is underdeveloped.

The protagonist of *Memorias* is unable to side with any of the public stances on the Missile Crisis. His very basic fear of the physical harm that the conflict may bring to him, emphasized by the physical materiality to which he has been clinging in his diary reflections, causes him ultimately to feel paralyzed and to abandon his diary. After the Missile Crisis is resolved without violence, Malabre's last words are, "Things and fear and desire suffocate me. It is difficult. Aside from that I have nothing to add. Finished. Man (I) [*sic*] is sad, but wants to live. . . . Go beyond words" (133). With this final surrender to silence, Malabre implies that intellectual activity is futile when one's most basic instinct, survival, is threatened. The book closes with the question of whether intellectual speculation is valid in the midst of the often adverse circumstances brought by a Revolution that challenges the world's most entrenched power structures. Such a question is never answered: it is up to the reader to judge whether it is a legitimate question that needs serious consideration, or yet another detail confirming that Malabre is an alienated bourgeois intellectual who is too concerned with his own self-image to take any action.

This ending has been interpreted by some as uplifting, rather than as an illustration that the Revolution has rendered obsolete the intellectual class that Malabre represents. For Erik Camayd Freixas, for instance, Malabre's diary and its abrupt ending constitutes, in fact, "an inconsolable memory of underdevelopment" that needed to be recorded. Malabre's documentation of the Missile Crisis serves as an individual's account of the crisis that precedes "the people's" elaboration of their own 'collective record' of the era" (Camayd Freixas 45). Though this reading runs counter to Malabre's solipsistic stance, it illustrates yet another attempt to reconcile the character with Desnoes's public image as a committed writer at the time.

In *Punto de vista*, a compilation of essays that Desnoes himself describes as *Memorias*'s "conscious expression in concrete ideas" (9), the author attempts to do away with the ambiguity of the text and to fix its elusive meaning. The collection of essays is a declaration of intentions, in which the author claims to have finally found "his point of view" (7). He makes allowances for the fact that "we are always two. The one who understands everything, justifies everything with a cold analysis of the inexorable history . . . and the poor 'I' who only has his individual life in the midst of the surprising and contradictory chaos of the Revolution" (10). But the firmness of his convictions in the rest of the essays suppresses the doubtful "I" with such assertions as "through culture, the Third World should aim at having Europe and the United States look at us with respect," and the idea that the intellectual should be "society's conscience" ("El mundo," *Punto* 105). With these comments, Desnoes refocuses the attention on Malabre as a would-be revolutionary writer, rather than as someone who resists that concept. As mentioned earlier *Punto de vista* serves as a companion volume to *Memorias*, and as such it seems an attempt to give proper direction to readers' interpretations of a text that may have caused significant anxiety to the writer.

The reader of *Memorias* should bear in mind both the institutional and the critical discourses it interpolates, rather than letting one cancel the other. By including the official critique of the intellectual as alienated and bourgeois, along with the assertion of the intellectual's right to criticize and remain aloof from the official mandates, the text refuses to advocate exclusively one position or the other. Desnoes's effort to explicate his novel in essays and interviews does betray a desire, however, to harness the possible meanings of the text and in effect force the reading that the revolutionary intelligentsia would approve. This gesture can be a result of what Mario Benedetti called the importance of "the attitude" versus "the letter"—the writing—of authors. In Benedetti's words: "Recently, some high Cuban functionary said this, in so many words, to various foreign awarding committees: 'We thoroughly admit criticism in the revolution; but to exercise that right one has to earn it first.' Will it be that what matters . . . is the *attitude* of the writer rather than the letter of his poems?" (quoted in Rama, "Norberto" 243). In public declarations, Desnoes constructed his "right to be critical" by assigning an intention to his texts that did not necessarily correspond to all of the interpretations the texts might yield. Beyond the exegesis of the text and the public responsibility of the author, however, the novel stands as a construction of the intellectual, in its different facets. Such a construction in itself vindicates the place of the intellectual that had been denied in public discourse. The next section proposes a reading of *Memorias* in terms of its body politics.

Malabre's Being-in-the-World: The Body and Its Fake Appearance

An important aspect of Malabre as an existential hero is the repeated reference to his body as the vehicle for his self-projection in the world. The diary contains many allusions to Malabre's body that are worth examining in the light of Sartre's *Being and Nothingness* (1943). As Gustavo Geirola has noted, this work profoundly influenced Cuban intellectuals in the 1960s (Geirola 109), and *Memorias* represents an original contribution to the discourse generated on this work in that era. At the same time, the focus on the body offers the narrator a way to state that alienation is not something exclusive to bourgeois intellectuals, but is a quality of being human.

For Sartre, the body is not the seat of consciousness, but consciousness itself. The body is one's way of "being-in-the-world," "it is a point-of-view and a point of departure" (Sartre, *Being* 331), in the sense that it is one's way of apprehending the world. One's body generates an order, or defines "what is," through the relationship that it has with "things." Malabre writes, "I have never felt that anything exists beyond my body. I think we are more of a machine than an embodied soul. The body is the only thing we have for desiring and hating others" (Desnoes 30). Note that Sartre also disputes the name *soul* to designate consciousness separate from the body. As his wife and family leave Malabre alone and he turns inward to reflect on himself, the awareness of his body is acute: he becomes very focused on the way his body manifests itself—thorough smells, secretions, gas, wrinkles—and, though he is sometimes ashamed of the way that these manifestations align him with animals, he reclaims the right to let his body express itself.

Since the body is the projection of one's self in a world where nothing exists prior to the body, Sartre emphasizes the primacy of one's senses as a means of getting to know the Other. At the same time, when one's senses fail or when one is in pain, one becomes acutely aware of one's own bodily existence, but also of one's vulnerability and contingency as a human being. Malabre feels a correlation between a sick or failing body and the fragility of the self, evidenced in his frequent comments on how his body is deteriorating or aging after his family has left him: "How can I explain what I feel today? It is as if I am collapsing inside. . . . I feel so sick that I do not want to speak or write" (11).

Whether as a celebration of one's way of being in the world or as an indication of one's own deterioration, Malabre's bodily discourse runs counter to the institutional discourse of the Revolution, where the body only appears as resistant, a force to be harnessed in the service of the physical demands of work and the duties of all citizens. As Geirola has indicated, institutional discourse imposed on the body what he characterizes as a "disciplina ignaciana" ("Ignatian discipline") according to the *Exercises* of the Spanish priest Ignacio de Loyola. Put simply, these exercises described a process by which the body would be subordinated to the soul, which would in turn be governed by a strict Other, usually a father figure such as God or, in revolutionary discourse, Fidel (Geirola 145). The dynamic of the exercises finds a parallel in Che Guevara's description of the formation of a guerrilla fighter in *Episodes of the Revolutionary War*, which describes a process of taming the body that fosters asceticism and "self-flagellation, martyrdom, sacrifice" (Geirola 170). This concept of the tamed body of the fighter was transferred to what was described later as the revolutionaries' commitment to self-discipline and asceticism. The state of virtual siege in which institutional discourse has kept Cuba since 1959 added reasons for the need to maintain the culture of sacrifice.

For Sartre, the body has a facticity, a materiality, that masks what the philosopher calls "the contingency of one's body in-itself," or the fact that one's body does not have an independent existence except through its instrumental relation to the world.[10] As Malabre reflects on his own bodily existence as a way to avoid his fundamental alienation, he shows that it is not the case, as in Marxist discourse, that only the bourgeois are alienated because they have lost the connection to manual labor. In the framework of existentialism, Malabre rewrites the institutional discourse of the Revolution, in that the stigma of alienation is no longer attached specifically to the bourgeois, and especially to bourgeois intellectuals, but to all human beings. Moreover, as Malabre's thoughts reveal, intellectuals as a class seem comparatively more aware of their alienation and perhaps eventually more able to overcome it.

Malabre makes numerous references to his body while he is alone, but his relationships with the other characters in the novel are also implicitly determined by his body. His reluctance to socialize can be explained by the way that his body becomes objectified under the "look of the Other," in Sartre's terms. What the French philosopher calls "the third ontological dimension of my body" is the idea that "I exist for myself as a body known by the Other"

(Sartre 351). Sartre calls the encounter with the Other "a shock," because it is "a revelation in emptiness of the existence of my body outside as an itself for the Other . . ." (532). In other words, in his fear of others, Malabre illustrates the fear of becoming objectified—made an object by the look of the Other—and thus losing his own "facticity in-itself," let us say, his own illusion of subjectivity.

For Sartre, the only way of avoiding the fear of being engulfed by the Other is by trying to "take the other's point of view in myself" or to act upon the Other's freedom of looking at "myself" as an object. Love, as defined by Sartre, is a way to appropriate the freedom or the point of view of the Other, by making "me" the center of the "Other's world." When the Other is in love with "me," "I am the absolute value," "the world must be revealed in terms of me," according to Sartre (369). This explains why Malabre, in his existential quest to find himself, does not seek the company of friends, family, or any other association, but courts women until they fall in love with him. With Elena, for instance, he stops the relationship as soon as he notices that he is falling in love with her: he states, "At the most [with her] I can be a witness, a spectator" (Desnoes 44), thus emphasizing the primacy of *his look.*

Critics who consider Malabre a negative symbol of the alienated bourgeois intellectual have remarked that his relationships with women are usually driven by sexual desire, thus illustrating a male chauvinist version of the impulse of capitalism, evidenced in his desire to consume women as objects (see Mraz 104, quoted above). This is a plausible interpretation, but attention to existential ideas yields a different analysis. For Sartre, sexual desire is a way to assert the facticity of one's body, in that sexual intercourse, the contact of surfaces, "reveals to me my body as flesh" (Sartre 389). According to Sartre, "Desire is an attempt to strip the body of its movements and of its clothing and to make it exist as pure flesh; it is an attempt to incarnate the Other's body" (389). Malabre as a fragile existential hero seeks to affirm himself through his body, by having relationships with women solely based on sex. He chooses beautiful women whom he dresses expensively as a way to make them objects to look at and to make himself always the bearer of that look, thus reasserting himself as a mere aesthetic observer.

The reading of Malabre as an existential hero through these references to the body also provides an explanation of the end of the novel, in which the protagonist is in bed with Noemí and listens to Kennedy's speech. Malabre experiences the announcement that the United States may launch missiles to Cuba as a threat to his body, and he becomes paralyzed. He states: "This is the end . . . Noemí by my side and I could not feel any tenderness, only fear. Instead of feeling my skin I felt my ribs and my lungs filling up and emptying with difficulty. We were naked in bed, defenseless, two animals without hair, without protection, destitute. Our sensuality turned into sadness. . . . The little breasts, Noemí's dark nipples disintegrate next to me" (Desnoes 121). As Sartre sees it, the human body is always covered to hide its own contingency, but there are moments when its nakedness is bared and the nothingness of existence is revealed.[11] This is one such moment for Malabre, who stops feeling desire and experiences the Other's body as a fragmented mass rather than as a firm surface on which to affirm his own materiality.

From this moment to the end of the novel, Malabre loses his sense of self. An emblematic scene that confirms the failure of his attempt to cling to his body as a means of deflecting his existential angst occurs when, after walking around Havana and feeling his fears growing, he says to himself: "I want to cling to things and nothing matters to me. I do not know what I am doing. I just put my pinky in my mouth and sounded my nail against the edge of my teeth. [I spent] several minutes like that. . . . I thought for a second that somebody was looking at me, I looked around and there was nobody . . . " (129). As Malabre tries once again to feel his body for confirmation of his own existence, not only does he become aware of the futility of the gesture, but he also feels "that somebody is looking at him." That is, he is aware of his being *an object* and no longer the master of his own being-in-the-world. This scene punctuates his definite downfall when he decides that he can no longer write. By making the connection between the body and writing, Malabre questions the notion that it is precisely in times of great physical danger—as Fidel quotes Martí saying—that the intellectual finds his voice (Castro, "Segunda" 91).

The introduction of a Sartrean theory of the body as the mode of being-in-the-world provides some additional clues as to how to account for the different readings of the text. For Sartre, one's being in the world entails what he calls "bad faith," or a state of self-deception about one's own being. One is aware that one's being is constituted by the look of the Other, and at the same time one is not that which the Other sees. As Sartre puts it, "We have to deal with human reality as a being which is what it is not and which is not what it is" (58). In that awareness, the human being is in a constant state of "representation": one is what one is by force of habit and due to the external characteristics of how others perceive him or her. According to Sartre, "It [my self as it appears] is a representation for others and for myself, which means that I can only be he in *representation*. But if I represent myself as him, I am not he; I am separated from him as the object from the subject, separated by *nothing*, but this *nothing* isolates me from him. I can not be he, I can only play at *being* him; that is, imagine to myself that I am he" (60).

Sartre's theory of being is striking in its theatricality, in its link to pose and artifice. As such, it is a productive metaphor for being in the Revolution, where the way that one acts and is perceived depends so heavily on prior assumptions of character and the need to define one's stance.

If one assumes that Malabre is indeed the representation of the being of a writer, riddled as he is with stereotypes and predictability, one can further speculate concerning the relationship between his character and the persona of the author, Desnoes. Malabre literally *represents* how Desnoes as the epitome of a writer in the Revolution is *seen*, so that the way he is interpreted ultimately reflects back the look of the Other, with his or her own political agenda. What Malabre says and what the author says in his essays to try and explicate this and other characters in his fiction are only part of that duplicitous persona, which one can call the author function—in Foucault's term—or the actor's act—in Sartre's term. The following section looks at the short stories appended to the end of the text and how they reflect on the idea of underdevelopment, placing emphasis on the importance of the figure of the intellectual. Masks, stereotypes, and representations abound in the stories, and all are characteristics of the narrator's productive "bad faith."

### *Memorias*'s Appendix: Further Reflections on Underdevelopment

The stories published at the end of the text of the first edition of *Memorias* are said to be of questionable quality and in need of revision. As they stand, the short stories can confirm the image of Malabre as a mediocre, "underdeveloped" writer, or point to Desnoes himself as having those flaws: the judgment will depend on whether one maintains the fictional biography of the novel or steps out of it. The comments in the edition in which they were published introduce the disclaimer that they were written by the mediocre writer protagonist. Whether or not Desnoes the author was proud of them, the stories contend with some points made in the main body of the text, which revolve around the issue of the difficult meeting ground between an underdeveloped country and a developed one. Malabre's paralysis after the encounter between the United States and Cuba in the Missile Crisis reiterates some of *Memorias*'s central questions: What are the a priori perceptions and assumptions when a meeting between a developed country and an underdeveloped one takes place? How does Cuba's status as an underdeveloped country, dependent on its relationship with the developed world, affect its present and future as a nation? Beyond the reality of the Revolution, how is Cuba likely to be perceived by the United States?

Before considering how these questions are posed in the short stories, two points deserve further attention. In setting up the dichotomy underdeveloped versus developed, Malabre/Desnoes thinks of Cuba and the United States, with the exception of the story "Créalo o no lo crea" (Believe it or not), which refers to Colombia versus the United States. Though in *Memorias* Malabre also speaks of Europe, most of his musings on underdevelopment are in reference to Cuba as defined against the United States, especially when he thinks of the cult of Hemingway in Cuba. Considering that Desnoes lived in the United States for a number of years and came back to Havana at the advent of the Revolution, it is understandable that the United States should be used as reference point. Further, the United States has been a constant presence in Cubans' attempts at self-definition, owing to Cuba's long-lasting economic dependency and the threat that the United States has posed to the Revolution. Whether viewed with veiled admiration mixed with jealousy, as in the case of Malabre, or with open hostility as seen in Fernández Retamar's "Calibán," the United States is an interpellating presence in intellectual discourse in the island. By taking up these questions, the narrator of *Memorias* represents the uncertainty felt in intellectual circles at the time about what would happen when Cuba severed its ties with the United States, and how this would affect the way that Cuba would be perceived. In short, Malabre/Desnoes is the victim of a sort of enduring intellectual dependency between the two countries.

It is worth noting that the short stories are situated in the prerevolutionary period and were written in the 1950s, according to Malabre. Regardless of possible revisions after 1959, at the point that Malabre is writing his diary, the stories pose questions on the relationship between developed and underdeveloped countries in the context of prerevolutionary Cuba and leave aside how that relationship plays out in the Revolution. But those questions do refer the reader back to the framework set up in the body of the text, where Malabre reflects on how underdevelopment leaves an indelible mark on intellectuals even after the Revolution. The stories reinforce what the character says in the novel, from the context of a different time frame. Because the stories have not been reprinted since the first edition of the novel, it is worthwhile to briefly summarize their plots.

"Jack y el guagüero" (Jack and the bus driver) is about an American (Jack) boarding a bus in Cuba and trying to make sure that it will take him to his destination.[12] The bus driver says in Spanish that he does not understand what the American is saying and Jack gets upset, insults the driver, and exits the bus. The bus driver complains that Cubans and foreigners always think bus drivers are dishonest, but in reality they are mere victims of stereotyping. A woman sides with Jack, arguing that it is nerve wracking to board a bus in Cuba without knowing where it will go. A voice closes the story by stating that "nobody is right, everybody is wrong" (139).

The story reproduces many of the stereotypical behaviors of people from the United States who go to visit Latin America: "the American" is only interested in going to the beach, he does not speak any Spanish and he insists Cubans should understand English. Jack insults the bus driver and extends his spite to all Cubans. In the essay "La imagen fotográfica del subdesarrollo" (The picture image of underdevelopment), compiled in *Punto de vista*, Desnoes comments on the idealized image of tropical paradise that many foreigners have of Cuba (86). The bus driver shrugs off "the American"'s attitude, does not realize the import of his insult, and uses this instance of verbal abuse as evidence of the incomprehension he suffers every day. Someone pities "the American" condescendingly. In its simplicity, the short story is highly resonant of the many times that this same scenario is recounted and the stereotypes it reinforces. In the context of Malabre as the author of the story, it can be read as evidence of the prejudices that mark the "underdeveloped intellectual," or the impossibility of communication between the two countries.

"¡Créalo o no lo crea!" (a reference to "Ripley's Believe It or Not") is the story of Pereira, a man caught in the Colombian Andes by an expedition of the Ripley's Museum and exhibited in American magazines and on television as the oldest man in the world, at 150 years old. A reporter of one of those magazines narrates the encounter between Pereira, himself, and other reporters and interviewers. From the barber who is at the time cutting Pereira's hair to the reporters and television impresarios, it is clear that they all want to use Pereira's picture to illustrate their own positions. He is exoticized as an indigenous person who needs an interpreter to translate his very rare dialect. Pereira subjects himself passively to the picture-taking session, but at some point he says in Spanish that he has a lot money and exhibits the few dollars and pesos he has in his pocket. After a female reporter poses with Pereira and remarks that "he is cute," the old man grabs her and screams that he wants to get her into bed. Some reporters separate them. The narrator leaves and as he reflects on Pereira he reads somewhere that a landowner in Medellín had claimed ownership of Pereira because he lived on his property. The reporter starts his article with the title "Who Owns the Old Man?" but decides to replace this title with "More Than One-Hundred-and-Sixty Years Old and He Still Likes Blondes" (146).

This short story once again represents an encounter between the "underdeveloped" and the "developed" world, where the former serves as an object of study or curiosity to the latter. The fact that Pereira is an indigenous man of old age resonates with the fascination of the "developed world" with the ancient cultures of Latin America. Like those ancient cultures, Pereira is valued for his alleged symbolism and exploited as a spectacular sight. The character is allowed no agency, and even when he speaks *in Spanish* nobody pays attention to him. For the implied reader, what Pereira says stands out among the narrator's musings and the comments of reporters in English. But Pereira's behavior contrasts with the idealized image that reporters have of him: he comes off as a pathetic figure, breaking the climax of the encounter with the "developed" world by exhibiting his money and asking for sex. The narrator's comments on the pictures that the reporters take, where he says Pereira looks either like a fetus or a chimpanzee, unequivocally portray him as "primitive." In his final decision on the title of the article, the narrator shows that he is not willing to let the readers reflect on the objectification that Pereira is suffering, but is instead complicit with Pereira's exoticization.

A similar reflection on how photography creates and fixes a certain stereotype of the so-called third world is contained in Desnoes's essay "La imagen fotográfica del subdesarrollo," also mentioned above, in which Desnoes states, "Most photographers, when they work outside their cultural milieu, [have] . . . a tendency to work with clichés and received ideas. Images can be resolved, but content is stereotypical" (Desnoes, *Punto* 85). In reference to the picture of a Peruvian Indian smiling while he plays his flute, he says it is idealistic and disregards the poverty that Peruvian Indians suffer (983). This essay influences the interpretation of a hypothetical reader of the short story, as it clearly expands the attitude of the reporters he is denouncing. Their condescension as they celebrate Pereira's longevity and declare that he is "cute" is further represented graphically in their pictures, in which he appears as a fetus or a chimpanzee.

The last story, titled "Yodor," is about a Cuban man who made "the first full robot in the world" (151). He thought of it as a business venture and tried to sell it to an American company that would use it to advertise cigarettes. His negotiations with the company failed because a bigger American company produced another robot that was less complete—he could not walk—but was good enough for advertising a brand of tobacco. The inventor then used the robot to tour Cuba and put on performances in small towns. People were delighted to see the robot, and there were comments of every kind, from those who thought there was nothing special about a robot that could do nothing more than a human being could, to those who mistook Yodor for a

Martian. But soon the authorities of several towns started offering resistance to Yodor's visits, on the grounds that he was a rabble rouser and incited people to protest against the government. The robot's fame declined, and eventually his inventor decided to destroy it. The protagonist ends the story, stating that "Yodor was too big for Cuba, it was very expensive, impossible to finance" (162).

The story is a good representation of the frustration experienced by the creator of something valuable who seeks recognition in the United States, does not obtain it, and sees his invention reduced to a curiosity exhibited in Cuba. The underlying assumptions are once again based on the imbalance between developed and underdeveloped worlds. The inventor wants to sell his product in the United States because he feels that country alone has the resources to put it to use, and he measures his success against the excellence of other teams of inventors he knows there. In contrast, in Cuba the robot is used as some sort of circus curiosity. The inventor feels that Cubans do not understand, or appreciate, the full value of his creation. Ignorance and lack of resources doom the product to fail in Cuba.

"Yodor" invites perhaps an easy, but useful analogy with what Desnoes attempts in *Memorias*. In a sense he, too, has found a doll to speak for him and, being a sort of automaton, Malabre cannot be held responsible for what he is saying. Like Yodor, Malabre can cite, seemingly using the author's own voice, different slogans for and against a cause. Like a ventriloquist's dummy, or a mischievous robot, Malabre can be counted on to discredit his owner. In addition, if Yodor speaks with his master's voice, one can wonder whether the oral account one reads in the story is the owner's or Yodor's. The same applies to Malabre's diary, which we know is fictional, and at the same time could perhaps be an account of the author's own life. Regardless of who owns the texts, the short story parallels the frustration that Malabre/Desnoes feels as a writer (creator) in Cuba: he measures his success against someone like Hemingway; his idea of himself is inflated at times, or alternately diminished when he is reminded that he lives in an "underdeveloped" country.

Overall, the style of the short stories is very different from the body of the text. As third-person narrations or first-person narrations with several protagonists, their points of view are not as seemingly one-sided as that of the main novel. The stories are also much more eventful and contain lively dialogue, in contrast to Malabre's slow, solipsistic account of his uneventful life. By the same token, the stories are predictable, thriving with stereotypes, thus rendering them more readable and mainstream. If one considers Malabre to be their author, the stories confirm the idea that he hammers on in his diary:

they are the product of an underdeveloped author. If one thinks of Desnoes as ultimately the writer of the stories, it seems that publishing them as an appendix to the fictional diary of a writer is a way to deflate responsibility as an author. In both cases, the stories prove the novel's assertions regarding the inequality between the developed and underdeveloped worlds, the impossibility of an instance of proper communication in an encounter between the two worlds, the unavoidable condescension and exoticization of the underdeveloped world in such an encounter, and the pathetic jealousy, admiration, and humiliation of the underdeveloped world in the face of the developed world in the same encounter. The stories refocus Malabre's reflections on himself and the Cuban nation in the light of these ideas, and they offer the United States as the reference point for the dichotomy of developed versus underdeveloped.

It has been noted that the stories lack originality and reproduce many commonplaces. One could argue that the stories consciously display many of the emblems used in a Sartrean poetics of the body: the stereotype, the picture as false depiction, or the puppet. According to Sartre, it is through these false representations that one's mode of being in the world is realized, since they are the materialization of what others expect of one. Thus one does not need to ask whether the reflection on underdevelopment is yet another obliged response to the institutional discourse of the time or an implicit comment on an author's frustration at being isolated from the developed world that had hitherto provided intellectual sustenance. The novel hints at the fact that discursive masks abound in Cuba and references to different camps constitute a writer's mode of being.

Most critics who have chosen a literal reading of *Memorias* see its protagonist as a bourgeois intellectual, where *bourgeois* is the most important term of the label given the lack of specificity accorded to intellectuals at the time. However, there is a shadow or alter ego of this intellectual as an existential hero who struggles with the idea of his role in the Revolution and reclaims for himself some sort of an identity. This shadow of the "new revolutionary intellectual" allows him to carve out for himself a place in a nation that had denied writers a specific role or a concrete mission. This intellectual dwells on the idea of underdevelopment not so much as a socioeconomic category, but rather as a state of mind. Not without self-loathing, guilt, and duplicity, both Desnoes as the persona of the writer and Malabre as the confused intellectual hold mirrors up to readers and writers in a revolutionary context. Malabre's refuge in the body and the ventriloquism of the short stories published at the end of the book contribute to the many-faceted picture of intellectuals that the novel provides. The novel does not just illustrate one point of view; it provides a textual summary of discourses, whose many voices can to a large extent be heard to this day. It also provides a convincing example of why the novels of this study attest to the construction not just of the New Man, but also of his shadowy Others.

# Harvesting the Nation

## How Cuba Became Unified in the Historical *Zafra*

The year 1970 has often been presented as the beginning of a time of greater orthodoxy in the Cuban Revolution, when the regime followed the Soviet model more closely and introduced more stringent rules in the field of cultural production (Pérez-Stable, *Origins* 118–20). The failure of the massive mobilizations and voluntary efforts put into place to achieve the goals of the 1970 Ten-Million-Ton Sugar Campaign no doubt played an important role in the decision to rely on more pragmatic Soviet-style policies. The Ten-Million-Ton Sugar Campaign was launched nationally on October 28, 1969, and came to an end in late May of 1970, with the official acknowledgment on July 26, 1970 of the failure to meet the goal. These dates mark one of the periods of greatest effervescence of revolutionary zeal and nationalistic euphoria in Cuba, when cutting cane became a patriotic duty that strengthened Cuba's sense of unity.[1]

As was the case with previous campaigns, the 1970 Sugar Campaign served to reinforce motifs that had become recurrent in institutional discourse, with nationalism taking center stage as a result of the fact that the whole country needed to take part in the campaign. If in the first decade the idea of the Cuban nation had been identified with the notion of Revolution, during the Sugar Campaign cutting cane was presented as *the* revolutionary task: beyond the dynamics of sugar production, there was no Revolution, there was no nation. In other words, official discourse at that juncture collapsed Cuba, Revolution, and Sugar into one and the same. If, according to revolutionary history, the Revolution was the culmination of Cuba's attempts at achieving the political independence that had been sought since 1898, the hypothetical success of the Sugar Campaign was seen as the signal of full economic independence. The campaign thus illustrated the tension between the need for both continuity and innovation in the motifs and images that the regime relied upon to create the feeling that the Revolution was both a fulfillment and a new beginning. Finally, if the Revolution operated on the idea of the unity of all Cubans at the expense of their diversity, the campaign carried this idea further, and ignored the protagonism of race in the tradition of cane harvesting in Cuba.

The post-1959 era does not necessarily represent a break with previous representations of the nation, but the Ten-Million-Ton Sugar Campaign is a key event in the archaeology of the concept of the Cuban revolutionary nation. If one assumes with Benedict Anderson that the nation of Cuba is, like all nations, a "cultural artifact," it is clear that this artifact or construct had been widely used since the nineteenth-century independence movement and had adopted several guises thereafter. Miguel Cossío Woodward's novel *Sacchario* (1970) was written as the campaign was taking place and thus provides a literary counterpart to the official representations of the revolutionary nation. In fact, *Sacchario* can be considered *the* novel of the Sugar Campaign, as the few other published texts recounting the story of the life of sugarcane cutters in Cuba do not refer to the 1970 campaign explicitly.[2]

Ambrosio Fornet, in his review of *Sacchario* as the 1970 Casa de las Américas Prize winner for best novel, wrote: "*Sacchario* brings up once again the possibility of an epic vanguard in the Cuban novel. . . . Narrated at times as an evocation and at times as a harangue, in the tone of a speech or a newspaper, the story of Darío [the protagonist] is fused with the story of the people; the individual is fused with the collective, in the leveling turmoil of revolutionary action" (Fornet, "A propósito" 184). For Fornet, Darío fuses with the revolutionary collective because he *develops* with the Revolution. Unlike the protagonists of other revolutionary novels, who had to shed their old bourgeois selves to become revolutionaries, Darío is a working-class man who suffered "the hardship and injustice of the prerevolutionary years," came of age in 1959, and immediately joined the ranks of the Revolution (Fornet 184). Thus, Darío illustrates three basic tenets of the Cuban revolutionary nation as represented in official discourse: his participation in the campaign is cast in the rhetoric of Cuba, Revolution, and Sugar as one and the same; his personal development illustrates the idea of continuity and innovation in history; and as a white male character, he epitomizes the questionable unity of the Cuban revolutionary nation.

The alleged fusion between Darío/the individual and the nation/collective is reproduced in the different meanings evoked by the novel's title. The word *sacchario* is a cognate for two terms in Latin: the word *saccarius*, which means "street porter, odd-job man, errand boy," and the word *saccharum* or "a type of syrup that Persians and Arabs extracted from sugarcane . . . and [was] used only because of its medicinal properties" (Valbuena 747). This title reveals how the novel seeks to give shape to the identity figure of the worker ("saccarius"), whose life is intimately connected with the sugarcane, and to traditional Cuban stories, which, like syrup ("saccharum"), are distilled from the plant. Because of his connection to the Cuban sugar tradition, Darío appears to be an amalgam of collective stories and can be likened to the syrup extracted from Cuban sugarcane. The character is so steeped in the official version of Cuban tradition forged by the campaign that it becomes almost impossible to distinguish him from the collective identity of cane cutters. Darío is thus emblematic of the Cuban revolutionary everyman as defined by the official rhetoric of the Sugar Campaign.

At times, the proposed identification between the Cuban worker and the Cuban tradition is questioned in the novel. This subversion can be explained by yet another ramification of the etymology of the word *saccharío*. In *Nuevo cataure de cubanismos*, Fernando Ortiz explains that the word *guarapo*, a beverage extracted from sugarcane, comes from the Arabic *xarabe*, a potion used as medicine (*Cataure* 277). The second meaning of the word *saccharum*, syrup extracted from cane, with medicinal properties, is thus related to guarapo or alcohol, as both are liquid substances with medicinal properties that are derived from cane. Indeed, at times cane syrup and alcohol seem to be mixed together in *Sacchario*: occasionally the narrator seems inebriated and carried away by the pleasure of the text, thus stressing his individuality and subverting the idea of a collective identity fostered in official nationalistic discourse.[3]

In this chapter, I will examine the different readings of this book in the context of the Sugar Campaign, but it should be noted that there were significant changes in the tone of the public discourse during the two years that the Sugar Campaign straddled, from October 1969 to July 1970. In most of the 1969 speeches, Fidel sounded very triumphant, boosting the nationalist ego, criticizing imperialism, and raising high hopes for Cuba's future. Every speech he gave that year, no matter the occasion, served to refer to the campaign and to exhort the people to meet the goal. By contrast, once the failure to meet the goal became apparent in 1970, Fidel adopted an apologetic tone and made the following surprising statement: "So we have lost the battle of the Ten Million to the sugar yield. . . . A basic fact is that the people have not lost the battle. . . . We, the administrative apparatus of the revolution, we, the leaders of the revolution, have lost this battle" (19700521).

The failure of the Sugar Campaign in fact marked the beginning of a new conceptualization of the nation, in which the responsibility of the Revolution would be placed largely on the shoulders of the leaders, rather than on the people. In other respects, the unmet ten-million-ton harvest signified, as Pérez-Stable puts it, "the end of the Revolution" (*Origins* 20), as it became clear that the regime had failed to generate the economic and political resources to realize its own form of Socialism. From that point forward, Cuba was compelled to follow the models of the Soviet Union and western Europe. The Revolution became institutionalized and the nationalist euphoria was muffled, as "the Soviet model with a Cuban face" was relinquished. My analysis focuses mainly on the speeches of 1969, which represent Cuban revolutionary and nationalistic discourse at its most expansive.

The Revolutionary Cuban Nation: The Sugar Tradition, a Halting History, and the Overcoming of Race

Because of Cuba's historical and economic development, sugar is often described as an essential element of the nation. For instance, Antonio Benítez Rojo wrote: "Sugar is and has been the one factor determining Cuban political geography and demographic composition, shaping as well its economic, social and cultural history. Sugar, in more or less apparent ways, has been the most powerful motive behind every war, intervention, revolution and crisis in Cuba, and on which its well being still depends" (Benítez Rojo, "Power" 13–14). In Benedict Anderson's expression, sugar production changed the "socioscape," or the landscape, the population makeup, and the distribution of wealth in Cuba (Anderson 32). The fact that Cuba had been a major sugar producer since the 1830s, and the effects of this culture on Cuban society and history, are often cited as marking the emergence of the Cuban nation.

In the year of the historical *zafra*, or harvest, the connection between the Cuban nation and sugar was particularly emphasized. For instance, the leading literary journal *Casa de las Américas* published the article "Desgarramiento azucarero e integración nacional" (Torn apart by sugar and integrated in the nation) by Manuel Moreno Fraginals, which traced a history of Cuba according to the development of sugar production. In that same issue, Edmundo Desnoes's "Cuba: Caña y cultura" (Cuba: sugarcane and culture) gave an account of the cultural history of Cuba by selecting works of art that represented sugar in one way or another. Desnoes explained the principle of his selection with the following argument: "The importation and voracious rootedness of sugarcane mark the economic and fundamental birth of Cuba. . . . Blacks are more Cuban than palm trees are, the Spaniards gave birth to *criollos*, and all of us bear sugar in our blood" (Desnoes, "Cuba: caña y cultura" 47). Note that Desnoes mentioned all of the Cuban ethnicities, with the glaring exception of Asian workers brought to harvest cane, who to a large extent failed to become integrated into Cuban society. The idea that all sectors of the Cuban population have "sugar in their blood" marks the Sugar Campaign as a decisive moment in the history of Cuba and in the development of the Revolution, collapsing Cuba, the campaign, and the Revolution into one and the same.

The equivalence between Cuba as a nation, sugar, and the Revolution is well documented in Fidel's speeches, in which he cultivated the moral support necessary to unite the nation in a single effort by presenting the success of the Revolution as contingent on the campaign. Upon launching the campaign, Fidel stated that "the revolution essentially depends not on the will of those who lead it, no; it depends on the will of all the people, what the workers themselves are capable of doing" (19691028). In 1969, cutting cane was presented as *the* revolutionary task: outside the dynamics of sugar production, the Revolution seemed to come to a standstill. What is more, in this symbolic collapsing, several of the characteristics associated with the Revolution shifted to represent the Cuban nation itself: in the same way that the Revolution was masculinist, that is, designed with a stereotypically masculine attitude, the Sugar Campaign was presented as a "male" endeavor. In Fidel's words: "It [the campaign] is a test of his [the cane cutter's] character, a proof of his will, a test of his integrity as a revolutionary and as a man. And the concept of man implies the disposition to face tests and labor. I am certain that work of this kind will serve to temper a man's spirit, to strengthen his character, to make him harder, to make him a better fighter. . . . It [valor] is what draws us closer to the true concept of the revolutionary, to the concept of manhood . . ." (19691106). As the "new men" of the Cuban revolutionary nation proved themselves in the fields, they were imbricated in the traditional discourse of "Cubanness," or the definition of what it means to be Cuban. In Martí's words: "In the gymnastics of nations, as in the case of individuals, one only starts lifting heavy weights after having lifted lesser weights (for an extensive period). . . . It is not this occasional, galvanic strength, fictitious and external, which nations need to prosper with certainty. Instead, what is required is one's own muscular strength, well-exercised, well-distributed, permanent, internal" (Martí quoted in Kirk, "José Martí" 102). True to his time, Martí associated moral fortitude with physical strength, and by implication he linked Cuban honor and dignity with the male character.

Building on Ernest Renan's theory that France was built on the tragedies of the past—the night of St. Bartholomew, for instance—Benedict Anderson claims that all nations are built simultaneously on a need to forget the past and an urge to constantly retell that same past. Hence the idea that every nation is constructed on the basis of "a tradition that is simultaneously remembered and forgotten" (Anderson 187). Indeed, in his speeches Fidel built the concept of a revolutionary nation on the tradition of struggle in Cuba;

the Revolution was thus situated in a line of continuity with the past. At the same time, the 1959 Revolution by definition inaugurated an era that represented a break with this line of history. In Hayden White's terms, the "mode of emplotment" of Fidel's concept of history is "Organicist" and "Romantic." It is "Organicist" because "it depicts the consolidation . . . of some integrated entity . . . whose importance is greater than that of any of the individual entities analyzed" (White 15). At the same time, it is "Romantic" because it is a "drama of the triumph of Good over Evil" (White 9). This triumph of Good, the moral redemption that the Revolution brought, allegedly became a reality in the "integrated entity" of the revolutionary nation.

In the context of the Sugar Campaign, the people of the revolutionary nation were the heirs of those who helped bring about this new era, and as such they were called to accomplish the same feats. According to Fidel: "It [the campaign] is what draws us closer to the fighters who gave their lives in the mountains during the war, or in the underground, the fighters who gave their lives in Girón, the fighters who gave their lives in Escambray, the fighters who gave their lives in Bolivia or in other places serving the cause of the Revolution. This is what draws us close to the great revolutionaries, the heroes, the martyrs of our country's history" (19691106). By pointing at the heroes of the Revolution, Fidel used a rhetorical strategy also similar to the one claimed by Ernest Renan, a classic theorist of the nation. According to Renan: "A heroic past, great men, glory, . . . this is the social capital upon which one bases a national idea. To have common glories in the past, and to have a common will in the present; to have performed great deeds together, to wish to perform still more—these are the essential conditions for being a people. Suffering in common unites more than joy does" (Renan 19). Renan and Fidel reached the same conclusion from two different ends of the political spectrum: both claimed a mythological past as a model to maintain a regime in the present. Renan, like Fidel, was bent on creating a national consciousness based on the spirit of sacrifice of the great epics of the past.

Following the motif of continuity with the past, the Sugar Campaign was appropriately threatened by U.S. intervention. In the same way that the Literacy Campaign was interrupted by the invasion of Playa Girón, the landing of some mercenaries on the beach of Baracoa and the killing of five Cuban fishermen interfered with the Sugar Campaign. This incident offered Fidel a unique opportunity not only to unite the Cuban nation against an enemy, but also to define the nation in terms of the campaign. At this point Fidel invoked what Benedict Anderson, citing Walter Benjamin, calls "messianic time," or past, present, and future in one, creating the idea of simultaneity that the nation is founded upon (Anderson 24). In official discourse, the confrontation on the Baracoa Beach situated Cuba in the coordinates of past, present, and future by linking the campaign with other campaigns in the past, reminding Cubans that others wanted to obstruct their hard labor in the present, and stating that Cubans were shaping their future while cutting cane. "We are working hard building our tomorrow," said Fidel, "defending our right to the present and, what is much more, defending our destiny—a destiny that has forced us to build with copious sweat—sweat is good, only with sweat can we create our destiny . . ." (19700421).

The continuity with the past was also illustrated in the speeches of the Sugar Campaign through the icon of the machete, which linked revolutionary Cuba with earlier feats of independence. Like Esteban Montejo in *Biography of a Runaway Slave*, whose account ends with him stating that, in case there were battles yet to come, "A machete will do" for him (Barnet 200), Fidel chose the machete to elevate cane cutters to the category of national heroes: "We shall keep the machete as a glorious reminder of two things: the charge of the *mambisa* cavalry [insurgents in the independence war against Spain] and the charge of the *mambises* of the twentieth century, i.e., the cane cutters, the charge of the ten million!" (19690714). The machete functioned as a sign of continuity in the struggle for independence. At the same time, this sharp tool symbolized the breakthrough that the Revolution caused. According to Fidel, if the campaign were successful, Cuba would replace machetes with machines, and the hardship of cane cutting with a machete would disappear.

Just as the machete was linked to the Sugar Campaign, so too were the *mambisa* cavalry, or the heroes of independence, who were in turn associated with the many rebellious slaves that integrated it. However, apart from the historical context of independence, during the Sugar Campaign Fidel did not acknowledge the symbolic connection of cane cutting to Afro-Cubans, as if their identity were also a thing of the past. The fact that there was not a single reference to race in Fidel's speeches displayed another constant of the Cuban revolutionary nation: the neglect of racial difference.[4] The idea of a color-blind society was replicated during the Sugar Campaign, with the result that Afro-Cubans—in spite of their protagonism in the history of Cuba as a sugar nation—were not explicitly represented in the ideal nation unified in the record sugar harvest. The speeches of the Sugar Campaign did not contain a single specific reference to the black roots of the culture of sugar in Cuba. The representation of the campaign participants as devoid of ethnic characteristics is echoed in the novel *Sacchario*, where the main character representing the revolutionary Everyman is, perhaps by default, white.

That the campaign represented a break with the past was also shown in the introduction of a new concept of time. As in the French Revolution, the Cuban Revolution associated every calendar year with a different name that indicated its focus: for instance, 1959 was "the Year of Liberation," 1960 "the Year of the Agrarian Reform," 1961 "the Year of Education," and so forth (Thomas 1436). In addition, owing to the demands of the harvest, Fidel proposed that from 1969 on the traditional Christmas holiday should not be celebrated until July, after the sugar harvest had been completed. According to Fidel, the Revolution would thus break with a tradition that was alien to Cuba, since Christmas was imposed either by Spanish or Anglo-Saxon cultures. The idea was that from that point in time onward, Cuba would advance according to its own calendar, based on the economic needs of a revolutionary country that was emerging from its dependency.[5] In this revolutionary time, which reaffirmed the image of the nation with its own historical plot on the path to a new era, the discourse of the leaders claimed a unique place economically and culturally for Cuba.

As explained in this section, the constants of the nation of Cuba in the speeches of the Sugar Campaign are the following: it is intrinsically connected to sugar and revolution, its history advances in a continuous and at the same time fractured line with the past, it is virtually silent about ethnic or racial identities. This representation of the Cuban nation offers only one version of Cuba and obliterates the existence of difference within the nation. As I will demonstrate, the constants and omissions of the revolutionary nation are both reproduced and subverted in *Sacchario*, whose protagonist exemplifies the revolutionary nation.

### The Cane Cutter as an Everyman: Darío Becomes "the People"

*Sacchario,* as a novel about the life of volunteer cane cutters, is divided into three parts titled "Morning," "Afternoon," and "Night," which narrate daily activities in the cane field. The text includes sections with omniscient narration in the present tense, creating the illusion that events are being narrated as they happen, and providing detailed descriptions of what the characters feel while cutting cane. The sections narrated in the present tense alternate with others written in the past tense that tell the story of Darío, the protagonist, and his fellow cane cutters. In addition, interspersed between the past tense and present tense sections are fragments of historical texts pertaining to the sugar tradition in Cuba, which are grouped under the heading "Sacchario."

The novel is framed by a conversation between a character "from another world" and Darío. The man "from another world" asks Darío, who is working in the fields, about the "meaning" of volunteer work in Cuba. This scene underscores the idea that volunteer cane cutting cannot be understood by outsiders, because only revolutionary Cubans would be willing to cut cane without material retribution. Hence, from the very beginning the text is construed to explain cane cutting as a defining part of Cuban history and tradition. The last part of this frame, where the stranger looks puzzled as the Cuban man explains about volunteer cane cutting, is repeated verbatim at the end of the novel. The image of Cuba that the stranger describes at the end has not changed: an underdeveloped nation where people harvest cane by hand, without receiving a salary. In the context of the novel the reader has just finished, this is a mistaken representation of the Cuban nation, but the conversation seeks to show that the perception of Cuba from the outside does not necessarily match the strong nation that the novel represents.

The frame of the novel and the sections with the heading "Sacchario" embody the identification between Cuba, sugar production, and the Revolution. The "Sacchario" sections consist of fragments of works representing the Cuban cultural tradition, particularly in its strong relationship with sugar, written by figures who could be called the Cuban nation's founding fathers, among others, Manuel Moreno Fraginals, Fernando Ortiz, Fernando Agete, José M. de Cárdenas y Rodríguez, Carlos Manuel de Céspedes, and Máximo Gómez. By virtue of being placed in the novel, fragments of their original works are rewritten and resemanticized in a new context, in which the 1959 Cuban Revolution completes the long struggle for recognition of the independence and cultural uniqueness of Cuba as a nation.

The first of these texts is a fragment of Fernando Ortiz's *Contrapunteo cubano del tabaco y el azúcar* (1940) (*Cuban Counterpoint: Tobacco and Sugar,* 1947), which refers to one of the few rebellions connected with sugar, known as the Demajagua Rebellion because it took place on a plantation of that name. On October 10, 1868, Carlos Manuel de Céspedes freed the thirty slaves he had on his plantation and issued a proclamation also remembered as the Grito de Yara: "We only want to be free and equal, as the Creator intended all mankind to be . . . we believe that all men are created equal" (quoted in Thomas 245). This rebellion and proclamation triggered a slave revolt, and both are considered the beginning of the wars of independence against Spain. Demajagua and Yara were also the first steps in the long process of the abolition of slavery in Cuba, which did not occur until 1886.

By selecting this fragment, the narrator highlights an aspect of the history of sugar in Cuba not emphasized at all in Ortiz's book. In fact, for Ortiz, the business of sugar was the antithesis of rebellion. According to Ortiz, sugar was associated with authoritarianism, as opposed to the tobacco world, wherein revolutions were constantly in the making. In Ortiz's own words: "There is no rebellion or challenge in sugar, nor resentment, nor brooding suspicion, but humble pleasure, quiet, calm, and soothing. Tobacco is boldly imaginative and individualistic to the point of anarchy" (*Counterpoint* 16). More explicitly, "It was not sugar, but tobacco smoke that wafted the breath of a new spirit through the Old World, analytic, critical and rebellious" (18). In inserting the fragment on the Demajagua Rebellion at the beginning of *Sacchario*, the author revises Ortiz's contentions in terms of the role of sugar in Cuban history: sugar production is radically represented as the place where rebellion starts, as it is similarly presented in the speeches of the Sugar Campaign and in the rest of the novel. Surprisingly, the racial implications of this revision are not brought up, either in the novel or in the speeches. For Ortiz, sugar was associated with the ruling class because it was white. In *Sacchario*, the resymbolization of sugar as the site of rebellion is not tied to its intrinsically *black* component, in that blacks did most of the cane cutting and it was the slaves who initiated the independence revolts in Cuba.

*Sacchario* also implicitly projects the consequences of the Demajagua incident quoted from Ortiz beyond the context of slavery toward the need for the 1959 Cuban Revolution: "The bell tolling in the sugar mill was substituted by the steam or electric whistle that now stridently calls workers in the sugar mill, like the whistle of a monstrous steel overseer" (Ortiz, quoted in *Sacchario* 17). In other words, since the Demajagua Rebellion only substituted the bell for the whistle, it did not succeed in liberating the Cuban nation, but the enormous voluntary effort of the Sugar Campaign in fact would signify the real liberation of Cuba. Once again, there is no mention of the role of blacks in achieving this liberation.

The opening of the novel with a reference to the Demajagua Rebellion was in line with Fidel's recurrent mention of "the hundred years of fighting" during the 1970 Sugar Campaign, "a theme of the historiography of the Revolution," according to Louis Pérez: "The centennial commemoration of the Grito de Yara (1868) served to define a unifying historical construct that gave decisive shape to Cuban historiography in 1968: *cien años de lucha.* The national past was set in a contextual sweep of a century-long struggle. A struggle in which successive generations of Cubans were summoned by history to dramatic action and heroic sacrifice" (Pérez 4). The centennial commemoration of the one hundred years of struggle coincided with the death of Che Guevara and had already been celebrated when the novel was written. To a large extent, the fact that the novel begins with a reference to the Demajagua Rebellion pays homage to the centennial, but more importantly, it emphasizes that revolutionary struggle is not over. After the death of Che Guevara, the Revolution experienced a loss of morale, and Cubans needed a boost of revolutionary fervor. The Sugar Campaign, apart from its economic motivations, represented an attempt at mobilizing the revolutionary nation and making it aware of the currency of the revolutionary values.

While the textual fragments cited at the beginning of the "Sacchario" sections reinforce the link between the nation of Cuba, Sugar, and Revolution, the narrator's peculiar use of personal pronouns and verb tenses in *Sacchario*, integrating and merging different points of view in the novel, creates a character who can be considered "universal": an empty "I" who is at the same time saturated with reference and stands for a speaker, an ideal reader, or an emblematic Cuban. The narrator's alternation of pronouns breaks the boundaries between a collective "they" and an individual "I" or "you." To use here the terminology coined by Benedict Anderson, the empty "I" in some of *Sacchario*'s passages thus conjures up "a world of plurals," it means "a young man who belongs to the collective body of readers," it creates "an imagined community" (Anderson 32).

For instance, the novel's opening paragraph offers an example of all characters, even Darío, being presented as a collective being, intricately connected with the events of the nation:

> The insistent sound of the whistle. They sleep soundly. Hunching. Bent in the hammocks. They snore. They sound like saws. El Moro traces some steps. Papaíto dances. The canes swing, they grow at a dizzying speed. . . . I try to make it through. But the cane forms a thick and hard screen. They have the size of skyscrapers. El Cantante is singing at a corner, playing his guitar. I call him. Help me. But he does not pay attention. . . . The cane grows like crazy. I cut and cut. We need to make a clearing. Paco and the barber follow me. . . . We need to open a clearing until our relief arrives. . . . Everything is dark and it smells of honey. The heat is scorching. . . . I must have entangled myself with the mosquito net. . . . El Cantante is giving a recital in the Teatro Mella. . . . An earthquake. Paco wants to get on the rocket. . . . The *persi* comes, gotta run. They sound the reveille. The whistle. The strident sound of the whistle in your ears. Cold. . . . Whistle. Arsenio's. Morning. The freezing air through the cracks, through the guano roof. Up! Up! Up! (Cossio Woodward 19–21).

This passage is worth quoting at length, because it displays a variety of narrative voices and techniques and alludes to some events that are significant in the novel. The staccato rhythm of this fragment reproduces the rhythm of the cane-cutting camp: every action is presented separately, as experienced by the characters, as a recurrent sequence of well-known events in the daily routine that is hammered into them. The narration of the crude reality of waking up in the barracks is interspersed with references to the characters' dreams, in such a way that at times Darío as an individual is indistinguishable from the other characters. The fragment introduces most of the characters of the text: el Moro, Papaíto, el Cantante (the Singer), Paco, el barbero (the barber), and Darío. Papaíto dressed as a babalao, el Cantante singing in the Teatro Mella, and Paco wanting to go in a rocket are all presented at the same level as Darío's being chased by the *perseguidora*—Cuban police ears, which were said to kidnap people in the Batista era—a fire that takes place in the field, which they all try to extinguish, and an earthquake as a natural phenomenon that affects a whole nation. The description of what the characters do ("They sleep soundly. Hunching") alternates with a first person ("I try to make it through"), which, we may presume, could be Darío speaking but could also stand for any other character. The narration thus migrates from the collective to the personal, creating the feeling that all characters fuse into one because of their shared experience of the daily routine and hardship.

While the mix of pronouns blends an individual with the mass of cane cutters, the alternation between past and present narration illustrates the idea of the suspended time of the nation or the "messianic time" cited above, in which different patterns of time become intertwined. There are sections of the text narrated in the present tense that give explicit details about the characters' thoughts while they are cutting. In these sections, the text creates the illusion that events are told as they happen and thus attempts to involve an ideal reader in the epic of the nation: "All the way at the bottom, Paco, that's right. . . . First you get rid of the leaves. You need to get rid of those additions. Bang! A strike at the center, how tough! . . . Pull it backwards, whack! I did such a good job! . . . You've got to bend your back well. . . . A *mache—tazo*!? [the last word simulates a big strike with the machete]" (Cossio Woodward 73). Interspersed with these sections in the present are different stories about the lives of the cane cutters narrated in the past tense. Together, the voices expressing what the characters are feeling and the stories representing the various "types" among "the people" provide the plot with a degree of descriptive thickness that represents the revolutionary nation.

Thus, for instance, el Cantante is a wandering singer and cane cutter who becomes a vehicle for the representation of the wealth of Cuban popular culture, expressed in the songs reproduced in the text and in the evocations of the natural beauty and culinary traditions of the places he has visited.[6] The barber Fígaro, in contrast, represents the person who "was stuck on the old ways," as he sympathized with the Revolution but was very fond of cockfights, which were forbidden once the Revolution was established.

The case of Papaíto, the only black character in the novel, deserves special attention. His individuality emerges because he is the best cane cutter of them all. His virtuoso skills could thus have been linked to the tradition of blacks cutting cane in Cuba, but there is no mention of such a tradition in the text. Instead, Papaíto's ethnicity is described as follows: "A black man like any other, who took life with an empirical and cheap philosophy, as it came, an advanced student at the 'University of the Street' to whom no one could give any nonsense . . .[a man] who would gain the heart of all the domestics and chicks of el Vedado" (41). Papaíto is thus characterized with a series of attributes that are stereotypically associated with his race. Papaíto, as "a regular black" is "like every other black," and within that group of people—synonymous with the lower classes in the worst sense—he has no individuality, except for his role in the Sugar Campaign. In contrast, it is Darío, the white protagonist of the novel, who—as a volunteer cane cutter—embodies the ideal of the New Man. This leads one to conclude that the novel is addressed to an ideal white reader who identifies with Darío and with the predominantly white nation evoked in the novel.

Comparable to the treatment given to ethnic and racial identity, gender difference was not foregrounded in revolutionary discourse. In like manner, women are completely absent in the revolutionary microcosm of the novel, their presence limited to the male characters' fantasies and recollections of past experiences with prostitutes. The construct of the revolutionary nation in Cuba was historically man-made and made for men. Thus, the novel does not mention the role of women in the Sugar Campaign, some of whom were cane cutters themselves or substituted for their husbands in their revolutionary duties in the city (Smith and Padula 101). Of those who substituted for their husbands, many abandoned their jobs in the middle of the campaign, as they felt their children needed them more. Despite their significant contribution to the campaign, women were excluded from institutional discourse, although they were invoked once again as a group at the time of explaining the campaign's failure.

The fact that women do not appear in the novel's figuration of the Cuban nation also has to do with the denial of difference in the concept of the nation itself, as the following text indicates: "The fatherland was something immaterial, intangible, [and] there was more to it than those lands and mountains and rivers and swamps that they were defending today . . . there was more to it than a government or an institution or a law written for all Cubans, there was more to it than the history gathered in texts, than the folklore and the *guajiro* thing, and the *décima* and the *guayabera*, the Valle de Viñales or Yumurí's; the fatherland was a regional concept of humanity" (Cossio Woodward 169).[7] Significantly, in this fragment, "the fatherland" is a collective identity that cannot be defined by the individuals that form it or the hegemonic institutions that regulate or control it. *Patria* is an entity where all identities are dissolved in favor of the concepts of "humanity" or "solidarity in struggle" that were fostered by the Revolution. Gender and race were of necessity dissolved in these abstractions.

Against the background of the collectivity, Darío emerges as the revolutionary everyman. His childhood, for example, is narrated with evocative detail, focusing on incidents and interactions that are supposed to represent the experience of "an average Cuban." From the sections narrating his childhood, we learn, on the one hand, about Darío's ambivalent attitude toward Cubans of Chinese origin and, on the other, about his respectful relationship with his elders. We also get a glimpse of the games he played with other children in the neighborhood. Darío's late adolescence coincides with the development of a political awareness and his involvement in the riots against Batista. Darío's revolutionary consciousness is taken up as he acquires a new revolutionary vocabulary:

> The first proclamations, the beginning of life, the bands of el Bejucal, the Granma landing, the sale of vouchers, the crazy youth, the domino games while conspiring, the swigs at Guanabo, the repression of the goons, the struggle, the danger, the insurrection, the triumph, the right to start, to say fatherland, agrarian reform, land, social justice, independence, freedom, sovereignty, words, words, repeated in this country throughout a century, . . . revolution, revolution, strong word, echo of rifles, of mountains, of planes, of cities, . . . raising a whirlwind of enthusiasm, turning them into men, giving them facts and rights . . . to breathe, live, grow, grow, be of age, be called Darío or Perico. . . *revolution, revolution, change, rupture, transformation of a people, of a society, of a life, of a man, of Darío* (102–3, emphasis added).

The events of Darío's life are narrated at a very a quick pace, similar to the rhythm of the passage I have just quoted. The cumulative rhythm of the narration juxtaposes one action with another, as if it were not necessary to dwell on details that a Cuban reader is expected to know from his or her own experience. Darío's life is evoked in order to establish continuity with the transformations experienced by the Cuban nation.

However, as I have already remarked in my reading of the speeches, the Cuban revolutionary nation is represented both in *rupture* as well as in *con-*

*tinuity* with the past. The epiphanic moment when Darío realizes that becoming a revolutionary entails a change of skin is paired with a description of the old collective identity, which the Cuban nation has to shed:

> Yes, it was necessary to change one's skin, to let slip that layer of "*Chambelona*" and politicking and deep skepticism, start getting rid of the insecurity, the [habit of telling a] cruel joke, the laughing, the cackle in the midst of silence, the mockery, the wit . . . the image of this island of sugar . . . the island of natives . . . the island of drummers, the island of voodoo and Santería, . . . the island of the happy man, . . . the weekend island, [the island of the] Hotel Riviera . . . , the island of the *sonsonete*, the island of tricks, the island of shit, the dirty island, the illiterate, backward, unemployed, lazy, ragged island, encrusted with that sick skin with which they were born. . . .[8]

This comment seems an ironic reference to the fact that race identities, metaphorized in the "sick skin," were also left behind in the institutional discourse of the Revolution. Since the island that is left behind after the revolutionary transformation is that of voodoo and Santería, it becomes clear that the black tradition is associated with the backwardness that the Cuban nation leaves behind.

As we follow Darío's development from novice to full-fledged revolutionary, his new persona becomes a metaphor for the highest point in the history of Cuban nationhood, which, according to the text, is embodied in the collective effort of the Sugar Campaign. The final section of the text narrates the last months before Darío joined the ranks of volunteer cane cutters and the end of the book therefore sends us back to the beginning of the central story in the novel, one day in the life of the volunteer cane cutters. In this circular movement the narrator invites us to note the transformation that Darío has experienced in the field: his maturity as a revolutionary would not be complete without his participation in the campaign. The contrast between the old Darío and the new Darío is constant throughout the text, as it alternates between present tense and past tense narration.

As for the other characters, their struggles in the field make them more politically committed. Since these characters are meant to be representative of most groups in the Cuban nation, Cuba as a whole emerges as a reconstituted nation after its collective involvement in the campaign. But it is Darío who, even as an individual character, embodies all of the characteristics of the ideal new revolutionary nation that emerges after the campaign: he represents all "new Cubans." At the end of the text, the revolutionary collective identity allegedly brought forth by the Sugar Campaign has no fissures: homogeneity and unity are the hallmarks of the new nation embodied in one character. And yet, as the next section shows, individual identity does not completely disappear in the ideal concept of the nation that the text attempts to create.

## The Narrator's Intoxication: Literary Creation and the Remembrance of the City

Revolutionary narratives require a straightforward style, a documentary technique that is as transparent and "truth bearing" as possible, in order to let the "facts" and "truths" of revolutionary ideology stand by themselves, as revolutionary commissars often noted. This explains Rogelio Rodríguez Coronel's prescriptions on the decade of the 1970s in Cuban revolutionary literature: "Those aspects [the concept of historical events and the projection of all current endeavors toward the future] will be devoid of all poetic magic [in order for authors] . . . to subject themselves to a more direct narrative discourse, leaving the parable aside, divesting itself of all mystification of reality" (*La novela* 168–69). In the novels of the 1970s in Cuba, the trace of the author as craftsman is often reduced to a minimum, as there should be no recognizable "mediator" between the "reality" of the text and the reader.

However, *Sacchario* strikes one for its *textuality,* since the narrative techniques employed in the text keep the reader aware of the fact that she or he is working through the fabric of the text. Such textuality also makes the *presence* of the narrator much more overt, as he seems to delight in the mixing of narrative modes, the deliberate fragmentation and the introduction of various time schemes and voices. There are three different types of sections in the novel, all woven together: in addition to the segments titled "Sacchario"—which are made up of fragments of essays on the Cuban sugar tradition—there are parts of the text that describe daily activities of the volunteer cane cutters and, finally, sections that evoke the past of these character's lives. There are seldom any transitions or apparent connections between these sections. The activities of the characters in the field do not necessarily connect with the reminiscences of their past. It is the reader who has to bridge the gaps and thus become aware of his or her role in the text.

Furthermore, *Sacchario*'s frame of retrospective reflections, which opens and closes the narrative, makes the reader acutely aware of the novel's status *as a text.* The fragmentation of the text, that is, the mixture of modes and the slippage of personal pronouns, makes *Sacchario* a readerly text, according to Roland Barthes's terminology, or one in which the reader *cooperates in creating* the text, since he or she needs to bridge the gaps and adapt him- or herself to the types of understanding required by diverse narrative modes.

The labor of reading *Sacchario* thus short-circuits the process of identification of the reader with the revolutionary hero, in spite of other rhetorical devices that the narrator uses to foster such identification. *Sacchario* contrasts
with the style of Socialist realist narratives as explained in my introduction,
which typically have a linear plot and a simple style of narration shorn of
the features of the readerly text in favor of facilitating a direct identification
between reader and hero.

In some passages of the novel the narrator remains an unobtrusive presence as he adopts a highly evocative, collective, or choral-like voice that alludes to characters, situations, smells, and feelings supposedly shared by his
fellow Cubans. But in these segments the narrator often provides detailed
descriptions of what one would presume to be his own experience, perhaps
overlapping with the author's experience as well. The wealth of detail offered
in these passages suggests that the narrator has a high degree of nostalgia
for an unrecoverable and pleasant prerevolutionary past. In particular, many
of these passages are devoted to reminiscing about Havana, reiterating the
significance of the city in the symbolic articulation of Cuba and the Revolution.

In the words of Guillermo Cabrera Infante, "Havana was a poetic reduction of Cuba, a metaphor" (Cabrera Infante, "La Habana" 125) situated at the
center of all of the drastic changes brought by the Revolution. In *La Habana
1952–1961*, Jacobo Machover explains that during the guerrilla war in the Sierra Maestra, Havana—though affected by numerous bombs, riots, jailings,
and executions—remained practically impassive. Even in those tumultuous
years parts of the city remained a haven for pleasure seekers enjoying its
famed night life in venues such as La Rampa, described in Cabrera Infante's
*Tres tristes tigres* (1965) (*Three Trapped Tigers*, 1971). With the advent of the
Revolution, the regime built hospitals, schools, and recreational centers in
many neighborhoods, but it gradually closed down all nightclubs. In those
early years Havana was offered as an example of the idea that the identity
of the New Man would be built on the basis of good health and education,
with the total eradication of all "ephemeral pleasures" (Machover 22). As
the Revolution attained worldwide recognition, Havana returned to center
stage, this time as the Mecca of all left-wing intellectuals who supported the
Revolution. Prerevolutionary Havana was represented not just as the site
of depravity and national humiliation, but as the place that epitomized the
social inequalities of the previous era, since the nightclubs were said to cater
exclusively to the elite.

Despite the cultural effervescence of the early years, it is significant that
it was the documentary *PM*, by Sabá Cabrera Infante and Orlando Jiménez

Leal, that unleashed a wave of stricter control over artists and intellectuals in Cuba. As described in chapter 2, this increased control started with the prohibition of the documentary, the closing of the weekly publication *Lunes de Revolución*, Fidel's speech "Words to the Intellectuals," and later the dissolution of the group called El Puente, along with the jailing of "antisocial subjects" such as Virgilio Piñera, José Mario, and Ana María Simó. The short documentary *PM* displayed a Havana whose existence the Revolution struggled to deny, a city where ordinary people also had their share in the night life. José Lezama Lima wrote about the sense of emptiness that the Revolution started to experience in the years after the crackdown on Havana's night life. "Havana still preserves the measure of all men. Man traces its contours, finds its center, grasps its areas of infiniteness and solitude where the fearful happens. That classical, neat measure of man drives him to renounce all night life. By chance, after midnight, Havana closes its flower and its marvels. . . . The lights of morning and dusk are now the dance of lights in Havana. The cold moon comes to our hearts and there it scratches and withdraws" (Lezama Lima, "Ritmo" 63). With his usual obliqueness, Lezama referred to the moralistic attitude of the Revolution, which used the concept of "classical measure" for the New Man," and chose Havana as the stage to show that Cubans were renouncing night life in favor of a strict work ethic.

Lezama's implicit nostalgia for the Havana before the crackdown on night life also appears in *Sacchario*, where certain places of the city are featured prominently. Such locations correspond to Pierre Nora's definition of the "places of memory," or the "vestiges, the ultimate embodiments of a commemorative consciousness that survives in a history which, having renounced memory, cries out for it." For Nora, at times when the collective of a nation is threatened by drastic political changes, it takes refuge in such places (Nora 6–7). In the case of Cuba, the national memory was in a state of flux after the Revolution, owing to the new revolutionary historiography and the historical rupture that the Revolution signaled. Therefore, the regime elaborated its own "places of memory" in connection with the icons and events of revolutionary history. But this did not prevent Cubans inside and outside the island from dwelling on memories of prerevolutionary Havana as a site for restoring lost identities.

The representation of Havana in *Sacchario* can be taken as an example of how Cubans inside the island remembered the city before the Revolution. In many instances in the first part of the novel, the narrator adopts a sort of choral voice that is deeply evocative of many characters, smells, and images of the former Havana. For instance in this passage: "At the Centro Gallego dances on Sunday evenings, where you had to beg the doorman to let you get in, . . . the orchestra all of a sudden would change the melody, and the refrain would ask 'let the ball stop,' . . . and they stopped, they laughed, . . . trying to follow the beat that now turned into a conga, one, two, three, what a cool step, forming a line, a parade, which ended up with a racket on the first floor, and the old woman looking for them, . . . to cross the Parque Central later, . going down the Calle Obispo, where they would stop to look at the windows of La Moderna Poesía, and La Rusquella . . ." (65–66). This passage does not condemn pre–Revolutionary Cuba as dissolute, a land of depravity, or the place where only higher economic classes could enjoy the night life. In this sense, such segments of *Sacchario* not only differ from other revolutionary novels of the time, but stand in marked contrast with other parts of the novel that explicitly criticize Havana's night life.[9]

In *Sacchario*, passages such as the one cited above have a subversive potential akin to the documentary film *PM*. The style of these evocations—with sites and names carefully noted—is also reminiscent of Cabrera Infante's *Three Trapped Tigers*, which painstakingly records the exact itinerary of the characters' cruising around in their car in the Havana night life of the 1950s. *Three Trapped Tigers* is undoubtedly much more experimental than *Sacchario*, but both novels share the narrator's attitude of rapture when remembering the city. In *Three Trapped Tigers*, the narrator states that Cué, the character who likes to drive around Havana, "had this obsession with time . . . [he] looked for time in space, and our continuous, never-ending trips were nothing but a search, one infinite journey through the Malecón . . ." (296). In the case of Cabrera Infante, who was already in exile when he wrote this novel, the detailed evocation of the Havana he knew may have responded to a desire to freeze time in order to keep the city intact in his memory.[10] As for Cossío Woodward, the romanticizing of the past in the evocative details of places visited, even within the limits imposed by a modest economic class, surely undermines the celebration of the Revolution as synonymous with liberation in Cuba. In *Sacchario*, the sections of the text written in the present—with the description of the hardship of cane cutting—contrast with these reminiscences, in which the narrator is carried away and seems unable to hide his own pleasure in recalling a prerevolutionary moment.

The first years of Darío's life, which are told retrospectively, provide the memories of pre-revolutionary Havana that the character supposedly will have to repress as he becomes a committed revolutionary. The section "Mañana" juxtaposes the narration of what the cane cutters are doing at that time of day with the account of Darío's rambling in the Alkázar movie theater, the Rex or the Dúplex, the bowling alley at Centro Asturiano, the Apple Club, Sloppy Joe's Bar, where they went to play the lottery, or the department store

El Encanto.[11] In those years, Darío dreams of being a character in an adventure novel or a comic book; his wish is to be famous and have his name appear next to those of the "heroes of the fatherland" (Cossio Woodward 30). The "Afternoon" section marks the moment of transition, when the places of memory of Darío's past gradually give way to the places of memory where the Revolution occurred. In these new symbolic spaces, Darío replaces the heroic language of youthful adventure stories with revolutionary rhetoric. At the same time, in this "Afternoon" section Darío's former life is reconfigured as a state of underdevelopment and lethargy, and the omniscient narrator seems to want to eliminate all previous pleasant memories, as is shown in this passage: " . . . that was what they were, miserable, deceived, exploited people without a future, crawling around. [They were] imitations of human beings, living in a backward state, in a lower state, lower than apes. [They were] like puppets, without conscience, [they were] drugged, in a drowsy state, those who had experienced, suffered, being shut up in a room in old Havana" (105).

At the end of the "Afternoon" section and through the "Night" section, Darío's individual places of memory are thoroughly replaced by the collective places of memory of the new historiography. These new places of memory situate themselves in a linear temporal succession expressing the setbacks that the Revolution had suffered and overcome, such as the Playa Girón invasion, the Missile Crisis, and Hurricane Flora. In the account of these feats, the reader notes that Darío does not exist as a character any more, but as a hero integrated in the new nation. Instead of narrating these events as experienced by Darío, the narrator gives a panoramic view of how they affected the different individuals who are taken as representative of the Cuban nation.

The narrator's "inebriation," as the etymology of the word *sacchario* and its associations with alcohol imply, is also manifested in certain passages in the text that catalogue some of the habits and beliefs that Darío had to leave behind when he acquired his revolutionary conscience. Unlike other revolutionary novels such as Daura Olema García's *Maestra voluntaria*, where mechanisms that censure the protagonist's doubts and "counterrevolutionary" criticisms are present from the very beginning, *Sacchario* is predicated upon a narrator who is carried away when describing habits he will end up criticizing later on. Such criticism, however, cannot cancel the impact that those enthusiastic descriptions have already made on the reader. For instance, the narrator states that Darío has to renounce his love for a woman, María, in favor of a full commitment to the revolutionary cause: he characterizes Darío's love as "selfish" and "ephemeral" in the face of the revolutionary task that Darío has ahead of him (148). Following this reflection, the narrator states that once Darío had acquired a revolutionary conscience, "his own reason for being only had meaning in revolutionary action, outside which he had nothing left but an abyss of repulsive reminiscences" (163). And yet, while evoking Darío's youth, the narrator surely relishes in the minute recounting of some of those "repulsive reminiscences," including the sexual encounters between Darío and María. The narrator's pleasure in describing the joys of sex and love lends little credit to his negative comments on those same experiences later on in the text, when Darío becomes a committed revolutionary.

In Cuban revolutionary novels, characters often present a split between their "bodily" and their "intellectual" selves. In order to complete their transformation as revolutionaries, they need to become detached from bodily needs and a sense of physical well-being and concentrate instead on their political commitment. For instance, Bruno, the protagonist of Cofiño's *La última mujer y el próximo combate* (1971) (The last woman and the next combat), has to repress his sexual urges as a "very masculine man" in order to focus on his revolutionary duties. Paradoxically in *Sacchario*, a narrative that aims at performatively constituting the revolutionary Cuban nation, there are many references to bodily pleasure that run counter to the allegedly stoic spirit of revolutionaries. In addition, while most revolutionary narratives vilify the prerevolutionary era as the time of moral dissipation, in *Sacchario* many of the narrator's pleasant reminiscences betray his inability to forge the story of Cuba's supposedly immoral past.

A narrative that constitutes the Cuban nation is necessarily a simplification. The leaders of the Cuban Revolution appealed to this simplification in an effort to unite the entire population around a common goal. Consequently, a vast number of people who participated in the campaign would not have seen themselves represented in the Cuban nation as described in the novel. The characteristics of the ideal new Cuba were chosen according to the needs of the moment: a revolutionary sugar-producing nation and a history of failed attempts at independence, culminating in the Revolution and in this campaign, aimed at making Cuba more independent economically. Most importantly, in 1970 the discourse of the revolutionary Cuban nation ignored race and gender because there could be no such distinctions in the face of such an enormous challenge.

These characteristics of the revolutionary nation are not exclusive to Cuba after 1959. In fact, they can be traced to Cuban nationalist narratives since the earliest independence struggles and especially to moments of crisis such as the 1940s, with the rise of Batista and the failure to enforce a democratic constitution. Among the metaphors of the Cuban nation that have prevailed since the 1940s is Fernando Ortiz's celebrated *ajiaco*, or Creole stew, with its delicate balance between the individual and the collective preserved in *specific* ingredients that float in the rich mixture without losing their characteristics (Ortiz, "Los factores" 168–69). Even though *Sacchario* reproduces the standards of homogeneity in the nation, it inadvertently recovers this aspect of Ortiz's image because the individuality of the narrator remains distinct. As Ambrosio Fornet has put it, *Sacchario* is indeed the product of the tension between the individual and the collective (Fornet, "A propósito" 184). But in contrast to Fornet's reading, this individual turns out to be not so much Darío, but the narrator, whose pleasure in the text prevents him from disappearing behind the unity of the nation he has created. That is, the textuality of *Sacchario*, the different layers and languages of the text, cause the narrator as craftsman to take central stage. Individual imagination and creativity rob the nation and the sense of community of their protagonism in the text. Beyond the author's political commitment to the Sugar Campaign, the task of the writer becomes prominent in this and other representations.

# Frustrated Mothers, Virgin Workers, and Masked Whores

## The "New Woman" at Work

Institutional revolutionary discourse often refers to men and "manly quali-ties" as those needed to sustain or advance the revolutionary project in its early years. For instance, during the Literacy Campaign, ascending the Tur-quino peak was a test of endurance for literacy teachers, and Vilma, the pro-tagonist of *Maestra voluntaria*, appears as an example of somebody who suc-ceeds in passing the test and frees herself from her "weak," "feminine" body. In the speeches of the Sugar Campaign, men were called upon to uphold the standards of the nation's honor and dignity by proving their strength in the difficult task of cane cutting. In Che Guevara's foundational document on "the new man," women seemed merely ancillary to the revolutionary project. In fact, Che's only reference to women is when he mentions that "the leaders of the revolution . . . have wives who must be part of the general sacrifice of their lives in order to take the revolution to its destiny" (Guevara, "Social-ism" 15). In this chapter I turn to the discursive production of the Federation of Cuban Women (Federación de Mujeres Cubanas, or FMC) and Manuel Cofiño's 1971 novel *La última mujer y el próximo combate* (The last woman and the next combat, henceforth *La última*) in order to learn more about the figure of the "new woman," who was constantly present but did not play a central role in official discourse.[1]

Cofiño's novel was published at a crucial time in terms of politics and revolutionary culture. Many scholars concur that the failure of the 1970 Ten-Million-Ton Sugar Campaign marked a watershed in the era (Pérez-Stable, *Origins* 118–20). The publication of Heberto Padilla's controversial poems also sparked a crisis in cultural policy matters during the same year. On April 30, 1971, Fidel gave an angry speech at the closure of the National Con-gress of Education and Culture, in which he stated that from then on literary prizes would be given only to *true* revolutionaries. *La última*, published in June 1971, responded to the strong need for commitment during those years as a novel that provided urgently needed female revolutionary role models; it was consequently awarded the Casa de las Américas Prize.

Though chronologically part of the decade following the publication of most texts examined in this book, *La última* is especially interesting for this study because it offers a reified version of gender politics during the first decade, and it also hints at some impending changes. Having been written after failed attempts to integrate all women into the Revolution, this novel aims at delineating the positive and negative female roles that had already been used in public discourse. Since this is an intensely cinematic text—in the sense that it relies strongly on the *visual* for characterization—I use theories of the gaze to examine female identification in the novel. This hotly debated issue in film theory deserves particular attention when one reads highly persuasive revolutionary literature.

Cofiño gives female characters in this novel a degree of protagonism that is exceptional in early revolutionary narratives. As Lourdes Casal has indicated, women were quite underrepresented in Cuban novels from 1950 to 1967, with a ratio of 1-2.4 in relation to men and a slight decrease after the onset of the Revolution (Casal, "Images" 31). Women almost always appeared as secondary characters, playing limited and restricted roles such as teachers, housewives, and prostitutes. While those restrictions still apply in *La última*, some of the female characters are more complex, and a new character emerges: the New Woman in the form of a female rural worker. The appearance of this character in this politically committed novel is due to the fact that toward the end of the first decade the regime set out to truly enforce the call to incorporate women into the labor force, especially when it came to working in the countryside, where there was a certain degree of hardship.

The central theme of *La última* does not appear to be gender. Rather, the state of the Revolution and the agrarian reform in the 1970s take precedence and define the situations in which the male and female roles of the characters come into relief. Gender stereotypes are thus naturalized in this novel, through what Kaja Silverman calls "the dominant fiction," or "images or stories through which a society figures consensus" (Silverman 34). Such consensus rests on binarisms, with male/female being the base upon which other binarisms stand. Thus, in *La última*, hero/enemy, civilized/ uncivilized, and revolutionary/counterrevolutionary are figured in good/bad, male/female terms. These are closely related to the positive and negative representations of women used in official discourse, examined in the next section.

Female Identities in Official Discourse: The Magazine *Mujeres* and Beauty in the Midst of Hardship

The women's movement in the first decade of the Revolution did not engage in a specifically gendered struggle, but was associated with enabling women to participate in the historic transformation of the country. Women were liberated from their oppression in that they were provided with education, health care, and certain reproductive rights that they had not enjoyed before, but they did not receive the benefits of what can be called a feminist agenda. This official posture can be seen in the words of Vilma Espín, the president of the FMC: "I believe in those feminist groups who tie the solution to the oppression of women . . . to the liberation of all the exploited. . . . The problems women face cannot be seen in isolation from other social problems, and they cannot be analyzed outside of their economic context" (Espín, *Confront* 55). The regime did not address the need to eradicate patriarchal attitudes, since class and economic needs took precedence over gender in public discourse, as they were given priority over race and other forms of difference as well.

The first decade of the Revolution saw very little activity in the FMC, a mass organization that regulated women's identities from the top down. Since its creation in August 1960, the FMC had met for one congress in September 1962 and a few small plenums before the second congress in November 1974. Legislation considered relevant to women's rights was not passed until the 1970s, including the Ley de la Infancia (Law of Childhood) in 1971, Reglamento de Círculos (Rules of Daycare Centers) in 1973, the Ley de Maternidad (Maternity Law) in 1974, and the Ley de Familia (Family Code) in 1975. The FMC was headed by Vilma Espín, Fidel Castro's sister-in-law, and its congresses usually ended with speeches signaling the institution's allegiance to Fidel, with the slogan "firm and determined, united by Fidel" (Espín, "Acto de constitución" 27). As Lourdes Casal explained, the FMC is not unlike other mass organizations in Cuba that "transmit directives from above, interpreting political decisions and mobilizing people for their implementation" (Casal, "Revolution and *Conciencia*" 200).

The magazine *Mujeres* (Women), published by the FMC, illustrates female identity figures promoted by the regime and the stereotypes and contradictions they entailed. *Mujeres* was founded in 1962 to replace *Vanidades*, published in the 1950s, and the short-lived *Romances* (1959–61), on the grounds that these two other magazines catered to the bourgeois woman. Surprisingly, though in the two previous magazines there were many more advertisements and references to the "American way of life," the structure of *Mujeres* was very similar, with the following sections: "General Interest,"

"Fiction" (romance novels, many of them of Soviet origin), "Women's and Children's Fashion," "Beauty," "Film, Radio and Television," "Cooking and Gardening." From the beginning, *Mujeres* cultivated an internationalist image, evident in a section included after 1963 called "Reportage," which had existed in the previous women's magazines. The focus of reportage after 1959 changed, however, to countries of the third world and the Soviet bloc.

The sense of mission of *Mujeres* was made clear in its first anniversary issue, dated November 15, 1962: "It is our goal to reach the widest strata of women, to reflect their wishes and their decision to fight in defense of the Fatherland, [to show] their fervent participation in the new society that is born, leaving behind an ominous past. [It is our goal to] underscore her participation in work of different types that dignify and become her. [It is our goal] to serve as cultural vehicle and entertainment to them, help them in their home tasks and their motherly duties, be the mirror of their beauty, and give guidance as to how to dress better and more simply" ("Primer aniversario de *Mujeres*" 1). This statement summarizes the irreconcilable characteristics of the images of women that the regime fostered: in contrast with prerevolutionary Cuban women, who were often referred to as having a dubious work life as prostitutes or as leisurely ladies of high society who did not have to do any work, the "new women" were supposed to work outside the house, but would continue to be excellent homemakers and model mothers who cultivated their appearances as well.

These contradictions at the basis of institutional gender discourse were displayed in countless examples, when a desire to wield what was considered a female empowering discourse was ultimately undermined by persisting stereotypes. An article titled "Ella y él" (She and he) for instance, starts with the following critique, "On both sexes and their diverse characteristics there is a whole facile rhetoric that is part of tradition" (16–17), only to reinforce that same stereotypical rhetoric by "proving" with photographs that women and men thread a needle, take off a sweater, sit down, and tie a knot differently.

The magazine published articles intended to educate women, including, for example, a series by Edmundo Desnoes on the representation of women in paintings of different epochs. For several issues from 1962 to 1963, a section titled "Círculo de estudios de la FMC" (Study circle of the FMC) published texts on historical events, such as one on "Feudalism," which came with a study guide, comprehension questions, and a bibliography at the end. Alongside these educational texts, however, readers found romance novellas with abundant stereotypes and masculinist assumptions concerning women.

While from the beginning the magazine included an initial section on female sports, presumably to show women's strength and ability to compete regardless of gender, this section would be followed by a fashion section, with the latest from Paris or Italy. The fashion section would be far longer than the sports section and would depict a very different type of woman. Styles for children, full of frills and accessories for every occasion, also seemed to reiterate traditional gender roles, as well as a wealthy lifestyle that was hardly supposed to have survived the Revolution. Children and women models were invariably white and fair, and the garments they wore were clearly marketed for an urban lifestyle.

In 1965 the magazine started to publish a special edition for the countryside, titled the "Campo" (Countryside) edition. One would expect that it would be substantially different from the edition distributed in Havana, given the gap between the countryside and the interests and lifestyle of a city that had remained fairly open to the outside world. Perhaps owing to the fact that most of the main cultural events of that decade took place in Havana, the sections on culture, reportage, and general education of women were removed from the Campo edition. As for the rest of the magazine, it was exactly the same as the one distributed in the city.

The paradoxes of the Campo edition became more striking after August 1966, the sixth anniversary of the creation of the FMC, when the regime initiated a strong drive to incorporate women in the labor force, especially in the countryside. In the corresponding issue, it was reported that a million women were working and had increased production to a billion pesos, with work in greenhouses, industry, truck driving, and so forth ("Un millón"). A few pages later, a section titled "Muestre una rodilla perfecta" (Show a perfect knee) included recommendations on waxing, making flexible, or tanning one's knees in the summer, and advice to "wear discrete clothes when going on an excursion" (24–25). This section, part of the Campo edition though clearly devoted to the image of a leisurely, city woman, ran counter to the identity figure of the rural worker that this magazine was fostering. An issue that published pictures of women working in farms and beating production records also featured advice to put makeup on legs, hands, and neck, and to cover up freckles ("Belleza" 26–27).

The permanence of masculinist stereotypes of the past may have been deeply entrenched among women themselves, which explains why the magazine was reluctant to give up the role model of a stereotypically bourgeois lifestyle, or a woman who would keep beauty among her priorities and allow herself money and time to care for her appearance. Compare, for instance, a poem by the celebrated Indio Naborí to a statement in *Mujeres* in 1969:

> In the past women were liked
> as a pleasant adornment
> as a servant for the master.
> More for their pretty hair than for their pretty thoughts.
> The Socialist woman continues to be a flower,
> But a thinking flower, who works and fights
> For the Land . . . for a world of justice and love. (Indio Naborí 59)

In this poem, the idea of women as beautiful objects is present, but is downplayed by the image of natural beauty and intellect. In contrast, the statement in *Mujeres*, in an article titled "Muchachas de hoy" (Today's girls) in the year of the Ten-Million-Ton Sugar Campaign, seems to be moving in a different direction.

> We are hard-working students
> Who can doubt that!
> [we are] girls who
> achieve the goals
> agreed upon
> by our
> youth organization
> but . . . we are also girls who continue
> to be vain
> taking care
> of looking cute and attractive
> in tune
> with what fashion suggests
> and what we are able to obtain. ("Muchachas de hoy" 19)

The statement did not display indifference to revolutionary duties, but it certainly did show a defiant desire to maintain an image of conventional female beauty, which the magazine was also endeavoring to nurture. The next section deals with the controlling images of women that both *Mujeres* and the discourse of revolutionary leaders made use of, keeping in mind some of the characteristics and assumptions just described.

Women Identity Figures: Stereotypes Live On

Owing to the radical changes and the sense of uncertainty in the first decade of the Revolution, the discourse on gender crystallized into what Patricia Hill Collins has called, in a different context, "controlling images" or stereotypical representations of gender identity that were routinely used in public discourse as a means to introduce changes starting from a familiar basis (Hill Collins 67). My analysis focuses on four of these stereotypical identity figures of women against the backdrop of the masculinist norm of the first decade of the Cuban Revolution, which displayed contradictions between Socialist ideals of women's liberation and strongly conservative, patriarchal notions of women's roles. The positive and negative role models of gender identity that the regime provided find an echo, as well as their ultimate subversion, in *La última*.

As the sections in *Mujeres* also illustrated, traditional gender stereotypes, such as the image of women marked by their "biological destiny" as mothers and fragile beings, remained largely unchallenged. For instance, in the opening statement of the FMC Constitution, Vilma Espín stated, "[This is a] message for Cuban women. Since the triumph of January 1, 1959, the Revolution has been refashioning a new Cuba, the Cuba that *our motherly heart* always dreamed of, a sovereign Cuba. . . . [Here is] where men have been given their dignity back, and where *our children grow* open to all horizons and blossom in creative work . . ." (Espín, "Acto de constitución" 9, my emphasis). As has been noted, the regime's emphasis on motherhood displayed reliance on a preconception deeply ingrained in Cuba, as in many other cultures. But it is remarkable that the FMC alleged "feminine discourse" was coated in a nationalist discourse in which motherhood was an important part of women's duty.

Women were responsible asa primary socializers in what Floya Anthias and Nira Yuval-Davis have called their "reproductive function" or "the reproduction of labor power or state citizenship...[as well as of] national, ethnical, and racial categories" (Anthias and Yuval-Davis 8). This explains why many sections of *Mujeres* were devoted to children and homemaking. As the regime strived to entice women to work outside the home, it did its best to provide adequate childcare, as public discourse always operated on the assumption that women's "natural responsibilities" with their children were the main obstacles in their transition to the workplace. But the daycare centers soon became unreliable and suffered from lack of resources, which affected women's performance at work. The dual role that the Revolution demanded of women is metaphorized in the emblem of the FMC, an image of a woman with a baby at her breast and a Kalashnikov rifle slung over her shoulder (quoted in Smith 3).

The regime's attempts to incorporate women into the labor force by strengthening their self-worth were simultaneous with the leaders' reliance on bourgeois Catholic notions of femininity—based on traditional motherhood, submission, and purity—which limited women's advancement. Thus, for instance, the model that the journal *Mujeres* needed to represent was "a woman who is full of tenderness, of love to humanity, truth, and beauty" (Espín, "Informe central" 26). Furthermore, the leaders of the FMC were allegedly especially suited for financial administration because "we, as housewives, observe this process very closely, and in the daily business of grocery shopping some new ideas may come to our minds" (Espín, "Informe central" 34). When Vilma Espín visited a factory, she wrote the following observations: "When we get to a factory, we find it clean, as clean as a dining-room table, and every nook and cranny is clean, and we look at how careful our comrade is, and she sweeps every corner of her factory with such love, with such conscientiousness that every job is important, no matter how humble" (Espín, "En el acto conmemorativo" 23). In the first congress of the FMC, Espín would refer to "the new woman . . . free of the domestic slavery and the weight of the prejudices of the past (Espín, "Informe central" 11) and then go on to say that "the ideal of the new woman . . . is that of a healthy woman, full of the joy of life, future mother of the new generations who will make Communism a reality" (Espín, "Informe central" 22), thereby robbing women of any role in the Revolution other than carrying children. The appearance of the New Woman in the novel *La última* resolves some of these contradictions, as it creates new guidelines for women.

With these masculinist views in mind, it should not be surprising that official discourse operated within a strictly binary concept of gender. Apart from the speeches at the FMC in which the centrality of women was justified, the emphasis on masculinity in public discourse was such that when there was any discussion of homosexuality at all, gay men took center stage while lesbians remained in the shadow. From a masculinist point of view, lesbians did not pose a threat, as long as the only acceptable choice left to women was marriage. As Marvin Leiner reports, lesbians in Cuba sought marriage as a way to gain social respect and have economic security (Leiner 23).

The lesbians who played important roles in the prerevolutionary clandestine urban struggle tended to have a masculinist ethic themselves, and therefore they did not identify with the oppression that gay men were subject to (Lumsden 61). Those who wanted to be more open about their sexual preference took refuge in institutions that promoted the arts, such as the UNEAC, according to Lourdes Argüelles and Ruby Rich (693). On the whole, lesbians were ignored by the regime, because women were considered childlike anyway, their sexuality not fully developed, and their sexual impulses somehow incidental. Unlike gay men, who had "betrayed their own kind," lesbians suffered from a kind of perversion that could be "corrected" (Smith and Padula 171).[2]

On the whole, lesbianism was either ignored or suppressed, particularly as the Cuban regime rested on a deeply patriarchal ideological basis. As Margaret Randall states, "Gay life profoundly threatens patriarchy, in which so much depends upon reproducing the nuclear family structure" (Randall, *Gathering Rage* 150). Indeed, in all representations of women in public discourse, and in the legislation that was passed to favor women, they were always thought of in connection with a family unit. Since my study works within the confines of the official revolutionary imaginary, I recognize the usual binary male/female opposition as a fundamental structure. However, in my analysis of the novel I will show that there is also a chance for resistance to this constrictive articulation of gender.

While Espín's speeches increasingly focused on the problems arising from women's multiple responsibilities in the early years of the Revolution, Fidel's speeches at the closing of FMC meetings were much more general and often not concerned with women's issues at all. In front of a large female audience, Fidel often rambled on about problems with U.S. intervention, or about improvements in production, without referring to how these problems affected women. In fact, he would often address the FMC crowd as "se-ñores" ("gentlemen")[3] and on only one occasion did he correct himself. His correction was received with good humor: "The Soviet Union has supplied us with our basic arms. And gentlemen—oops, in this case, I mean ladies [laughter and applause]. . ." (19700824). Fidel generally took up the role of educating women regarding issues of national importance, such as defense, productivity, or ideological commitment. More often than not, he played the role of a figure of authority who calls on someone and performatively bestows identity on that person. In the speeches, Fidel *named* what women's function in society was through their role in a given campaign.

Regardless of Espín's and Fidel's different styles in addressing women, they fell back on "controlling images," to return to Patricia Hill Collins's expression, referring to positive or negative role models used to prove a particular point. One of those images, as I have noted, was the mother in the wide sense of caregiver and homemaker. In addition, there were three negative images—the housewife, the prerevolutionary woman, and the prostitute—and a positive one—the woman worker.

Throughout the Revolution there was a tension between women's duties as mothers and homemakers, which were taken for granted, and the notion that household tasks were an obstacle for women's accomplishments in professional and revolutionary duties. In other words, the traditional image of the woman as caregiver clashed with the Marxist definition of human beings as producers in society. In the document of the Cuban Communist Party Congress, which formalized the attitude of the regime toward gender identity, the figure of the housewife was the object of an intensely misogynistic impulse that made her the embodiment of many of the conventional female vices. The document quotes Lenin's writing on homemakers: "notwithstanding all the laws emancipating woman, she continues to be a domestic slave, because petty housework crushes, strangles, stultifies and degrades her, chains her to the kitchen and the nursery, and she wastes her labor on barbarously unproductive, petty, nerve-wracking, stultifying and crushing drudgery" (quoted in Stone, 99). As Julie Marie Bunck has noted, institutionalized discourse appropriated the terms of women's emancipation to mean integration in the Revolution (Bunck, "Women's"). As years went by and the need to incorporate women in the work force became more pressing, the regime's rhetoric turned increasingly negative toward household chores by minimizing the importance of homemaking duties in society and resignifying the life of the housewife as "idle" and "drudgery."

For instance, housewives were largely blamed for the failure of the Ten-Million-Ton Sugar Campaign. As Smith and Padula report, in this campaign housewives stayed in the city to fill the jobs that their husbands left vacant when they went to work in the fields. The fact that many of these women returned home shortly afterward, to tend to the needs of their children instead of remaining at their husbands' workplace, was cited as confirming their inability to join the national effort at any level. The labor minister, Jorge Risquet, called housewives "a dense layer of idle women which was intolerable in a country struggling for national development" (quoted in Smith and Padula 100). The word *idle* is key here, as anti-loafing laws were applied mainly to men whose being "idle" was interpreted as disaffection for the Revolution.

In contrast to their "unimportant" home duties, the revolutionary project was said to offer women proper challenges.[4] The FMC registered the stress resulting from the coexistence of old and new attitudes toward women, and women's triple schedule of home, paid work, and volunteer work. *Mujeres* began to teach women ways to achieve their maximum at home, so that they could be more productive outside. But both this magazine and movies such as Pastor Vega's *Retrato de Teresa* (1975) (Portrait of Teresa) represent the gap between women's experience of life at home and official representations of housewives as idle. Even after the implementation of the 1975 Family Code, which declared that household duties should be shared by men and women, women were far from idle at home, as the demands of children and homemaking did not diminish and were placed largely on the mother's shoulders.

The second negative image that was presented in official discourse is the prerevolutionary woman. Official discourse focused on the negative image of pre-1959 Havana as the destination of gamblers and sex tourists, with the Revolution bringing a time of dignity and moral cleansing. This situation was said to have impacted women particularly in terms of how their place in society was regarded.[5] According to Ana Ramos, before the Revolution most working women were maids, and for middle class women "there was no choice in an underdeveloped capitalist society that viewed women either as decoration or as a vehicle for pleasure" (Ramos 63). Pérez-Stable's list of jobs available to women is a little more extensive, including domestic servant, teacher, and manufacturing or clerical worker, but she states that before 1959 only 13 percent of women held a job and their choices were very limited (Pérez-Stable, "Cuban Women" 53–54). All critics agree on the high incidence of prostitution before 1959, though the actual number of prostitutes is hard to determine.

An illustration of the way in which most women working prior to 1959 were allegedly forced to become prostitutes or do other degrading work was presented in the article "Retrospectiva de la mujer cubana" (Retrospective view of the Cuban woman), published by A. Soto Cobián in *Mujeres* (1969). It included personal and commercial advertisements from *Diario de la Marina*, a journal published in Cuba between 1832 and 1962. From descriptions of female slaves in 1848, to maids in the 1950s, to a personal advertisement seeking "girls who look good, for several bars," the author spun a narrative of the absolute lack of choices for women in the past: "Humble young women in a rotten society, who began like that, at a bar in Guanabo, where they would be made presentable and be offered 'room and board, an attractive salary, commission and tips,' can you imagine why the 'commissions and tips'? And after starting at the bar, what was their life? The street and their miserable home . . ." (5). This view was reinforced by ample reports in the magazine on the present efforts of the Revolution to rehabilitate maids and prostitutes with groups such as the Ana Betancourt Brigades, which schooled these women and trained them to become seamstresses.

The reduction of working women's roles in the era before the Revolution was also reflected in the post-1959 novels set in those years, in which the few women characters who appeared were for the most part prostitutes or shallow ladies of high society. The focus on these controlling images is strategic in its narrative potential, since the ladies of high society often were transformed once they devoted themselves to the new revolutionary duties, as is the case, for instance, for Silvia in David Buzzi's *Los desnudos* (1967) or Teresa in Hilda Perera Soto's *Mañana es 26* (1960). In turn, prostitutes were rehabilitated with the Revolution, as is the case with Yolanda in José Soler Puig's *El derrumbe* (1964) or Elsa in Manuel Granados's *Adire y el tiempo roto* (1967). Although these fictional characters were evil, the romantic image of a leisurely, completely white, bourgeois woman did live on in the collective unconscious, as the models and advice of *Mujeres* referred to above demonstrate.

Working women of the Revolution, in contrast, always offered positive role models as long as they held positions deemed "appropriate" for them. Fidel assigned what he considered "difficult tasks" to men, because "where nature has established some difference, society must establish some difference which is not of a legal, moral, or intellectual character, but of a social character" (19650220). The "natural" differences between men and women originated, once again, in women's supposed biological destiny as mothers. The demands of the FMC that Fidel was willing to satisfy were those affecting women as working mothers, such as providing better day-care centers and schools, or addressing special medical needs, such as building better hospitals. His conservative opinions concerning women were clearly displayed even into the 1970s, when there was a conscious effort to change the dominant discourse on women. Thus, in a speech at the FMC's second congress, in 1974, Fidel stated that, because of their being mothers and "physically weaker," women needed to enjoy "special considerations" in society (quoted in Stone 68).

The first decade's intense debate on the role of women in society showed its results in the 1970s, in the form of a series of significant documents, including the Family Code (November 1975), the document for the "Comisión para el pleno ejercicio de la igualdad de la mujer" (Committee for the Full Exercise of Women's Equality, December 1975), and the 1976 Constitution. While several of these documents categorized household duties and parenthood as the shared responsibilities of men and women, the language that articulated the new regulations revealed that the leaders themselves failed to believe in that sharing. Thus, the introduction of regulations governing part-time jobs, longer hours for grocery stores, and improved day-care centers, and so forth, were explicitly said to aid *women* as the sole responsible partner.

Most importantly, the fact that women were defined according to their role as mothers was revealed in Resolution 48 of the 1976 Constitution, which stated that women needed to hold jobs appropriate to their physical makeup. In addition, Resolution 40 of the Constitution effectively barred women from some three hundred jobs owing to their allegedly harmful effects on women's reproductive organs (Casal, "Images of Women" 188). The list of jobs, Casal adds, is rather "odd," perhaps motivated by the belief that work outside the home was more suited to men, and men were considered a potential danger to society if unemployed (198). This list was fortunately brought down to twenty-five jobs in 1985, thanks to pressure from the FMC (quoted in Pérez-Stable, "Cuban Women" 61).

But if official discourse was not honoring its promises, or had not yet resolved its contradictions, there were hints in some forums such as the arts that new concepts of men and women were emerging. Hence Milagros González's poem:

> What difference to you
> that the children make their beds
> pick up their shoes
> and help me dry the dishes
> if you study for your next class
> in the most comfortable chair we have
> and keep your fear in shadow, almost hidden
> so no one will discover the *macho* at the base of your spine!
> . . . Now that your specialty
> is breaking your balls for Future
> . . . Learn then to heat your food while I study
> . . . because Revolution is . . . more than Congress, Assembly,
> . . . Revolution is also we who make and do
> . . . [it is you] sitting next to me,
> as dishes are unwashed
> and there is a smile when duty calls
> and we share the difficulty of leaving bed. (quoted in Randall, *Breaking*
>     176–77)

As the poem shows, the New Man that women envisioned, the "whole Human Being" as Milagros González called him, was brought down from his pedestal and turned into the cooperative husband, transformed by love. The discrepancy between individual or non-hegemonic conceptions of gender roles and official discourse has continued through the Revolution, and as I will show below, the contradictions at the foundation of revolutionary discourse themselves speak against the apparently seamless construction of gender in official discourse.

After looking at the representation of mothers, housewives, and women workers, I turn now to the last identity image I include in my analysis, which operates in the framework of the document "On the Sexuality of Women," issued by the Grupo Nacional de Trabajadores en la Educación Sexual (National Group of Workers in Sex Education), or GNTES. This document was published in 1977, but it represents an attitude already manifest at the time when *La última* was written. The GNTES protected the family as the primary social unit, while it also focused on the high demands of female sexuality and tried to instill the idea that men needed to satisfy women sexually. The promotion of this "new female eroticism"—as Smith and Padula term it (175)—confirmed the stereotype of women as bodies and recuperated the old-time myth of the Cuban *mulata* for official discourse. At the same time, the GNTES document sought to contain women's sexuality within the boundaries of the family unit, and it still worked with a traditional heterosexual norm, where women played a passive role in lovemaking.

The recurrent representations of women as idle housewives, as sexual objects, or industrious mothers who bear the responsibilities of home and work outside the home are not exclusive to the dominant ideology of revolutionary Cuba. Moreover, the striking absence of lesbians in Cuban public discourse is a characteristic of all masculinist societies. Some feminist critics caution that different standards should be applied to Cuba, owing to the special economic and cultural circumstances of Socialism.[6] Still, the FMC cast age-old stereotypes of femininity in the language of women's emancipation and fostered a traditional division of labor that retained fundamental inequalities, in the wider interest of the Revolution. The marked gap between the discourse of the FMC, other instances of official discourse on women, and the ways that Cuban women are evolving at present was already apparent in the formative years of the Revolution, which laid the foundation of the discourse of gender. As Maxine Molyneux states, the FMC has served to maintain the place that women's organizations have enjoyed since before the Revolution in Cuba. But its failure to carry out the promise of a radical transformation of gender attitudes, its bureaucratization, and its position as an open ally of the state have rendered this organization almost irrelevant (Molyneux 305). One has to look beyond the FMC, to the representation of women in literature, to see the subversion of gender stereotypes.

The Eye in the Text: How Women's Bodies Appear

As do many politically committed novels, *La última* relies on stock characters and conventional gender identities. The protagonists are arranged in triads of men and women, with women as supporting characters to their male counterparts. Bruno is a revolutionary hero, and Mercedes, the model worker, gives Bruno the chance to display his moral rectitude. Siaco, the counterrevolutionary, displays his cruelty and aggression against his wife, Claudia, the frustrated and hysterical housewife. Clemente, the indifferent individual turned New Man by the end of the text, is married to Nati, representing the stereotype of the femme fatale, who as a consequence of an early sexual awakening has an insatiable sexual appetite. Nati elicits Clemente's compassion and, as Siaco's lover, she is the object of his "animalistic" instincts. In spite of their stereotypical roles, women in *La última* signal some changes as they reveal the erosion of the spatial organization of gender that was prevalent in Cuba. Instead of having men and women split between "the street" and "the house," as Lourdes Casal puts it ("Revolution and Conciencia" 18), only the negative characters, Claudia and Nati, are confined to the realm of the home. Mercedes works in the fields, thus representing the new ideal of the revolutionary woman worker.

In synthesis, the plot of the novel revolves around Bruno as a supervisor of agrarian reform who goes to a little town in the Sierra Grande in order to put an end to certain irregularities committed against government plans in the area. During his stay, Bruno makes the town "more modern" as he installs electricity, builds roads, and introduces elements of city life such as ice cream and movies. Bruno also rids the town of many "counterrevolutionary" elements, except for a group of men, Siaco among them, who resent Bruno and want to leave on a raft bound for the United States. At the final confrontation between these two parties, Bruno and Siaco die.

*La última* is mainly narrated by an omniscient voice that recounts the events of the characters' past and present. Occasionally this voice gives way to the interior monologues of the protagonists or of anonymous characters in the village. In some sections of the text, the voices of the villagers tell the implied reader about their superstitions or traditions. This collective voice is meant to provide a choral commentary and a thickness to the events of the plot, while also displaying the transformations that the isolated town is experiencing with the arrival of Bruno and revolutionary plans for the area. In terms of point of view, however, the narrative technique of this novel is monologic, in Bakhtin's sense: the narrator's perspective dominates over the voices of the other characters, as far as gender representations are concerned.

For most of the novel, Siaco and Clemente serve as background to bring the character of Bruno—the epitome of the New Man—into relief. Clemente stands out only at the end of the novel, when he is distinguished as a good revolutionary and given a position as a supervisor of deforestation plans. Siaco, as a counterrevolutionary, operates mostly in the shadows, at night, or in the woods. While Bruno arrives with the rainy season and purifies the corrupt area he is assigned to as a supervisor, Siaco is associated with the dust and dryness that prevent the village from making progress. With their lust and "counterrevolutionary" behavior, Siaco and Nati represent resistance to the modernizing impulse of the Revolution, epitomized in turn by Bruno and Mercedes. As Nissa Torrents notes, Siaco has a lot in common with the traditional "bad guys" of the thriller and counterespionage novels that proliferated in Cuba in the 1970s (Torrents 180).

In contrast with Siaco, Bruno illustrates how a revolutionary, while still being "a man," can channel the force of his temper and sexual instinct through the rule of law. Bruno is attracted to Mercedes, but this does not become an obstacle to his mission in the Sierra, since their love is only platonic. He describes the revolutionary's relationship with women in the following terms, which in turn explain the title of the novel: "Here we think of the last woman we had, and the next combat" (Cofiño 253). Bruno's discipline corresponds to his role as the bestower of "order and civilization" in the wilderness. However, the fact that Bruno clings to his dedication to the Revolution over a passionate involvement or married life displays the ideological paradoxes of this novel, where the role of the New Man as a rational, dedicated worker coexists with highly sexualized images of women.

That Bruno is desexualized to emphasize his qualities as a revolutionary is revealed in the fact that only emblematic fragments of his body are represented, and then they are used as symbols of revolutionary commitment. For instance, like Siaco, Bruno has aggressive instincts, but they are restrained and sublimated in his revolutionary mission. His aggressiveness is never manifested outwardly, except for a little detail that the narrator insistently reports to us: the vein in Bruno's forehead seems to swell and throb whenever he is tense. In addition, there is a scar Bruno feels for whenever he needs to reinforce his values. A memory of his past, when he came home from the Sierra and saw that his wife had abandoned him, is recurrent in Bruno's mind: his own image in the mirror, with his leathery face and emaciated look, his beard and the mane of hair that confirmed him as a rebel. That memory and the allusions to Bruno's scar serve to remind him that the Revolution does not succeed without sacrifice. In sum, as Hernán Vidal puts it, Bruno confirms that scars, blood, and sweat are monuments to the Revolution.[7]

So far I have been delineating the gender images that the text proposes, which are designed to offer negative and positive models of behavior for readers. However, if one wants to escape the dynamics of reader complacency, or the belief that a text always achieves its intended aim, one needs to focus on aspects of the texts that are not part of a dominant reading. *La última* is a strikingly visual and, if we think of how films have been conceptualized in theory, a very cinematic text, in that women are characterized according to how men *see* them. Initially, the novel shows great resemblance to Laura Mulvey's characterization of Hollywood movies, in which a central male figure "is the bearer of the look of the spectator" and women are reduced to spectacle (Mulvey, *Visual* 20).[8] The male gaze is sadistic/fetishistic, because it delights in seeing women punished, as well as scopophilic, because it turns women into sexual objects "to-be-looked-at" (21). Much has been written about Mulvey's perpetuating rigid gender roles in her characterization of spectators and denying women any part in the dynamics of pleasurable identification.[9] My use of her theory does not take for granted her generalization that all movies presuppose a male gaze against which females are powerless, but I find it fitting to use her description when considering the way that Cuban official discourse conceptualized gender. It must be said that in this novel there is no single masculine gaze, though all of the masculine gazes correspond to the rhetoric of gender used in the Revolution. Bruno's gaze constructs the revolutionary woman, pure and virginal; the omniscient narrator's gaze, aided by the voices of anonymous characters in the village, constitutes women as objects of desire, or Nati as the epitome of exuberance. My next step is to look at the way that these masculinist gazes portray the female figures in the novel.

Claudia is a negative role model, as a woman who never succeeded in becoming a mother. After several miscarriages, she gave birth to a baby who lived only four months. The narrator returns over and over again to Claudia losing her children and withering away as a result: "She could never avoid the anguish that gripped her when she felt life forming in the depth of her flesh, and it grew and grew like a bush, like ivy through her veins, rooting itself in her bosom until it escaped through her mouth in a blooming branch. . . . She knew that, inescapably, days after, months after, she would feel her womb open as if slit by a knife, while that which had been forming itself inside fell between her legs, like a withered leaf, before it was born. *Claudia vegetates, hardly aware of what she does or does not do, instinctively resigned to her grief and abandonment*" (Cofiño 82, my emphasis). The image of the ivy tree and intricate, leafy bushes are used frequently in the novel to express Claudia's state. The first time that image appears in the text is when the reader is told that Claudia used to meet Siaco under an ivy tree (112). Since that day, Claudia has the shadow of a creeping bougainvillea in the depth of her look (59) and at the end, when Siaco leaves her, she seems to turn into a withered ivy tree herself: "Her body dries out by the minute, it hardens, until it seems made of wood" (310). Claudia's destiny was shaped by her relationship with her man: her life with Siaco left indelible marks on her body.

In Mulvey's terms quoted above, the narrator does not "fetishize" Claudia's body for its beauty, but for some morbid repulsion in the way she is somehow rotting or consuming away, as the image of infertility (Cofiño 310). The narrator's gaze thus confirms the official revolutionary claim that women's destiny is to be mothers: a woman's body, always blossoming and beautiful at a young age, is consumed if she does not have any children. In addition, Claudia is the image of the inactive and hysterical housewife who frequently appeared in official critiques as suffering the drudgery of life at home, metaphorized in the novel by her feeling that the walls are closing in on her (140). Significantly, she feels liberated at the end of the novel when Mercedes takes her out of the house and treats her "as if she were her daughter" (236).

Nati, the exuberant female, is Claudia's antithesis in terms of how her body is described. Her behavior is explained, rather simplistically, by a dark past: she was raped by an old landowner at the age of fifteen, and this led her to become sexually insatiable and to constantly seek sex from strangers. The tone of the narrator in describing sexual scenes with excruciating detail, especially the violent scenes of her early years, is indeed sadistic: he relishes in representations of the female body dominated by male sexual violence. For the narrator, Nati *invites* sexual assault: "Nati, I don't know what that woman has . . . one cannot see her walk, move the way she moves, without thinking that all men follow her dragging themselves on their stomach, trying to kiss her calves . . . without realizing that she is more female than all the females here together; that she has to feel the heavy breathing of all the men who follow her, the lips of all the men who want to get to her hips, the tongues of all the men who want to lick her calves. . . . One looks at her and feels that that woman will always be naked in front of all men. . . . That woman. . . . I don't know what she has: she is like a destiny" (28–30). Through the generalization of what Nati represents for all men who look at her, the narrator implies a "masculine reader," understood as a conventional heterosexual male. There are innumerable scenes where Nati is used and abused by all the men in the town. She fulfills an "iconic role," according to Mulvey, displayed constantly in the text for the gaze of masculine readers that the text constructs (Mulvey, *Visual* 21). In the words of the critic Ernesto García Alzola, "Nati is a character that we have seen a lot, that exists everywhere: the woman who drives us crazy" (110). In the wider context of the Revolution, Nati fits the stereotype of the sexually overcharged woman, which triggered the campaigns of sexual education aimed at harnessing this "female eroticism" within the family unit.

The importance of Nati as the object of a masculine gaze is also evident in her only possibility of "redemption," which, like her fall, came from a man. Mario frequently visited Nati at the bar where she worked, and Nati liked him "because he never looked at her" (Cofiño 248) and did not defile her like the other men through a gaze that inflicted violence. Once Nati was "disembodied" because this man did not look at her, she offered to go with him wherever he wanted and "be good" (249), thus giving him the promise of complete domination.

However, the image of Nati as submissive is hard to picture. Though she is confined to the home and keeps house for her husband, she clearly subverts the stereotype of the housewife. For instance, she uses an emblem of home, a red and white checkered tablecloth, to signal to her lover when she is available. Her role as wife is subordinated to that of mistress or an archetype of the Goddess, as she spends most of the day outside, experiencing sensual pleasures and reminiscing about previous sexual encounters in which she seemed to take the lead.

For her part, the character of Mercedes is constituted by the overlapping of the narrator's and Bruno's masculine gazes: "Bruno turns around and looks at her from head to toe. . . . *With working clothes, she looks like a young man except for her little breasts that insinuate themselves under her shirt, and the slight curve of her hips. . . .* Bruno watches her blond hair over her shoulders. The yellowish light of the street lamp illuminates her green eyes" (215, emphasis mine). Mercedes's role in the novel is to be a revolutionary worker, and in that her sexuality seems to be beside the point. As the above passage shows, Mercedes's sexual attributes are not prominent, especially because they can hardly be noticed through her ample work clothes. Mercedes's body is not desirable in a conventional way, though she is still defined by her "to-be-looked-at-ness," in Mulvey's terms (*Visual* 21). Instead, Bruno focuses on her long, blond hair and green eyes, and relates to her only platonically. As Roberta Salper puts it, it is as if "knowing that one cannot treat a woman like that [a worker] the same way as others, the revolutionary man does not know how to deal with her" (Salper 65). In Mercedes we clearly see the split that the Revolution required of Cuban women: their femininity was constructed according to the usual masculinist stereotypes, but in their role as revolutionaries they were required to downplay those "feminine" features.

Mercedes is what Casal calls "the idealized female," in that she is fragile, virginal, and unconcerned with sex ("Images" 38). Mercedes dreams of kissing Bruno but never actually thinks of him sexually. What defines Mercedes as a woman—apart from her work, where her conventionally feminine features are suppressed—is her being in love with a man. In fact, the narrator reports how Mercedes's gender identity was questioned before she loved Bruno, which is shown in the fact that her coworkers asked her, "Mercedes, you are not some sort of butch, are you?" (Cofiño 102). But in her role as an exemplary female worker Mercedes is the new figure that the regime wanted to promote and that was starting to appear in the novels of the era. By being young and unmarried Mercedes avoids the problems of triple duty that revolutionary women suffered. However, the conventional representation of her *femininity* shows the fundamental confusion of revolutionary discourse at the time, which did not effectively break with stereotypes about women but relied on a few select notions of how women *should* be different in order to integrate themselves in the work force.

Bruno's death at the end of the novel provides a makeshift solution to the contradictions inherent in the ideal images of men and women involved in a romantic encounter. Mercedes and Bruno never consummate their love, and they do not become a couple. Mercedes is deprived of her "feminine" charms and is very focused on her work. As for Bruno, he cannot be cast in the role of a partner, a father, or a husband, nor can he appear as the stereotypical womanizer since, as Guevara stated, men's involvement with women and family was subordinate to their duty as revolutionaries. In Guevara's own words: "They [our vanguard revolutionaries] cannot descend, with small doses of affection, to the level where ordinary men put their love into practice. The leaders of the revolution have children just beginning to talk, who are not saying 'daddy.' They have wives who must be part of the general sacrifice of their lives in order to take the revolution to its destiny" ("Socialism" 15).

Most importantly, the novel offers a contrast between Bruno's and Mercedes's platonic relationship and Nati's and Siaco's carnal exchanges that has much to do with race. Mercedes fulfils the stereotype of the angelic (white) beauty, and the narrator often describes her as delicate and pure. For instance: "Mercedes flies through the patio, barefooted, with her blond hair floating over her back. . . . Drops of dew shine on the yellow and milky spots of her ankles. . . . She stops, lifts her arms, breathes in deeply and her nostrils flutter" (Cofiño 144). By contrast, the narrator makes constant references to Nati as a "mulata jíbara" (*jíbara* meaning "peasant" in a derogatory way, that is, "ignorant and brutish") and she is often described as if she were "in heat": "The wind tosses her hair. . . . Her violently tossed locks suggest impulses of fear and escape. . . . Something is heavy in her body and her blood. She lifts her arms and in her armpits one sees two tufts of blackness. The wind lifts her skirt and caresses the start of her full, brown thighs. . . . Nati feels the desire that dilates her nose and makes her shake" (94). As Roberta Salper has noted, representations of women with animal features are frequent in Cofiño's narratives (Salper 63). Both Mercedes and Nati manifest their excitement with a flutter of their nostrils, like some animals when they experience something new or sense danger. But Nati's "animality" is combined with the narrator's underscoring of her dark features, as well as her *sexual* excitement. Her beauty is different from the type of beauty represented in the magazine *Mujeres*, for instance, wherein women were fair and pretty but never eroticized. Nati is associated with the icon of the mythical Cuban *mulata*, the epitome of woman as sexual object. In contrast, Mercedes, as a female *worker*, corresponds to an image of careless femininity and is characterized as a female angel, a delightful object for a stereotypically male looker, but certainly not approachable as a sexual object.

Claudia, indolent and hysterical because she cannot be a mother, and Nati with her sexual obsession, offer *negative* models for the reader, or examples of what women should *not* be. In contrast, Mercedes, the sexually unapproachable figure of the new revolutionary woman, is the main role model for the female reader. By revolutionary standards, Mercedes is the only accomplished woman in the novel and she is also the hero's object of interest, even though that interest is platonic. Mercedes's body is disguised or distant, in order to fulfill the revolutionary need for restraint. Following Mulvey's theory, female readers are left with masochistic identifications with Claudia and Nati or with sexless identifications with Mercedes, who as the new ideal woman is liberated from being an object of desire by becoming disembodied or virginal. If one considers reading as an "encounter" where identities are performatively constituted, however, one can postulate a divergent reaction to these performances, which may in fact allow female readers to opt out of the constrictive gender discourse of the Revolution.

## Nati's Body and the Final Masquerade

As the narrative approaches its end, the polymorphous Nati can take on various meanings. First, as the abused body of a woman, she can be claimed as an ambiguous symbol of the Cuban nation. As Doris Sommer has noted, women's bodies as a representation of the nation are commonplace in Latin American literature and are used as emblems for the land that the masculine might of a usurper took from colonized people (xii). Vera Kutzinski states that in Cuban literature *mulatas* are often represented as symbols of racial harmony, but they are often the object of the narrator's desire rather than true subjects. All of these stereotypes resonate in Nati, whose body history is seen as a parallel to the history of the Cuban nation.

As shown in the previous chapter, in the revolutionary master narrative, Cuban history is the result of the struggle for independence from Spanish and U.S. colonial powers, which finally ends with the liberation brought by the Revolution. When read allegorically, Nati's body is used first by the colonizer, represented in the figure of the Spanish landowner Alejandro de la O, and then by Siaco, who has dealings with the United States. One could expect that Nati's body would achieve liberation at the end of the novel, after she has freed herself from different powers. She, like the Cuban nation and the rest of the town, would be expected to take part in the Revolution and be relieved from the domination of all other men except her husband, who becomes an exemplary revolutionary. But at the conclusion of the novel Nati is neither a revolutionary nor a counterrevolutionary; she remains a mystery. Since she resists interpretation and parades her femininity and sexual desire so shamelessly, the identity Nati performs can have potentially liberating effects for a female reader. I now turn to a critique of Laura Mulvey's work in order to explain an interpretation that may allow female readers of *La última* an opportunity for resistance.

Mulvey has been criticized for giving great prominence to women as the object of the gaze and yet denying them any participation in the dynamics of pleasurable identification. Even in a postscript to *Visual and Other Pleasures* (1989) titled "Afterthoughts on 'Visual and Narrative Cinema' Inspired by *Duel in the Sun*" (1990), where she made an effort to give women spectators a more active role, Mulvey stated that a female gaze presupposes a masochistic position (identification with a suffering female body) or a masculinization of herself (in the identification with the male hero). In identifying with Nati, female readers may indeed give in to a masochistic pleasure. Bruno may invoke identification, thus achieving the masculinization of the female reader, which is already elicited by Mercedes. Without denying these subject positions of the spectator, it is possible to claim Nati as a figure that goes beyond the dominant male gaze imposed on her.

As Jackie Stacey has stated, in order to provide women spectators a different position, one has to be able to see a character "through a woman's desire" (Stacey 253). The fact is that in addition to the sadistic depictions of Nati being raped in the mud, the reader witnesses Nati's sexual enjoyment and the power she experiences by choosing her sexual partners. Her sensual delight can be characterized as homoerotic, in scenes such as when she runs naked in the rain, laughing and making provocative movements that are aimed at nobody but herself and her own enjoyment. Though she may be sexually objectified by a male gaze, I want to reclaim the liberating component of her solitary scenes of imagined copulation in nature. As Stacey also claims, it is difficult to revindicate the cinematic pleasures of women without working within the mainstream frameworks that are offered (Stacey 255). As I will explain below, there is a liberating element in Nati constantly parading her sexuality in front of strangers, but what is unprecedented in official revolutionary discourse is the appearance of (literal) homoeroticism. If these scenes are read in a certain way, and I reiterate that these readings will have to coexist with the stereotypical ones, Nati can signify the appearance of lesbian pleasure, in herself and perhaps in a queer reader who may identify with her or see her as an object of desire.

As Flora González has noted, Cuban *mulatas* as represented in literature are characters doomed to fail. Nati is the embodiment of what she calls "the spectacular *mulata*," sexualized and racialized to the extreme, and as other *mulatas* who try to destabilize the patriarchal order, she ends up being marginalized (González 543). But Nati has a lot in common with Ochún, the *orisha* or Afro-Cuban deity who dwells in the river and who is the goddess of sexual love and a consummate prostitute. Nati chooses to receive her men in the river and experiences great pleasure in the water. The final scenes of the novel offer clues to the liberating effects of these characteristics.

The image of Nati's naked body, when she emerges out of the house in ruins where she had first been raped, is the last one in the novel. She bares herself in the presence of a group of men and goes to a nearby puddle to wash herself. When her husband tries to force her to go with him, she refuses and says, "I am pure as water" (Cofiño 333), thus defining purity in her own terms. The very last look of Nati that the reader is offered is of her being wrapped in a sheet, after which some neighbors force her into a car. All of these images of Nati are given to us interspersed with the comments of two men watching her. For instance, while she is washing herself in the puddle, one of the men says to the other, "We did not see her as female, as a woman. I don't know how to tell you. It was like a force, like something already not from this world" (332). And later, "And when they wrapped her up in a sheet, when the shape of her wet body was marked in the fabric, it was then that we saw her naked again. You see, it was all very weird" (334).

According to the narrator, all men see Nati constantly naked, no matter what she is wearing. With this she is defined as an archetype of the female body, always under the male gaze. But in the above passage there is a moment when she is "seen" literally without clothes, and at that moment she is no longer a "female" but "a force," she is not from this land, she is uncanny. Nati's multiple faces are synthesized in that last line of the book: "it was all very weird" (334).

In terms of the cinematic theory of the masculine gaze, Nati is subversive because she flaunts her femininity and elicits the gaze of everyone in the town. As a hyperracialized and sexualized *mulata*, she produces herself as an excess of femininity and thus masquerades the role of supreme womanhood. Nati's masquerade culminates at the end of the novel, when she ceases to be an object of desire for men—which is metaphorized in the fact that the two men no longer could see her naked—and she becomes a subject, the performer of her own identity. In Mary Ann Doane's words: "The masquerade, in flaunting femininity, holds it at a distance. Womanliness is a mask which can be worn or removed. . . . *To masquerade is to manufacture a lack in the form of a certain distance between oneself and one's image*" (185, emphasis mine). In the passage above, the moment when Nati's body is marked in the sheet wrapped around her is thus emblematic: Nati's nakedness shown in the wet sheet marks her detachment from her own image, her resistance to having a body present-to-itself. For a female reader who is open to questioning the female identity that the Revolution prescribes, Nati is subversive because she exposes the farcical aspect of women's stereotypical roles.

To conclude, in this chapter I have reviewed some of the positive and negative roles offered to women in the official discourse of the first decade of the Revolution, such as the mother, the housewife, the worker, and the object of desire. I have shown that there is some continuity between the representation of those roles in official speeches addressed to women and female roles in a revolutionary novel. This continuity is not seamless, in that there is no exact parallelism between representations of women in speeches and in the novel. In political speeches, representations of women emerge matter-of-factly: women are the object of revolutionary policymaking, and as such they are generally flat characters. Women as constituted by revolutionary leaders are afforded only the characteristics that are needed for the particular task they are asked to do, and they are not complex enough to rebel against their creators. In *La última*, Claudia and Mercedes are also flat characters, endowed only with the few attributes that constitute them as frustrated mother and revolutionary worker. Nati, however, escapes the mold that constricts her, because the narrator's infatuation with her unwittingly gives her more attributes than he can control. If one considers the reaction of a queer reader or a non-stereotypical female reader who sees her own femininity not as an identity but as a masquerade, the gender economy that the text constructs in the framework of Revolution becomes undone.

This is how a close reading of *La última* can explain the official gender discourse that more recent writers have been trying to deconstruct, but the novel also lends itself to a theoretical reading uncovering the points of resistance that are used by those same authors. In the end, the crucial element is a performance that poses many challenges to a liberating gender discourse, but which can be appropriated and refashioned by female readers who will not be denied pleasure.

# Toward a Revolutionary Utopia

## Fluid Identities in a Child's Account

In his seminal essay "El nuevo mundo, la isla de la utopía y la isla de Cuba" (1965), ("The new world, the island of utopia, and the island of Cuba"), Ezequiel Martínez Estrada made the controversial claim that Thomas More's *Utopia* (1516) represented Cuba as the idyllic place described in Pedro Mártir's *Ocho décadas del Mundo Nuevo* (1493–1526) (Eight decades of the new world) (Martínez Estrada 90).[1] Martínez Estrada went on to state that despite that first favorable representation of the island, utopia was not truly realized in Cuba until 1959, once the concept of utopia had evolved from that of a bourgeois liberal state to a Communist one (Martínez Estrada 107–8). Martínez Estrada was one of many intellectuals who voiced their enthusiasm for the Revolution in its early years by expressing their belief in a utopia made reality. Yet even in those years there was little reference to the fulfillment of utopia in the official discourse of the Revolution, which focused instead on what remained to be done and a tentative promise of a better future. The key to utopia's banishment may be found in Che Guevara's essay "Socialism and Man in Cuba," which criticizes "an ideal society, almost without conflict or contradiction" as a vain illusion, and urges Cubans—to be more specific, writers and artists—to engage with "the real problems of man and his alienation" (Guevara 11)

A study of the novels sanctioned as revolutionary texts in the first decade of the Revolution reveals that many of their authors followed Guevara's recommendations for a "committed" art, as they represented the painful transformation process required to constitute the New Man. The characters appearing as true revolutionaries in these novels, such as Vilma in *Maestra*, Bruno in *La última mujer y el próximo combate*, and Darío in *Sacchario*, experience rites of passage that reveal the many sacrifices needed. My focus in this chapter is the novel *Los niños se despiden* (1968) (The children say good-bye, henceforth *Los niños*), by Pablo Armando Fernández. The text is exceptional in the first decade of the Revolution, not only because it is one of the very few representing utopia, but also because it advances the controversial idea that utopia cannot be built until revolutionary identity or the New

Man is deconstructed. My reading of this novel is therefore not contrasted with political speeches, since to a large extent this text serves as a counterpart to all of the speeches concerning the New Man that I have cited. It is in *Los niños* that the message implicit in all of the other novels is promoted more clearly. The novel is structured in such a way as to lead the reader toward a final, triumphant voyage to utopia, represented as the advent of a radical revolution. But before that end, the basic pillars of revolutionary ideology, such as a unified identity and the notions of Truth, Authority, and History are debunked.

My interpretation of *Los niños* might seem paradoxical to readers acquainted with Pablo Armando Fernández's long-term commitment to the Revolution. The fact that Fernández was awarded the National Prize for Literature (1996) and proclaimed Cuba's poet laureate after Nicolás Guillén should not prevent one from observing the relentless criticism underlying Fernández's first novel. It is important to keep in mind that intellectuals experienced a great deal of agitation in the years before and after this book was published. The threat of censorship had loomed over Cuban letters following Fidel's injunction, "Within the Revolution everything, against the Revolution, nothing" (June 1961). In addition, the closing of *Lunes de Revolución* (August 1961) affected Fernández deeply, since he was the director of the journal along with Guillermo Cabrera Infante (Fernández, "Autopsia" 52–62). In a recent interview, Fernández revealed the harsh way the authorities treated him when he was forced to return from London, where he had been assigned after *Lunes* closed, without an explanation. Upon his return, Fernández was told that the Ministry of Culture could not offer him a position, and he remained unemployed and isolated until 1971. He stated that, until 1978, "very few people visited us" (Báez 110).

The reasons for Fernández's isolation may be related to the Padilla case, which began to unfold in 1968. Fernández was in fact cited in the Padilla hearings as one of those intellectuals who were "embittered, disaffected, sick and sad, and therefore counterrevolutionary" (Padilla, "Intervención" 115), and certain voices in *Los niños* do indeed allude to the atmosphere of tension experienced as early as 1968. For instance, in the midst of the euphoria of the trip to Sabanas, or a utopian land, the narrator issues the following angry warning:

> And I want you to understand me very well, . . . with many words, but all very clear words . . . , that this is how it is . . . , and he who dares remove an iota from everything that has been written in this book is very wrong, . . . and very mistaken indeed. . . . And in this book ev-

erything is written, everything that the little opportunists, the petty, shitty liars, and the little goody-goodies in behavior, heart, and mind, the insignificant starched shirts, listen to me well, do not want to read. They, who are shocked with the terrible and wondrous pages of this book that says everything, . . . and when it has nothing new to say, words and syllables and letters make a Revolution inside the book and say everything again but in another way, in a different way (Fernández 534–35).

The voice in the text just quoted is obviously trying to guard the novel against censorship, and the irate mention of the "opportunists," "liars," and "hypocrites" is perhaps an allusion to the writers who had hitherto towed the line of official cultural dictates. One should also remember that by that point certain writers who were critical of the regime were already publishing abroad, such as Reinaldo Arenas, whose *El mundo alucinante* (*Hallucinations: Being an Account of the Life and Adventures of Friar Servando Teresa de Mier*, 1971) questioned the notion of a linear history, and was published in France in 1968. Additionally, Arenas's *Celestino antes del alba* (*Singing from the Well*, 1987), which promoted subversive writing in various ways, was published in 1967 by Unión, but in a limited edition of two thousand copies (F. Soto 345). The mention of "a Revolution inside the book" in the passage also marks Fernández's contribution to a debate that was going on at the time, pitting two kinds of literature against each other: committed literature or literature that was revolutionary in content, versus literature of the Boom or literature revolutionary in form.[2]

In my reading, *Los niños* bears a strong resemblance to the tradition of Thomas More's *Utopia* (1516) though not, as Martínez Estrada would have it, because both of them represent Cuba as a utopia. On the contrary, both More and Fernández are critiquing a contemporary situation that they deem dystopic and presenting an alternative ideal that may somehow resemble the place wherein the author writes but that does not quite exist. This tradition of critical utopia corresponds to Peter Ruppert's definition of the genre: "Structured and organized as dialogues, utopias set out to engage their readers in a dialogue on social alternatives and social variations. What initiates this dialogue is the experience of non-coincidence between social reality and utopian dream, the incongruence between what is and what ought to be. This non-coincidence produces thoughts, stimulates desires, makes us dissatisfied with the way things are" (ix–x). For Thomas More, the dystopic situation is Tudor England, in which poverty, corruption of morals, and selfish individualism were rampant. The text is written in the form of a dialogue, with several points of view: More himself and Peter Gilles appear as characters who express the conventional ideas of the time, while a Raphael Nonsenso is a traveler who has been to Utopia and voices quite revolutionary views. In More's dialogic text the author guards himself against censorship by trying to "talk sense into" Raphael Nonsenso, while the latter's critical opinions are made clear in the text. Like More's utopia, Sabanas or the utopian region toward which the characters travel at the end of *Los niños*, is constituted by the desire for a better world. Fernández's text is not written in the form of a dialogue, but it is as multivocal as More's, with some voices quoting the official ideology, and others questioning it completely.

Both Fernández and More were constrained by restrictions on what could be said. As Antonio Vera-León puts it in his reading of other revolutionary novels, Fernández was writing "on the state's stationery." In these circumstances, "writing, memory, self and narrative desire are constituted in, and by, the state papers, in compliance with the requests of the state" (Vera-León 67). That is why the critique of the Revolution in the late 1960s, the present time of the author, is disguised in *Los niños* as a commentary on the prerevolutionary years.

Since Fernández was still committed to the Revolution in its original utopian aspect, he balanced his strongly critical attitude by appropriating many of the topics, motifs, and images of revolutionary novels, to such an extent that readers and critics interpreted the text as denouncing the chaos of the prerevolutionary years and unconditionally supporting institutional discourse. In fact, the novel was awarded the Casa de las Américas Prize, which was generally awarded to revolutionary texts. In that same year, the winners of the poetry and drama awards—Heberto Padilla's *Fuera de juego* (1968) and Antón Arrufat's *Los siete contra Tebas* (1968)—were eventually published with disclaimers from the UNEAC owing to their alleged counterrevolutionary slant (Casal, *Caso Padilla* 57–60). That the revolutionary commissars overlooked the many subversive aspects of Fernández's text may be explained by its fragmentary and multivocal character, and by its allegorical as well as ambivalent dimension, all of which leave room for conflictive interpretations.

The novel opens at day's end when a group of children are saying good night to their parents before going to bed. The fact that the title is "the children say good-bye" makes it sound as if the characters are leaving in a more definite way than just going to sleep, giving the rest of the novel the quality of a voyage or a vision. The narrator of this section is one of those children, who tells of this and other childhood experiences retrospectively. Among those experiences is the day that a relative of the narrator's came back from a long stay in New York. When the recollection of this homecoming begins, the narrator and this other character, called Alejandro, are two different people. But all of a sudden, without a change of style or any indication of a change of voice, the narrator and Alejandro merge into the same character. The narrative continues with Alejandro and the former child narrator as one character providing the implied reader with the account of his youth. In this account, Lila, who was also present in the reminiscences of the previous child narrator as an invisible friend, appears as a sister. Another character with a changing identity in these memories is Salvador, who serves as a friend, a lover, or a double in different parts of the plot.

In his narrative, Alejandro/the child narrator says that in order for Sabanas, a utopian world, to come into effect, Lila had to destroy Earth and create it again. The control of the narrative is gradually assumed by an impersonal narrator who explains that the Sabanas Lila created was a failure and was soon ravaged by the avatars of Cuban history. Alejandro/the child narrator's family is then chosen to travel up the Río de la Luna in a boat like Noah's Ark in order to establish the town of Sabanas. At this point the narrative jumps back to the moment when Alejandro was leaving *el batey*, or the sugartown, to go to New York, and he prolongs the farewell with memories and reflections on what it means to leave Cuba.

The second part of the book begins in New York, where Alejandro is discussing a novel he is writing with Salvador. By the description of the text, this novel is *Los niños*. The entire second part is devoted to Alejandro recounting his experience in New York, especially his love affairs and his struggle in writing the novel. These accounts are interrupted by sections titled "Jardín," presumably a reference to the Garden of Eden, which describe the excitement, illusions, and fears of the people on their way to Sabanas on the always traveling boat. The child narrator in the "Jardín" sections corresponds to the narrator in the first part of the novel. The style of the second part is not very different from the first part, and there are numerous references to Alejandro's/the child narrator's family and Lila in the second part, but the account of Alejandro's life in New York introduces many characters and conflicts that have no relation to the first part, or with the trip to Sabanas.

The narrator of *Los niños*, despite his fragmented identity, is *one*, though he adopts multiple personas and registers. The narrator alternates between first and third-person narration, and ventriloquizes with voices that express contrary views. There are sections such as "Miscelánea" (Miscellaneous) that do not have a narrator because they are factual descriptions; an example is the minute description of a sugar-grinding plant. Occasionally, other voices emerge in the narrative, such as Nana Ianita's (102–8). But there is one narrator, one voice at times a child or a young man, who weaves the plot and makes constant appearances in all of the sections of his narrative.

According to Seymour Menton, the title of *Los niños* explains its chronological framework, since it refers to everything that young people had to part with following the beginning of the Revolution (Menton 59). Though the time coordinates of this novel are quite difficult to determine, Menton states that *Los niños* narrates life in Cuba mainly in the 1930s and 1940s, and the references to the building of Sabanas bring the reader to the utopia that the 1959 Revolution was attempting to realize. Notwithstanding the references to the infamous pseudo-republic, the text possesses an implicit link to the present time of the author. For instance, according to Menton, Alejandro's departure to the United States refers to the prerevolutionary exodus from Cuba in the 1930s and 1940s, but it can also serve as a comment on the large number of people who left Cuba in the first five years of the 1959 Revolution. For Menton, Fernández describes New York as a "den of iniquity," representing the center of the dehumanizing, imperialistic, materialistic power that Cuba had tried to confront since the beginning of the century. But as with the narrator in *Sacchario*, despite his negative comments about the city, the narrator can hardly hide his fascination with the city he is describing.

One third of the book is devoted to the narrator's life in New York, in spite of the fact that it has very little connection with the rest of the plot. One can speculate that the second part of the book represents an opportunity for Fernández to express his own divided identity, his love for Cuba and at the same time his infatuation with the city where he spent his youth, as he has expressed several times in interviews (with Font 44–45; with Bejel 87). Ultimately, after a leap in time, these sections illustrate the divided identity of revolutionary Cuba, in a wider understanding of the term *revolution*. As Fernández himself explained in an interview: "Well, the Revolution is the Literacy Campaign, but it is also the Mariel; it is the conquest of the means of production of the country, but it is also Camarioca. I mean, the Revolution is everything. . . . I do believe that in the United States we have had something very beautiful happen among the Cuban youths who have delved into the root of our country. . . . We have always had them visiting at home, these children who wander around everywhere. And they are adorable human beings, because they have come to get to know Cuba's roots, through its literature, music, and country essence, through its true culture" (with Ibieta 62). The narrator's account of life in New York represents "the other Cuba," the life of Cubans outside Cuba after the Revolution. Fernández displays feelings of love and hate similar to those experienced by many Cubans who have lived in the United States, long before and after the 1959 Revolution.

But because that love and hate is enduring, and the novel was published in 1968, it can be interpreted as referring to the years after the 1959 Revolution.[3] If, as Menton suggests, the utopian world in *Los niños* were a metaphor for the advent of the Revolution after the Machado era, there would be a wide time gap between that time and the 1959 Revolution, which would rob the idea of a utopia of its usual immediacy to the time period of the author.

Some elements in the text do provide evidence for Menton's interpretation, such as the dialectic concept of history or the trip to Sabanas as "the Revolution of the young people" (*Los niños* 313). Most importantly, the joyous climax at the end of the book (541) wherein Lila summons the "Light of Yara," Martí and Fidel to lead people into Sabanas, is a clear reference to the founding elements of the Revolution and its official discourse. The "Light of Yara" is a reference to the rebellious spirit of the Grito de Yara, a proclamation issued by Carlos Manuel de Céspedes that was said to have initiated the first war of independence against Spain on October 10, 1868, after Céspedes liberated his slaves at the Demajagua plantation. Martí was proclaimed Mentor of the Cuban Revolution after Fidel said in "History Will Absolve Me" (1953) that he had been the inspiration for the July 26 attack on the Moncada Barracks (219–20). When Lila summons Fidel, he appears in the text as follows: "Behold him sitting on a white horse. He is called Faithful and Truthful, and struggles and judges with justice" (Fernández 541). With this epic representation of Fidel the narrator of *Los niños* allies himself with countless other narrators of revolutionary novels, in which the explicit appearance of *el líder máximo* was a given.[4] By tracing a line of continuity between the Light of Yara, Martí, and Fidel in 1968, Fernández commemorates the hundred years of the initiation of the independence movement and presents the Revolution as the culmination of that struggle.

And yet, the indeterminacy of the timeline in *Los niños* is such that despite these references to official discourse, it can represent many other aspects of Cuba circa 1968. My next section is devoted to showing how, against the official cultural discourse that derided most literature as escapist and promoted a committed literature, the narrator of *Los niños* used precisely that literary tradition to undermine revolutionary principles.

## Tinkering with Literary Tradition: A *Bildungsroman* and a *Künstlerroman* without a Protagonist

According to Edward Said, a beginning is a "first step in the intentional production of meaning" (5) that establishes the rules of pertinence of a text, its "authority," or the organizing principle that makes sure that all words belong to the whole of the work (16). The narrator of *Los niños* plays with this notion of beginnings by securing a firm footing on the well-established literary traditions of the *bildungsroman* and the *künstlerroman* and subsequently disappointing the horizon of expectations that these genres set up. The child narrator at the beginning of the text is modeled out of the narrative of self-discovery or education, which describes the child's process of maturation and enlightenment through a series of trials. One can cite other Cuban novels such as Alejo Carpentier's *El siglo de las luces* (1962) (*Explosion in the Cathedral*, 1962), Reinaldo Arenas's *Celestino antes del alba* (1967) (*Singing from the Well*, 1987) or even *El mundo alucinante* (1968) (*Hallucinations: Being an Account of the Life and Adventures of Friar Servando Teresa de Mier*, 1971), and José Lezama's *Paradiso* (1966) (published in English with the same title in 1974), all published in the same period, as examples of narratives that begin with the story of a child's life.

The tradition of the *bildungsroman* was loosely adapted in many of the narratives of the Revolution that contained the voice of a protagonist telling his or her story of transformation from a bourgeois skeptic into a convinced revolutionary. These fictional autobiographical accounts focused mainly on the self that the revolutionary left behind, as well as on the new aspects of his or her revolutionary identity. In the words of Antonio Vera-León: "Self-narration may thus be taken as a special zone of the post-1959 Cuban social text, a zone in which forms of subjectivity have been and continue to be negotiated, where 'old' forms of *cubanidad* are represented in tension with, or superseded by, new forms and values sanctioned by the revolutionary state" (Vera-León 65). No matter how much wavering there was along the way, at the end of these narratives the revolutionary identity was fully constituted. Such is the case, for instance, of Vilma in Daura Olema García's *Maestra voluntaria* (1962), whose transformation into a model revolutionary occurs when she goes to the Sierra Maestra to serve as a volunteer teacher. The beginning of *Los niños* thus creates the expectation that the young protagonist will come of age and renounce his comfortable life as he embraces a life of struggle.

The beginning of the text also sketches the tradition of the *künstlerroman*, or the story of the making of a writer. The child narrator reveals his fascination with words in a scene that is typical of the genre: "Words seduce me like the most succulent and elaborate delicacy, first they fill my eyes, then my mouth, then my stomach. . . . The fact is that I am doomed to smell them and taste them forever. . . . Doomed to listen to them, to say them, to write them, aware that these exercises will not make me a more intelligent, more prudent, wiser, happier man" (Fernández 29). This character is comparable to José Cemí in Lezama's *Paradiso*, another *künstlerroman*: "As he listened to the succession of the names of marine tribes, . . . the words themselves rose up, lured up out of their own territory, artificially grouped, and their joyous movement was invisible and ineffable as it penetrated his dark channels. . . . He felt the words taking on substance and he also felt a soft wind on his cheeks shaking those words and giving them movement" (*Paradiso*, trans. Rabassa, 172). Beyond the obvious differences resulting from the diverse styles of these writers, it is clear that a boy developing a taste for words is a familiar occurrence for a reader, and both the *künstlerroman* and the *bildungsroman* chart a path with a clear beginning and an end. Sooner or later, after the protagonist has accumulated some life experience and undergone some trials, it is expected that he will become a writer.

In the literature of the Cuban Revolution there are several other novels that respond to the tradition of the *künstlerroman*, such as David Buzzi's *Los desnudos* (1967), which describes the making of a revolutionary writer. The protagonist of this novel, Sergio, goes from being "a bourgeois writer" to a "committed" one, and at the end of this process he describes his newfound identity in the following terms: "If you knew how clearly everything looks to me now. This is life, Servando . . . to add to the words I join together, one after another, the action of one man. . . . I. A man without fear of saying 'I,' because I understand things in terms of 'we': we have to fight, . . . we" (Buzzi 297). Sergio's new identity is that of the intellectual who unites action to writing. As a writer representing those who fight for a just cause, he earns his sense of identity, his "I" through a kind of writing that links him to the community.

Sergio's idea of the writer as a mouthpiece of the masses coincides with the concept of the revolutionary writer as defined by Alejo Carpentier in "Papel social del novelista" (1971) (The social role of the author): "They [the writers] understand the language of the masses of men of their time. They are thus capable of understanding that language, of interpreting it, of giving a form to it, . . . by practicing a sort of shamanism, that is, by putting a message in understandable language. . . . [They are] receiving the expression of human movements, verifying their presence, defining, describing their collective activity. I think that in this . . . we find the role of the writer in our time" ("Papel" 166). The writer protagonist of a revolutionary *kunstlërroman* is allegedly bound to develop this special voice.

In the traditions of the *bildungsroman* and the *künstlerroman* the new identity develops linearly and completely from childhood to maturity, running parallel to the mastery of language. In *Los niños*, however, after the voice of the child protagonist has situated the narrative within these traditions, the identity of the narrator becomes fragmented. The child who is supposed to mature as he grows up, the budding writer, suddenly disappears, leaving a young adult who had previously appeared as a different character. The child and this other character, Alejandro, are different and yet the same person, since they share certain childhood memories. This is the moment when, after the narrator underscores the physical resemblance between the two characters, they merge: "I felt that his gaze and his voice were starting to irritate me. I discovered that his eyes were a shade of gray very similar to mine. I discovered that his voice and mine were not very different. . . . I also verified that my imitation skills became better next to him" (38–39). This scene constitutes the identity of the child narrator as fluid because the reader pictures the image of the child narrator only as he sees himself reflected in, and gradually merging with, Alejandro. The child narrator's name and a description of his appearance are not provided until this moment. There is some indication that Alejandro might have felt as if he had never left Cuba, and thus he meets a younger version of himself at the time of his homecoming, but in terms of characterization and plot, Alejandro and the child narrator remain two characters, or a character with a split personality.

As for the fledgling writer, he does not achieve success as an author, as would be expected; on the contrary, the reader is made privy to his feeling of failure, his writing difficulties, and his ignorance. Furthermore, the novel's authorship is disputed by two characters: Lila and Salvador. Lila—the narrator's sister/childhood friend who is also described as a color, a mood, and a real character—is at times said to be dictating to the narrator what he is writing.[5] Salvador accuses Alejandro of wanting to *be* him, and of pretending to be the writer of the novel that only Salvador was able to write.[6] Fernández himself stated on one occasion that Alejandro wrote Salvador's novel (with Font 45). The narrator's split personality casts doubt on the very notion of identity on which the Revolution is based, and since the narrator is not fully in control of his voice, there is a high degree of skepticism toward the role of the writer in the Revolution.

The fluid identity of the narrator of *Los niños* extends to the protagonist's gender identity. Thus, at a certain point in the narrative, Alejandro states: "I love and fancy people, I take pleasure in the things in my memory. I like that woman, I would want that man. . . . I would like to be that woman, I like that man. Everything mixes joyously, the absent and the present. Let us suppose that I do not understand the joining of these desires, that I do not distinguish them. Let us suppose that I imagine them to create different situations" (Fernández 325). In this passage, the narrator plays with gender identity in a way that illustrates Judith Butler's notion of the performativity of gender, as he shows an awareness that such an identity is constituted in the act of performing it. In Butler's words, "The substantive effect of gender is performatively produced and compelled by the regulatory practices of gender coherence. Hence, within the inherited discourse of the metaphysics of substance, gender proves to be performative—that is, constituting the identity it is purported to be. . . . There is no gender identity behind the expressions of gender; that identity is performatively constituted by the very 'expressions' that are said to be its results" (Butler 25). As a writer, the narrator represents his gender identity as a product of his imagination, fashioned through his memory. In Butler's terms, the conventional "practice of gender" in the citation above is desire for a man or a woman, and the narrator desires both; he can imagine himself performing several gender identities metaphorized through the exercises of writing, imagining, and remembering.

By having the narrator as writer perform different gender identities, the role of the heterosexual male, or the usual authoritative voice of the narratives of the Revolution, is called into question. The appearance of fluid gender identities overturns attempts at forging "a new man" with any degree of permanence; indeed, it calls into question the idea of "man" altogether. As one reads the novel, the presuppositions of the *bildungsroman* and the *künstlerroman* are abandoned. They occasionally resurface, only to be subverted again.

Contrary to Edward Said's theory of foundational beginnings, in *Los niños* the elements of *bildungsroman* and *künstlerroman* that appear at the beginning of the novel not only "do not belong" there later, but are in fact displaced. The notions of character, character development, potential writer/actual writer, and gender identity are also compromised. The sense of certainty inherent in the *bildungsroman* and the *künstlerroman* is thwarted, casting doubt on any discourse with claims to truth. If the reader takes this text seriously, he or she may wonder: How can any ideology have the final word? How can any author claim full authority for his or her text? How can one presume the constitution of a fixed identity? The metafictional aspects of the text respond to all of these questions in the negative.

Metafiction and the Undermining of Revolutionary Discourse

Metafiction encompasses narrative techniques that make writing self-referential or self-conscious. Its use has been common in experimental novels that seek to question ideological constructs. In Patricia Waugh's definition: "Metafiction is a term given to fictional writing which self-consciously and systematically draws attention to its status as an artefact in order to pose questions about the relationship between fiction and reality. In providing a critique of their own methods of construction, such writings not only examine the fundamental structures of narrative fiction, they also explore the possible fictionality of the world outside the literary fictional text" (Waugh 2). This self-conscious fiction is therefore a good antidote to any discourse seeking to establish a clear difference between "the fictional" and "the real," implicitly defining the latter as what corresponds to the acts and values espoused by a dominant ideology. The metafictional character of *Los niños* exposes the textuality and to some extent fictionality of what we consider real, as well as the vulnerability to subversion of the texts that make up that reality.

The self-consciousness of *Los niños* is displayed in a conversation between Alejandro and his friend Salvador about the novel Alejandro is writing. The weak points that Alejandro criticizes in his text can be applied to *Los niños*: for instance, he fears that his novel is a "narrative failure" because "the double personality of the protagonist, difficult to identify for the reader, obscures the plot without providing any clear sense, making it chaotic, false, implausible" (Fernández 330). This double protagonism refers to the merging of Alejandro and the child narrator at the beginning of the novel. By expressing doubts about the novel he is writing, the narrator challenges the authoritative voice that the author is usually endowed with and by implication the authoritative voice of the Revolution. As González Echevarría puts it, when the author ceases to be the "author-dictator" or the "author-rhetor" and shows himself as a "weak and fragmented *scriptor*," the figure of a political authority that holds the reigns of the state is deposed ("*Biografía*" 71). The images of Fidel as a leader and mouthpiece of the masses, the *maestro* of communication whom Che Guevara so much celebrated, is defaced when one sees that a writer cannot extinguish his own doubts and disowns his authority by denying authorship of the text we are reading.[7]

In addition to the intrusive narrator who discusses the writing of the text, Waugh points to two other characteristics of metafiction: self-consciousness concerning language and literary form; and playfulness of style (Waugh 2). An example of the latter is the incorporation of the language of comics and movies in the text. The protagonist, Alejandro, and his friends impersonate famous characters, mixing up historical or fictional figures with actors, thereby elaborating their own version of reality: "And he also mixed up cartoon characters with the generals, statesmen, and heroes who waged war: Sir Neville Chamberlain with Pancho el Largo with Gary Cooper; Hitler with Pedro Harapos with George Raft; John Wayne with Douglas MacArthur with the Magician Mandrake . . . Paul Henreid with Tarzan with Mussolini; Joseph Stalin with Charles Boyer with Benitín . . . Chiang Kay-Chek with Terry with David Niven . . ." (Fernández 241–42). In this passage, the narrator is not only once again questioning the notion of authority, but is also parodying a concept that revolutionary discourse often invokes, that is, history. When Stalin is placed at the same level as Charles Boyer and Benitín, historical figures of the Revolution can also be equated with movie actors and characters in a comic strip, and their feats are reduced to fiction or play rather than celebrated in the annals of history. As Vera-León puts it, referring to Jesús Díaz's *Las iniciales de la tierra* (1986) (*The Initials of the Earth*, 2006), in which the language of comics is also used, the character is enmeshed in a number of different languages, and each of those languages defines the self at different stages in life (70). Ultimately there is no definite language that takes the dominant place among others, and there is no unified self constituted by a dominant discourse.

The ruptured plot and apparent lack of planning in the narrative also draw attention to the status of the text as text. One reads the comments of an intrusive author who plays games on the reader in order to make him or her aware of the writing process. For instance, the same dialogue as to whether it is best to "leave" or "come back" appears twice, with only a few words changed (Fernández 257–61). When asked about this novel in an interview, Fernández himself described its haphazard quality: "I wrote *Los niños* as if I had been singing in a park alone. I did not intend to have a concrete structure, or a concrete style, nor even a linear or logical plot. Some things I wrote from memories I had, . . . and the book started to take form. . . . [This novel] was like a big bag that all the words were falling into, until it flooded" (with Gabriella Ibieta 49). One striking effect of the textuality of the novel is that, unlike other revolutionary tales of identity, it precludes identification between the reader and the characters that revolutionary narratives tend to foster. Further, in the fragmentation and discontinuity of the plot, *Los niños* rejects the notion of linearity. The story of a given character is often told in several ways, revealing an awareness of the many possibilities of emplotment. An instance of the latter is when the narrator traces the history of Sabanas in three different ways, all of which lead to different understandings of Cuban history. The next section will further examine the subversion of history and other pivotal notions of revolutionary discourse in the novel.

Family, Home, Nation, and History as the Cores of Identity:
Fernández's Debt to Lezama

At the beginning of *Los niños* the concepts of family, home, nation, and history constitute the child narrator's sense of self. He reports that when children went to bed at night, parents all around Cuba would start telling stories about the past. The notion of family was created through the stories that parents told of their ancestors, and thus history was inextricably linked to family life. Parents boasted about their family's participation in the building of the Cuban nation through heroic acts in the wars of independence. Family pride was exclusionary, for all mothers and fathers claimed to descend from "pure Spaniards" or "pure *criollos*," the offspring of Spaniards born in Cuba. The narrator implicitly states that if there were any other races or ethnicities in the family, they were not part of the stories told.

Once this image of a thick web of simultaneous conversations establishes the concept of family at the beginning of the text, the narrator launches into an account of the particular history of his mother's and father's families respectively. These histories are exhaustive, with family trees and different voices telling long stories of love, war, and betrayal. Family history is also influenced by traditions and the different homes ancestors lived in, some of them now destroyed.

Family, home, nation, and history are considered part of the collective identity of Cuba, or *cubanidad*. As the narrator recounts: "Papa started to tell the history of the splendor and the privation of our ancestors. We were Cuban, born of Cuban parents, children of Cuban parents, children of Cubans born in the island, and that was our glory. Papa spoke slowly and carefully about their lives and their feats, with the same nostalgia with which he heard the very same stories from his people. The important thing was to be Cuban, to feel Cuban, and *that,* only our geography, its climate and its nature could determine" (Fernández 13). The notion of history is important only insofar as the family was implicated in it; that is why a sense of place, of geography, and the family's roots in Cuba are more important than the notion of grand history itself.

The topoi used at the beginning of *Los niños* may once again remind the reader of José Lezama Lima's *Paradiso*, since both texts trace the history of a family and a home as involved in the past and the destiny of the Cuban nation. In fact, both novels construct and deconstruct these notions, both willingly or unwillingly seek the notion of a core identity based on family, home, nation, and history, and both inevitably fail in their quest.[8] The reason for these affinities between the texts lies in two similar aspects of Lezama's and Fernández's work: the notion of "un sistema poético del mundo" (a poetic system of the world) and the concept of the father as the bearer of the Word. A brief comparison between the treatment of these concepts in the work of Lezama and Fernández will illuminate some important aspects of the latter.

In his essay "Coloquio con Juan Ramón Jiménez" (1937) (Colloquium with Juan Ramón Jiménez) Lezama defined what he called the "mito de la insularidad" (myth of insularity)—subsequently called "teleología insular" (island teleology) and a "sistema poético del mundo" (poetic system of the world) in "La expresión americana" (1957) (The American expression). According to Lezama, the myth of insularity represented a return to the origin, to a purely American expression. This language exclusive to America (understood as the Americas), would allegedly turn the marginal *americano* into the center that appropriated any other influences and would create a poetic world that replaced empirical reality. For Lezama "island expression" ("insularismo") was designed to combat the pessimism of the epoch and the dependence of Cuban letters on European or Spanish precedents.

According to Cintio Vitier in *Lo cubano en la poesía* (1970) (The expression of Cubanness in poetry), the pessimism Lezama alluded to in "La expresión americana" was the result of a long-felt stagnation in the era of the pseudo-republic in Cuba (1909–33), which was marked by corruption and contempt for the arts (Vitier 462). Perceiving a clash between history and poetry, Lezama made a choice for the latter, advocating a poetic "imago" that imposed itself on reality by transferring it into the reign of the metaphor, or "el reino de la absoluta libertad" (the reign of absolute freedom), as Lezama called it in another essay ("Imágenes posibles" 159). In the face of frustrations with the "historic destiny" of Cuba, the "absence of finality" in history, and the profound disorientation of the era, Lezama chose poetry as a way to return to a time before history; he tried to rescue Cuba as described in Columbus's first written account, where Cuba was likened to the island of Utopia. Lezama estimated that the infinite possibilities of a utopian world were opened through poetry, as a verbal incantation of reality.

Though Lezama's refuge in poetry took place in reference to a previous moment in Cuban history, this attitude was constant in his writing, and is also applicable to the post-1959 era. One of Lezama's few explicit comments on that time was the following: "Among the best qualities of the Revolution . . . is the fact that it brought again the spirit of radiating poverty, of the poor that is superabundant in spiritual goods. . . . We start to see the results of our spells and the kingdom of the word half-opens in absolute time. When the people are inhabited by a living image, the state achieves its form . . ." ("La cantidad hechizada" 838–40). Lezama equated the Revolution with a new era of poverty, in the sense of frugality and spirituality, rather than material- ism. For the celebrated Cuban poet, this era opened infinite possibilities of expression that generated a sort of poetic utopia. In effect, Lezama's *Para- diso* proposed a poetic revolution that transcended the Revolution, went beyond the political rhetoric, and ultimately supplanted it.

*Paradiso* culminates with the moment when Oppiano Licario introduces the protagonist to the poetry of totality, a moment that, according to Julio Ortega "suggests the deep joy of the world as the recovery of innocence, as the founding of the paradise of verbal creation" (Ortega 54). The realm of the word as the refuge of innocence, the idea of poetry as the "foundation of paradise," and the turning to poetry as an antidote to one's sterile reality are key topics for establishing a comparison with Fernández.

In a 1979 interview, Fernández stated that he was attracted to the Revo- lution "as a poetic phenomenon" (with Font 42). Like Lezama, Fernández sought refuge in the poetic text as he strove to focus on the creative po- tential of the historical moment. But unlike Lezama, rather than focusing on a poetic utopia beyond or parallel to the Revolution, in an institutional sense, Fernández elaborated this utopia from the deconstruction of some of the ideological foundations of the Revolution. For Fernández, poetic utopia went hand in hand with sociopolitical utopia, and both were created from the impulse to make the Revolution better by critiquing it from inside. It is for these reasons that Sabanas, the mythical state of utopia, is created only at the end of the novel, once some of the constrictive aspects of revolutionary identity have been deconstructed.

Like Lezama in *Paradiso*, in *Los niños* Fernández situates a child figure as a recurrent presence in the narrative and stresses the importance of inno- cence and candor in the construction of his poetic utopia.[9] But in *Paradiso* the child Cemí strives for the restoration of the father figure as an organiz- ing center in the elaboration of this poetic utopia; Fernández's utopia, on the contrary, cannot be built until the father figure is destroyed. In Lezama's case, as Arnaldo Cruz-Malavé puts it, "restoring the paternal world of pro- portion, or . . . the *logos spermatikos* or seminal reason, is the aim of *Parad- iso*" (71). In principle, the lost paternal *logos* in *Paradiso* is recovered through writing, and a sense of history is regained through the son's transcription of family history, which is also an allegorical history of the nation. However, for Cruz-Malavé, the narrative of *Paradiso* deliberately fails to restore the father figure despite its initial plan, because Cemí chooses the path of "the breach between the creator and the creature, the father and the son, the I and its successor" (102). Ultimately, the text deconstructs the concepts of subject, family, and nation because they are built on "the unproductive [in the very literal sense, as "non-procreating"] homosexual eros" (90, parentheses mine). *Los niños*, in contrast, does not even attempt to restore the father figure, but instead stages a deliberate parricide in all senses: as I demonstrated above, the narrator undermines the figure of the author as the master of the text and deconstructs any voice with claims to authority.[10] By implication, the authoritative and paternal voices of revolutionary discourse are also called into question.

When questioning the father's narratives, the narrator questions the narratives that the Revolution itself has passed on, in particular the narratives on the constitution of the revolutionary nation. For example, if in the citation above the father is the definer of *cubanía*, the narratorial voice soon rejects what his father has taught him, casts doubt on the family history that has been passed on to him, and revises the entire history of Cuba to include what his parents chose to ignore. The narrator bitterly detaches himself from the Spanish ancestors that his parents celebrated and asserts that Cuba as a nation was formed by the Indians that the Spaniards massacred:

> I would like Mom and Dad to see the things I see, know everything I know, so that they do not open their mouth again to mention those people [his ancestors, the Creoles]. They only speak about what happened here from the great war to the present, and then it seems, to those who have to listen to them, that the whole history of their family is made up of heroes and martyrs; all brave, all honest, the best people, just and fair. But all the Indians are dead and all their rivers only flow with stones. . . . Looking at the night . . . I have seen how my family killed the Indians. . . . Things will never be the same as before, as when the Indians owned them, but we once and for all will be like them, all Indians, not Galician or Polish, or Arabs, or blacks, or Americans, but Indian. All *siboneyes, taínos, guanajatabeyes* . . . (Fernández 89–90).

The nation is thus redefined by "the minus in the origin," as Homi Bhabha puts it, or "what is forgotten at the beginning of the nation's narrative" (*Nation* 160). This version of nationalist discourse is quite contrary to the revolutionary one, where difference was neglected in favor of the much needed unity of the Cuban nation. Fernández's turn to the Indians is the return to prehistory, to a prelapsarian past, or perhaps to the irrecoverable "essence" of Cuba in the peoples who inhabited it before any foreign influences.

As the narrator subverts the narratives that were passed on to him, he parodies revolutionary narratives, especially the grandest narrative of them all, history itself. As published in 1968, the novel does pay tribute to the

"Hundred Years of Struggle" beginning in 1868, summoning the spirit of the Grito de Yara or cry for independence for the founders of Sabanas on their way up the Río de la Luna.[11] At the same time, the text parodies the grand history of the nation, mainly by tracing the history of Sabanas in three different ways that lead to different understandings of Cuban history. All attempts at building Sabanas as a utopian town fail, and as a result Sabanas stands as a mythical state of being yet to be realized on Earth, rather than an actual place:

> Sabanas will not be taken by surprise, or on a day-trip, by the members of a family . . . who want abundance and well-being . . . for themselves. . . . Sabanas is something that needs to be built, erected, established, and sustained with everyone's help, with everyone's love, with the generosity and the respect and the understanding and the humility of everyone. Because Sabanas is not an ideal, it is not a promise, it is not in the pages of any human or divine book. Sabanas is . . . from Earth and it is on Earth, for all men alive who work and meditate, who sing and cry. . . . Sabanas is being in full, without fear or suspicion, without shame. Because Sabanas is Humanitas, Felicitas, Libertas, and even in Sabanas men are sad and die (Fernández 192).

As in Carpentier's *El reino de este mundo* (1949) (*The Kingdom of this World*, 1957), the narrator invokes in Sabanas an effort to "do good," which, although it can be identified with a Christian ethic, builds the kingdom of *this* world, rather than the kingdom of heaven. The spirit of Sabanas has many of the characteristics of the revolutionary spirit as defined by the leaders, such as love, generosity, and sacrifice.[12] But, unlike the Revolution, Sabanas is a poetic utopia, the kingdom of the Word. The next section expands on the description of Sabanas.

### *Los niños* and the Lost Utopian Spirit

Despite the absence of the notion of utopia in most revolutionary narratives, Fernández's novel manages to rescue the utopian dimension of the Revolution and carry it further. Though built on a Marxist model, Fernández's utopia succeeds in transcending the totalitarian threat that applied Marxist models have yielded. Consequently, Derrida's theory in *Specters of Marx* (1994) illuminates Fernández's utopia. Derrida borrows Marx and Engels's image of the ghost in "Manifesto of the Communist Party" (1848) as a metaphor of the spirit of Marxism, and turns Marx himself into a ghost from the past haunting us in the form of an ethics or a principle of justice that has not yet been realized.[13] According to Derrida, the ghost that haunts us in the present is like the ghost of Hamlet's father, who beckons him to follow it. This ghost comes from the past but it projects us into a future, with a sense of anticipation.

Derrida's ghost can be a model for Fernández's spirit of utopia: the spirit of Sabanas is a *reviant* (Derrida's word, alluding to somebody who "returns") from the past, because the novel shows the long history of attempts to bring utopia to Cuba. In addition, like the ghost of Hamlet's father, the ghost of utopia that beckons an ideal Cuban reader of *Los niños* demands responsibility from him or her: the implied Cuban reader is to somehow repair the mistakes of the past and avenge Cuba's failed attempts at achieving utopia. Like a ghost, Sabanas is never "felt" as a real presence because it is linked to a promise and a perpetual deferral, it is a present that announces the yet-to-come.

Utopia as the yet-to-come is explained by Derrida with the following lines from Hamlet: "the time is out of joint/o cursèd spite/that ever I was born to set it right!" Derrida brings up Heidegger's use of the Greek term *a-dikia* to describe the time Hamlet is referring to: the present is out of joint and it is marked by injustice. The two translations of the term *a-dikia* applied to the present signify, first, that the present is out of joint because it is permanently transitory, a passage to some other stage. In Derrida's words: "The present is what passes, the present comes to pass, it lingers in this transitory passage, in the coming and going, *between* what *goes* and what *comes*, in the middle of what leaves and what arrives, at the articulation between what absents itself and what presents itself.... Presence is enjoined, ordered, distributed in the two directions of absence, at the articulation of what is no longer and what is not yet" (Derrida 25, emphasis in the original). Second, the present is the space of injustice, but it constitutes an anticipation of justice. The disjointed present that Derrida alludes to explains the metaphor of the boat to utopia in *Los niños*. The time in the boat is described as follows: "One time is all time.... All times are the same time. One is born and dies at the same time, one destroys and builds at the same time, one laughs and cries at the same time.... Now, here and in the boat.... And when time runs out we will look for more time and we will begin again to turn everything around. And when there is nothing to turn around, we will turn around what we turned around before" (486). The boat is traveling in an endless present, but that present is a transition to a state that never becomes a state in an institutional sense, it remains "the not-yet." Unlike the Revolution, which had become fairly institutionalized by 1968, the time on the boat to utopia is constantly in revolution. The trip to Sabanas announces continuous improvement, the never ending effort to realize a more just society.

For both Derrida and Fernández it is important that the future with the anticipation of justice remain a possibility, a hope. In Derrida's words: "We are asked . . . to turn *ourselves* over to the future, to join ourselves in this *we*, there where the disparate is turned over to this singular *joining*, without concept or certainty or determination, without knowledge, without or before the synthetic junction of the conjunction and the disjunction. *The alliance of a rejoining without conjoined mate, without organization, without party, without nation, without State [sic], without property . . .*" (Derrida 29, emphasis mine). Both Derrida and Fernández avoid the idea of a consolidated revolution, because of the threat that institutionalization poses to a liberatory politics, focusing instead on a utopian principle as a potentiality for change. Sabanas is a liberatory state that one should strive for, but at no point is it a finished product. Like Sabanas, the Revolution remains in the realm of the impossible, which operates on the possible.[14] In Lezama's own formulation of utopia, "The impossible, when acting on the possible, begets a *potens*, which is the possible in the infinite" (Lezama, "La cantidad" 839). Fernández's role in building the revolutionary utopia, like Lezama's, is to leave open the possibility of a better society, without tying it to a given form of government or state. It is for this reason that the trip to Sabanas is not characterized as progress but as a process. Sabanas, like the act of writing for Lezama, is a "free zone," without a paradigm, but within history.

An important element in Derrida's concept of utopia is the opening to "the other," not only in a discursive sense, but also in terms of "the other" whose difference cannot be overlooked, according to the principle of justice. Striving for an adjoined time of equality should not prevent one from leaving room for the "asymmetry of the other" (Derrida 22). *Los niños* includes several attempts to give voice to "the marginal," "the other," without erasing difference in the totality of the nation. As mentioned, the narrator revises history and revindicates the indigenous roots of Cuba (89–90), but there are also passages where the plight of the black slaves is heard (98–99), and at the end, when Lila is giving instructions on how to build Sabanas, there are invocations to the gods of El Monte, thus referring to the rich Afro-Cuban tradition and its resistance to injustice (536–39). In addition, there are five sections in the text titled "Baldío," wherein the narrator addresses Ianita, a black slave. The narrator also reflects on the performativity of gender and opens the possibility of choosing roles that run counter to the heterosexual compulsion. Finally, by describing his life in New York in minute detail, the narrator implicitly gives voice to vast number of Cuban exiles in the United States.

It is important to note, however, that in *Los niños* "the other" does not emerge "as a group." The others in *Los niños* are the individuals that disrupt unity. They make brief appearances, but they do not have a prominent presence in the text. Moreover, if Sabanas were made up by "the other," if indeed the boat to Sabanas were populated entirely by "the minus in the origin" in Homi Bhabha's terminology (Bhabha, *Location* 160) or by those who do not have a place in the nation—such as nonwhites, women, nonheterosexuals, nonrevolutionaries—the other would be reified, it would turn into "an identity." But that is not the case. The other in *Los niños* is a surplus, a supplement that, as in Bhabha's interpretation of Derrida's notion, *interrogates* the totality: "[The supplement] intervenes or insinuates itself in-the-place-of. . . . If it represents and makes an image it is by the anterior default of a presence . . . the supplement is an adjunct, a subaltern instance. . . . As substitute, it is not simply added to the positivity of a presence, it produces no relief. . . . Somewhere, something can be filled up of itself . . . only by allowing itself to be filled through sign and proxy" (quoted in Bhabha, *Location* 154, emphasis in the original). As noted above, identities are deconstructed in *Los niños* and reconstituted as fluid, indeterminate, changeable. Sabanas is a state of becoming, a trip in which one's identity is constantly remade. Identity is a momentary state: identity is what one is now, at this moment in the present, and it is subject to constant change. Identity does not bring answers in the search for an origin, though it has a relation with the past. Identity does not imply a projection into the future, though if one decides to take the utopian challenge, one's identity is situated in a continuum of future improvement.

In elaborating the notion of a fluid identity, *Los niños* questions revolutionary discourse with its emphasis on the New Man. Instead of constructing a stable model identity, the promise of a radical revolution is placed in an attitude of constant self-improvement and revision. The novel thus represents a principle of hope against the strictures of an institutionalized revolution. Above all, it shows that one needs to have the trust of a child in the ideals of a perfect society. Fernández's text advances the belief that only by holding on to that trust and the drive to constantly become better, as if following the specter of justice, can a radical revolution be effected.

In many ways *Los niños* closes the first decade, loosely defined, or the first era in the literature of the Cuban Revolution (1959–1971). True to its disruption of chronological time, the novel was published before that era ended, but it represents the most thorough attempt to critique the Revolution from inside, that is, to preserve one's allegiance and enthusiasm, and yet be unforgiving of the Revolution's mistakes. Thus this text encapsulates the spirit of the early 1960s, with the young uninstitutionalized Revolution that still believed in promises and hoped that serious mistakes would not undermine its faith. As previous chapters have shown, later novels such as *Sacchario* (1970) and *La última mujer y el próximo combate* (1971) would be much more militant and rigid in their representations of revolutionary identity and offer glimpses of alternative identities only "in spite of themselves." The year 1971 ushered in what has been called "the five gray years," which many critics have claimed is an inaccurate estimation, as that period actually lasted much longer. My last chapter offers an epilogue by turning to the most recent decade of the Revolution, after the Special Period, as one in which the spirit of the 1960s is being revived in some ways. Thirty years later, however, the New Man and his ideals have aged, and he is far more cynical and miscreant.

# Epilogue

# Identity and Its Discontents

## Leonardo Padura Fuentes Looks Back at the New Man

As the previous chapters have showed, the 1960s witnessed the construction of the idea of the New Man as the allegedly novel identity of the Cuban Revolution. The fictional texts that attempted to reproduce this figure displayed enthusiasm for but also fear and resistance against the new person Cubans were called to become. In this chapter I travel almost thirty years into the Revolution to look at another author who reflects critically on the figure of the New Man from the context of a more relaxed cultural policy and the benefit of several decades of hindsight. Leonardo Padura Fuentes—a recognized Cuban author who has been a member of the editorial board of well-established journals such as *El caiman barbudo*, *Juventud rebelde*, and *La Gaceta de Cuba*, of which he was the editor-in-chief from 1989 to 1995—is credited with the rewriting of a long tradition of detective novels in the island, with a series of texts in which the emphasis shifts away from intrigue to probe a generation's past and future: his tetralogy or series of four detective novels with the same protagonist includes *Pasado perfecto* (1991) (Past perfect), *Vientos de cuaresma* (1994) (Winds of Lent), *Máscaras* (1995) (*Havana Red*, 2005), and *Paisaje de otoño* (1998) (*Havana Black*, 2006).[1] With his distinct sense of failure and yet a glimpse of hope in the value of social solidarity, Mario Conde, the protagonist of these novels, may very well represent the impact of the ideal of the New Man for a large sector of the Cuban population raised in the Revolution.

To note the importance of Leonardo Padura's tetralogy in the current Cuban cultural scene, one must describe the development of the detective novel in the Revolution. According to the Cuban literary critic José Antonio Portuondo, Lino Novás Calvo was the first author to attempt producing a novel of this genre under the direct influence of the North American models and their Latin American versions, popularized by Jorge Luis Borges and Bioy Casares's *Seis problemas para Don Isidro Parodi* (1942) (*Six Problems for Don Isidro Parodi*, 1981) (Portuondo, "Astrolabio" 107). While detective novels by North American authors or their imitators where widely read in Cuba during the 1950s and 1960s, there really was not a distinctively Cuban detective novel until 1972, when what came to be called "the Socialist police novel" was born. In the First Congress of Culture and Education after the Padilla case, when Fidel proclaimed that literary prizes would only be given to true revolutionaries and that literature should serve the purpose of educating the masses, the seed was planted for a literary contest commemorating the anniversary of the Revolution. The contest was eventually called "Concurso aniversario del triunfo de la Revolución" or "Anniversary Contest for the Triumph of the Revolution," and it was instituted to reward the best works of the Cuban police novel. As the minister of the interior declared: "The competition is directed at developing this genre in our country, so the works that are presented will be on police themes and will have a didactic character, serving at the same time as a stimulus to prevention and vigilance over all activities that are antisocial and counter to the interests of the people" (quoted in Braham 29). The police novel became quite successful in Cuba, accounting for 25 to 40 percent of published titles between 1971 and 1983, with editions of 20,000 to 200,000 copies sold within a short time of their publication (Braham 32). The popularity of these novels can perhaps be explained by the fact that they were very readable and provided a comforting sense of community and belonging by appealing to a revolutionary spirit shared by everyone. In that respect, the police novels of the 1970s are comparable to the revolutionary novels of the 1960s I have examined, with regard to popularity and degree of commitment.

If the North American model of the detective novel exposed certain problems that were typical in a bourgeois model of society and were solved when the criminal was brought to justice, the Cuban detective novel represented the social instability created by counterrevolutionary elements in a Socialist society. Rather than a monument to the exceptional intelligence and intuition of the detective who solved the mystery, the Cuban detective novel was about a policeman as part of an efficient body of officers relying on Comités de Defensa de la Revolución (neighborhood committees in defense of the Revolution, or CDRs) and government agencies to restore the desired order in the Revolution. The Cuban police novel was a celebration of the Revolution as collective, and it appropriately depicted political crimes in the strict sense, or crimes against the Revolution rather than against individuals.

As a result of the ideological commitment of these novels, influential critics such as Portuondo decried them as representing the kind of literature produced in "the gray five years," because they were often unabashedly propagandistic of the dominant revolutionary discourse and therefore predictable and formulaic. However, some Socialist police novels did manage to avert the style that Portuondo calls *teque* or straight defense of revolutionary values. Critics coincide in naming Daniel Chavarría's *Joy* (1978), Luis Rogelio Nogueras's *Y si muero mañana* (1978), and Nogueras's and Guillermo Rodríguez Rivera's *El cuarto círculo* (1976) as among the best exponents of the genre.

The fall of the Soviet bloc in 1989 brought disillusionment in revolutionary ideology and a weakening of formerly strict cultural policies, which resulted in a revision of the police novel. Leonardo Padura's series of four novels introduced great innovation in the popular genre. The *neopoliciaco* (new police novel), as the new genre has been called, was significantly influenced by seminal writers of detective fiction, such as Paco Ignacio Taibo in Mexico, and other representatives of the North American "hard-boiled" detective novel, such as Dashiell Hammett. And yet Leonardo Padura and other writers who are practicing this genre in Cuba—Padura himself cites Rodolfo Pérez Valero and Justo Vasco as examples (with Epple 58)—have gone far beyond these models, using them as vehicles to turn the former Socialist police novel on its head and reflect on the current state of the Revolution.

The hard-boiled North American novels were created in the 1920s and achieved popularity after the Second World War, with the rise of crime and the corruption of the justice system (Braham xii). The hero of these novels was a cynic, who shared a lot of the marginal characteristics of the criminals he was investigating. The settings of these texts were cities in which chaos prevailed and the corruption of the moral fabric of society was apparent. Intrigue was often subordinated to social criticism and the description of daily life in the city.

Leonardo Padura uses the hard-boiled novel to reflect on the decadence of the ideals of the Revolution and the corruption of the former vanguard classes. His novels take place in Havana, the administrative and cultural center of the Revolution. In addition, the post-Soviet new police novels are critical of the current state of affairs in a way that runs counter to the traditional Cuban police novel: rather than have an individual's revolutionary record be the guarantee of his innocence, the new novels unmask people with flawless revolutionary records who then turn out to be criminals.

If in the classic police novel, according to Alejo Carpentier, "the detective is to the criminal what the art critic is to the artist; the criminal *invents*, the detective *explains*" ("Apología" 464), in Padura's case the detective struggles to explain not just the roots of crime, but his own past. For that purpose, Padura rescues a character of the 1980s Socialist novels: the young student of the "becas" (a sort of boarding school offering the best education to exemplary students and revolutionaries) who begins to reflect on the clash between inherited values and present reality (Padura, with Epple 51). In the novels of Padura, this character is Lieutenant Mario Conde, who has constant flashbacks to his high school years and tries to reconcile the gap between the ideal future of his generation and what he and his fellow students have become. In that respect, Conde once again defies the model of the classic Cuban police novel: instead of the police and the revolutionary community as protagonists, the detective reclaims center stage as an individual who tries to understand himself with every case he attempts to solve. And yet, Conde also defines himself against a collective, a certain class. The next section takes up the character of Conde, featured in every novel of the tetralogy, and his connection to the critique of the New Man.

### Conde as the Central Enigma of Padura's New Police Novel

The series of four novels that comprise *Las cuatro estaciones* (The four seasons) are set in the year 1989, when the so-called Ochoa case unfolded in Cuba. Arnaldo Ochoa, a high-ranking official who had been repeatedly decorated, was accused of corruption, embezzlement, and drug-trafficking, along with the minister of the interior and fourteen other officials. There was a strong suspicion, however, that the real reason for Ochoa's arrest was that he was conspiring against the regime. According to Padura himself, it was a year "when I as an individual, and I think Cuban society to a great extent, lost a lot of hope" (Padura with Epple 58). Each of the novels of the series takes place in a season of that year: winter (*Pasado perfecto*, 1991); spring (*Vientos de cuaresma*, 1994); summer (*Máscaras*, 1995) (*Havana Red*, 2005); fall (*Paisaje de otoño*, 1998) (*Havana Black*, 2006). All of these novels feature a murder case or disappearance that Conde solves and that somehow has a direct link with Conde's past. The fact that these novels take place in 1989, right after the Ochoa case and the fall of the Soviet bloc, sets the mood for the onset of a period of decadence, both in economic and in moral terms, whose causes and effects the narratives try to elucidate.

While each of the novels spins a new plot about one sector of society and its problems, there are recurrent elements in every novel that lend complexity and credibility to Conde as a protagonist. As is the case with each of the revolutionary novels examined in this book, the protagonist of each text stages a performance of his own identity. *Identity* is the key word here: though Conde's concerns seem highly personal, he reveals himself as having a symbolic value as a character, in a similar manner to revolutionary characters of previous novels. However, the characters of revolutionary narratives of identity that I have examined, such as Bruno, Darío, Vilma, and to some extent Malabre, remember their past only to be more reaffirmed in their present, which serves as the ultimate stage of their development as revolutionaries. Conde, in contrast, appears to be in some stage of transition between a past from which he has not successfully distanced himself, an alienating present, and a future in which he feels compelled to be different from the way he is now. Rather than having reached a climax of maturity, all of the elements of Conde's personality seem to illustrate the idea of an identity in flux. Another fundamental difference between the heroes of previous revolutionary novels and Conde is that in the protagonists of novels of the 1960s the dissatisfaction with the present is paired with an almost blind hope in the better future that the Revolution would allegedly bring. Conde's alienation in novels set in the late 1980s is revealing of the fact that the Revolution did not fulfill the promises issued in the early years.

Each of the narratives of the tetralogy introduces Conde as the opposite of the traditional revolutionary hero. The name given to the character is in itself significant, as there is no connection between "El Conde" meaning "the Count" and his actual nature or character: there is nothing distinguished or noble looking about this man. Each of the novels of the series begins with Conde vomiting or feeling really badly owing to a hangover: from the beginning of the narrative the character is associated with the individuals who were considered marginal in the Revolution, and as such they were often rounded up and jailed, or brought to justice in previous police novels. Additionally, Conde is known for his negativity concerning the current state of affairs in Havana, an attitude that would have been considered counterrevolutionary in previous times. As he struggles to get out of the house and go to the police station every day, Conde's nostalgia for a better past and his frustration for unmet expectations are invariably triggered. Conde's wellbeing ultimately depends on fulfilling basic needs, such as eating, smoking cigars, and drinking coffee. The narratives illustrate that on the eve of the 1990s, the scarcity of goods shifted the focus of revolutionary discourse from ideology to basic survival.

As popular detective novels, Padura's narratives use the formula of the love affair between the protagonist and a woman, and the latter is often used as an entry point into the corrupt societal circles that each of the crimes exposes. Contrary to the characters in previous revolutionary novels such as *La última mujer y el próximo combate*, Conde does not succeed in keeping his distance with women, and he becomes hopelessly smitten with love. The story of the detective's love affairs and the intensity of his emotions become as important in the novels' plots as the cases he is solving, which signals the preponderance of individual identity alongside the usual abstractions of class. Each of the women with whom Conde has an affair also bears a relationship with an aspect of his past that Conde is trying to resolve. For instance, *Pasado perfecto* brings back for Conde the years of his high school. As he has an affair with the wife of a former classmate, an exemplary vanguard revolutionary now turned corrupt politician, Conde uncovers the decadence of a privileged class that both the politician and his wife represented. In *Vientos de cuaresma* Conde falls in love with a woman and imagines a perfect picture of stability with her, only to discover that she enjoyed that very stability with the husband she cheats on to be with him, who is now absent. The narrative establishes a parallelism between the mysterious woman, who resists commitment with Conde, and the victim of the crime he is investigating: it is hinted that both may be *jineteras*, or hustlers, and therefore part of the underground world Conde is uncovering. In *Havana Red*, there is a clear satire of the revolutionary intellectual class and the isolation of gay intellectuals. It is in that novel that Conde comes to terms with homosexuality and stereotypical male roles in general, and it is interesting that women are almost completely absent. An exception is Conde's lover, whom he not coincidentally calls "culito de gorrión" (sparrow's bottom), referring to the anal sex that he enjoys with her: Padura thus gives the reader a homoerotic wink. Finally, in *Havana Black*, Conde gets a glimpse of the class of revolutionaries in charge of expropriating the personal possessions of Cubans who exiled themselves with the advent of the Revolution; those government officials ended up seizing most of those possessions, particularly houses and artworks, for themselves. Conde covets the wife of one of those officials, but like many prized works of art found after many years in hiding, she is inaccessible. She turns out to be as false as many of the artworks passed off as authentic by the people who sold them.

Apart from Conde's women, his reliable sources of affection and inspiration include his boss, Major Rangel, and a group of friends from the old gang in his high school years. Rangel manages what seems to be an all-male police station with the exception of a single female investigator, La China (the Chinese lady), who has a cameo appearance in *Pasado perfecto*. Among Conde's friends, two are especially relevant in the narratives: Carlos el Flaco (Carlos the skinny one) and Andrés. The former is Conde's best friend, and they both enjoy an emotional bond with Flaco's mother, who manages to assemble and prepare culinary feasts despite severe food shortages. The fact that Flaco is confined to a wheelchair owing to the loss of a leg in Angola gives Conde a chance to lament the futile military campaigns of the first revolutionary decades. Andrés, for his part, is a busy doctor and a happily married man with children; the group of friends consequently regards him as a success story. And yet, Andrés is the one who voices the most criticism and actually provides the key to Conde's feelings of nostalgia and frustration. But before resolving Conde's enigma, one needs to look more closely at the crimes perpetrated in the novels.

The "New Man" Is Dead: The Criminals of the Revolution

The four books of the series expose what are arguably four of the most important symbolic pillars of the Revolution: the Ministry of Finance, the school (recall Che's definition of "society as a gigantic school"), intellectuals, and the patrimony of Cuban exiles. Each of the novels takes on one of these groups and relates it to Conde's own development as an individual.

*Pasado perfecto* tells the story of a Rafael Morín Rodríguez, an official in charge of the department of imports and exports in the Ministry of Industry, who has gone missing. But more important is the fact that Morín was a classmate of Conde who always served as an example for everyone in the school, and the woman who became his wife was Conde's erstwhile adolescent crush. As Conde investigates the crime, he finds out that this eminent revolutionary and exemplary man was taking money from the ministry in the form of gifts, and trading with foreign governments as an individual, not in accordance with his position. Conde had always envied this man, even though he always represented the hardest line of the Revolution, and the investigation becomes a search not only of whom Morín was in reality, but also of whom Conde has been and whom *he* has become.

Conde remembers that Morín was the president of the Student Federation of their high school and a member of the Municipal Youth Committee. Shortly after Conde wrote a short story for a little journal they were publishing at the school, it was Morín as president of the student association who spoke at the meeting and said that the journal would close owing to the lack of revolutionary commitment in its pages. Conde could never forgive him, for this and other interventions in his life. Now, Morín, with his trips to foreign countries and his luxurious house, represents the elite status that some exemplary revolutionaries have attained. Tamara, Morín's wife and a former friend of Conde, confesses to being extremely attached to luxury and the comfortable life they lead.

From his initial conversations with Tamara until he ends up in bed with her, Conde seeks to understand his past and the gap between what he thought he would become—a writer like Hemingway—and what he is now, a bitter policeman ("What have you done with your life, Mario Conde?" *Pasado Perfecto* 56). Though he does not explain the failure that he feels his life has become, Conde does come to realize that Morín was a fake and did not deserve the admiration that many people professed for him. It is interesting, however, that Conde's rivalry with Morín is expressed in terms of Conde's relationship with Morín's wife as it unfolds. As is the case in institutional discourse, a man's dignity is based on his ability to perform his revolutionary duties as well as his physical strength, in this case translated literally into his sexual prowess. During the period when Conde feels inferior because he compares himself to Morín, he is not able to satisfy Morín's wife sexually. However, once Conde has uncovered Morín's corruption, he is able to satisfy Tamara in bed—we are told that he makes love to Tamara several times in the same night—and he declares that he has "vanquished Rafael Morín" (211).

In *Vientos de cuaresma* the case is about the murder of a teacher at the high school that Conde attended in his youth. This lady, who was awarded several distinctions as a model revolutionary, turns out to have shared exam questions with her students so that she could beat records of excellence. The model teacher also slept with her young students and held parties where marijuana was smoked. Conde uncovers a marijuana ring and exposes the current school principal, who, in his mid-life crisis, had fallen in love with the victim. The novel represents some aspects of the underground world of drug users and hustlers whereby the image of respectability that Conde has cherished of the school of his youth is shattered by the many new allegations of corruption. The clash between the attitude of the youths he sees at the school and the way he remembers himself and his friends as they were students makes Conde especially aware of the changes that have occurred in Cuba.

*Havana Red* to some extent is the central book of the tetralogy, as it lays out a new concept of identity and takes up a class of revolutionaries whose mistakes seem to have been particularly influential in Conde's own life: intellectuals. The text also delineates a crucial distinction, implicit in all four novels, between the mask as a way to play with identities and the mask as a marker of falsehood. In this book Conde steps out of his ultra-masculine world to question gender identity, and thus Padura Fuentes's irony as a writer who usually situates his characters in a very male-oriented world is laid bare.

The case Conde solves in *Havana Red* offers the chance not just to satirize the intellectual class of the Revolution, but to somehow rehabilitate those who were ostracized despite the fact that their work really mattered for people who were interested in literature regardless of political commitment. It is the story of Faustino Arayán's son, Alexis Arayán, who is murdered in El Bosque de La Habana—a park in Havana—while dressed as a transvestite.

A good friend of Alexis who lived with him at the time, Alberto Marqués, is Conde's main witness. Marqués is a flamboyantly gay man who initiates Conde in different types and meanings of transvestism, as well as in the history of homosexual artists such as himself who were *parametrados* after 1971, with their careers ultimately destroyed. *Parametración* was a legal process by which some intellectuals, many of them homosexual, were accused of not being sufficiently involved in the Revolution and banned from public positions. The character of Marqués is modeled after Virgilio Piñera, as they share many characteristics (Bejel 173–74), and the narrator mentions that Marqués was the designer of a dress for Electra Garrigó, a character in a play of the same name by Virgilio Piñera. Alexis, Marqués's friend, was wearing that dress when he was killed. Marqués also tells Conde of his trips to Paris with a certain Recio, which is probably an allusion to Severo Sarduy, during and after May 1968.

The case of Andrés Arayán, as usual, reveals many aspects of Conde's life. The way that Marqués's brilliant career was curtailed with *parametración* is paralleled by the frustration of Conde's first literary attempt. As shown in the first book of the tetralogy, Conde published a story in *La viboreña*, a small journal founded by a group in his high school, which was then banned owing to its alleged lack of revolutionary commitment. For Conde, this episode seems to be emblematic of the fact that the system prevented him from becoming what he wanted to be, "a writer like Hemingway," and led him to become what he had never thought of being, a law enforcement official. As Conde gets better acquainted with Marqués, he overcomes his initial resistance to the fact that the character is gay and comes to feel "a furtive rebel solidarity" with him (*Havana Red* 58). Conde actually feels increasingly attracted to Marqués as a person, and his preconceptions about homosexuals change as the narrative progresses.

The fact that Marqués and gay life in general are depicted in a positive light in *Havana Red* is actually quite a significant change from the precedent of previous Cuban police novels. As Braham indicates, the antisocial elements of the MININT (Ministry of the Interior) police novels were "deformed" individuals, "individualists, prostitutes, blacks and mulattos [despite the official anti-racist stance], Cubans of Chinese descent and Jews, and above all, homosexuals" (Braham 46). Criminals in these novels were described as pathetic, weak, and cowardly, and this behavior was equated with effeminacy and a lack of manliness. In fact, as Braham indicates, it is not an accident that the Cuban police novel with its effeminate villains was instituted as a genre in 1972, as this immediately followed the repressive purges of intellectuals and artists—some of them homosexual—and the banning of effeminate behavior as counterrevolutionary. A statement issued after the First Congress of Culture and Education in 1971 declared that "the cultural media cannot serve as a framework for the proliferation of false intellectuals . . . who want to convert snobbism, extravagance, homosexualism, and other social aberrations into expressions of revolutionary art" (quoted in Arias 28). The fact that some relevant writers and artists who were homosexual were not particularly committed to the Revolution—such as the members of the group El Puente, José Lezama Lima, Virgilio Piñera, Antón Arrufat, José Rodríguez Feo, and Reinaldo Arenas among many others—often led political leaders to make a link between intellectual life, homosexual orientation, and disaffection with the Revolution. As Desiderio Navarro has put it, intellectuals were considered the Other of "the people," and as such they were identified with the "homosexual, the 'strange,' and the unworthy of political or moral trust" (D. Navarro 704).

Padura undermines the macho metaphor of the previous police novel and replaces it with the masquerade. The many allusions to life as theater and the idea that revolutionaries wear masks advance a critique of the current ideological state of the Revolution. More importantly, there is extensive commentary on the meaning of transvestism in this novel, which poses the idea of the performativity of gender. In the theory of Judith Butler, gender is constituted through the performance of certain "acts, gestures, enactments," prior to which there is no ontological gender identity (Butler 136). It is the self-conscious, parodic performance of these acts and gestures that exposes the constructed nature of gender and offers a way out of the tyranny of gender dichotomies. In Padura's novel, the transvestite illustrates gender as a performance, a disguise worn for the sake of the spectacle, which constructs gender but deprives it of any essential characteristics: "As far as he was concerned . . . *á la limite* there is no woman, because he knows . . . that he, that is to say, she, is an appearance, her fetishistic realm and power concealing an irredeemable defect created by an otherwise wise nature. . . . [The transvestite] is an appearance, a perfect theatrical masquerade, . . . the very essence of performance . . . the transvestite as an artist enacting himself" (*Havana Red* 38). In this quotation there is a celebration of transvestism as an uncovering of gender as performance; the allusion to the "otherwise wise nature" that critics such as Emilio Bejel have interpreted as dismissive (Bejel 177), on the contrary refers to the fact that the transvestite would like to be what he apparently is not, that is, it is a rather ironic understatement. For the narrator in Padura's novel, transvestism is an image that surpasses its model, or it can be a provocation, but above all, "the question was not to be, but to look like; it was not the act, but its representation; it was not even its end, but the means as an end in itself; the mask for the pleasure of the mask, disguise as a supreme truth" (*Havana Red* 73).

Thus Padura situates himself in a similar line of criticism as Cofiño and Fernández, whose novels I have examined. If in the 1960s Nati in Cofiño's *La última mujer y el próximo combate* parades her naked body and exposes gender as a masquerade, if the narrator in *Los niños se despiden* displays a playful attitude toward gender and sexual orientation, in the 1990s, Padura can afford to carry the criticism much further by introducing a transvestite character whose life and career are devoted to mocking gender practices. Given that masculinity is crucial to the concept of the New Man, Padura's total deconstruction of gender seriously questions revolutionary identity at this stage of the Revolution.

No matter how much the novel celebrates identity as performance, however, a crucial distinction is made between identity as performance and what Conde calls "the moral mask" (*Havana Red* 166). The disguise of the transvestite does not seem offensive because it stays in the category of play, whereas the moralistic mask of the corrupt judges of culture during the *parametraciones* is objectionable because it is used to deceive and condemn others: "Parisian transvestites had given me the final key to that spectral metamorphosis which magnifies the supreme aspiration of performance, when the actor dies beneath the garments of his character and the performance ceases to be a passing, carnivalesque act and turns into a another life, all the more real for being more desired, consciously chosen and not assumed as mere conjectural concealment" (*Havana Red* 162). This is where Conde draws the line between a postmodern idea of identity and the necessary condemnation of the falsehood of "conjectural concealment," or changing one's identity according to what becomes politically or financially more advantageous.

At the end of the novel it turns out that Alexis's father murdered him out of shame because of his homosexuality and because he had threatened to reveal that his father, an eminent revolutionary, had lied about fighting against Batista. The moral repulsion of this crime drives Conde to write, once more, and to wish he could stop being a policeman. But he is not able to do that until the next novel, the last in the tetralogy. In *Havana Black* Conde solves a case about Miguel Forcade, an official in charge of expropriating artworks in the first decade of the Revolution, who then immigrated to Miami with his wife. When Forcade returns to Cuba for a visit after many years, he is found dead in the sea, with his genitals cut off. With this case, Conde uncovers the corruption and falsehood of those responsible for managing the patrimony of the former moneyed class, those who made themselves rich and became the new elite. The third-person narrator refers to all of the goods that went through the hands of this man "with the promise of a revolutionary redistribution that was never effected" (43). Forcade had caught his wife, Miriam, and her lover in bed together, during a recent visit to Havana. Forcade's future murderer turns out to be his wife's lover, who had been been in love with Miriam for years, and Conde laments that the only clean man he met in the case is the one who will end up in jail.

At a personal level, in *Havana Black,* Conde undergoes the usual revision of his own life, with increasing doubts about his professional calling, up to the moment when he offers his resignation and becomes a writer. He makes clear that his first novel will be *Pasado perfecto*, the first in Padura's tetralogy. Apart from this hint of an autobiographical link between Conde and Padura, Conde makes a statement about writing as the only means to work out his existential crisis and the pain inflicted by the corruption of Cuban society. The novel is open-ended, once Conde refuses to move in with Tamara, his former sweetheart, as she has suggested. Instead, he takes up refuge at home in the face of a rapidly approaching hurricane. He takes in a stray dog and begins writing, signaling a new epoch in his life in which he will try to heal his own wounds and come to terms with who he is. Rather than a happy ending in which Conde's idyllic visions of a stable life are fulfilled, his sense of self or identity remains open, fraught with contradiction, and in need of revision.

If the tetralogy exposes exemplary figures of the Revolution, if it indeed implicitly proclaims that the mythical New Man never existed, it does not end without hope or belief in some of the ideals of the Revolution. The next section returns to the idea of the lost generation and its potential for a rebirth from its own ashes.

## The "Lost Generation" and Its Future

More than forty years into the Revolution, Padura looks at the unfulfilled promises of what was supposed to be a bright future, and the sense of frustration of a generation of people who devoted their young years to the effort of building a revolutionary nation and now find themselves still struggling. Andrés, Conde's only "successful" friend in *Havana Black*, provides the definition for the *hidden generation*, a term on which the four narratives hinge: "We are a generation that obeyed orders. First, our parents gave us orders, to be good students and citizens. We were ordered around at school, . . . and then we were ordered to work where they wanted us to work . . . but nobody ever thought of asking us what we wanted. . . . Everything was pre-planned, wasn't it? From playschool to the spot in the cemetery assigned for us, everything was planned for us, . . . that is why we are a pile of shit, because we don't dream, we just exist to carry out our orders . . ." (*Havana Black* 12). At the end of the novel, Andrés announces that he is leaving the country with his family, as he wants to prevent his children from becoming "the second round of the hidden generation. . . . In the end they'd be as fucked up as I was, faceless no-hopers with nothing to tell their own children" (250). Conde confesses that he should leave too, but that he has a pathological need to belong somewhere (251).

The repeated reference to the "hidden generation" in the tetralogy ironically echoes the "lost generation," as the generation of the 1950s was referred to. There clearly is a reference to Cuban intellectual history in this label, as Andrés says to his writer friend, "Do you remember that, Miki, the hidden generation?" In a 1962 article in *La Gaceta de Cuba* Virgilio Piñera initiated a controversy regarding the generations prior to the Revolution by referring to writers who came of age in the Republic at a time when literature was depoliticized and there was general contempt and indifference toward the arts. At the time, many writers were exiled and became unknown in Cuba. Most likely with irony, or perhaps not knowing yet the full impact of the Revolution in subsequent years, Piñera stated that the lost generation had now come back to Cuba and would somehow be rescued in their commitment to the buoyant revolutionary period.

However, in *Havana Black*, Andrés is not referring to the generation of the 1950s, but to his own: the people who were in high school in the 1970s, for those are the years he and his friends shared. Andrés's reference is not so much to an intellectual generation but to all Cubans who lived through the strictest years of revolutionary commitment in Cuba. If the 1960s were partly a time of euphoria and the formative years of the New Man, the 1970s were devoted to enforcing this ideal of revolutionary identity, and young people were the main objects of this enforcement. The reference to a generation for whom everything was planned, to the point that individuality was threatened, is a comment on how the New Man made a whole generation of people feel that they never existed for themselves, but only in the name of an ideal. Andrés and Conde are frustrated because they feel that incarnating the New Man has not brought promised benefits.

At the end of the tetralogy, when Conde decides to resign from his job as a policeman and become a writer, he explains that he will write about the feeling of frustration that Andrés was referring to, "the great experience of this generation, which was so well nourished that it grew with every year, and he concluded it would be good to put it in black and white, . . . as a practical way of reaching once and for all the diffuse kernel of that whole unequivocal equivocation: when, how, why and where had it all began to fuck up?" (*Havana Black* 15). At the end of the novel, Conde sits down to write a novel with the same title as the first book in Padura's series, which adds to Padura's own declaration that "Conde is very much like me. . . . He is a fictional character with his own history, but we share a lot of characteristics. He grew up in a neighborhood that was worse than mine, was raised in a way similar to mine, with friends similar to mine. And somehow, Mario Conde's sadness, skepticism and melancholy are mine too" (interview with John Kirk, December 2000, quoted in Kirk n.d., "Symbol" n. 28). We can thus assume that Padura's four-book series is devoted to rescuing the generation that suffered the consequences of a strict ideal of revolutionary identity or the New Man. The tetralogy clearly advances a criticism of model revolutionaries, as the perpetrators of the crimes Conde solves are always men and women with flawless records as revolutionaries. Thus Padura presents the New Man either as a fake in himself or as an ideal with few positive consequences for Cuban youth.

The very concept of a stable identity in itself comes under attack, as the cases prove that a person has multiple facets that are often contradictory and irreconcilable. At one point, for instance, when investigating a man who has disappeared, Conde wonders whether he is getting to know the person better, from what others tell him, or perhaps "he is a circus phenomenon with a thousand faces" (*Pasado* 86). Although the multiplicity of faces is often associated with the false lives led by criminals in the high echelons of the Revolution, it also applies to the metaphysical confusion that Conde's generation experienced. In relation to the weariness of revolutionary ideology starting in the recent decade, Conde talks about having to get rid of his other, corrupt self in order to "begin to be himself" (*Havana Black* 225).

All four of Padura's Mario Conde novels display a desire to "be authentic" and to have the opportunity to start from scratch, but such desire is curiously disconnected from the idea of a new identity. Instead, the novels featuring Conde as a protagonist show a deep nostalgia for recovering the dreams of the hidden generation. The old gang gets together and recalls what each of them wished for themselves, as their lives now diverge widely from those dreams. Ironically, the 1970s perpetuated what Piñera called "the lost generation" of the 1950s: those writers who came back to Cuba after 1959 would in fact have to emigrate again or become more isolated during the first roughly twenty years of the Revolution. The generation of Conde experienced a sense of loss similar to that of the Republic. The idea of the repetition of certain events or cyclical time is quite present in the tetralogy, and in every book there is a natural phenomenon, such as a hurricane or strong winds, that threatens to destroy Havana but is welcomed as a promise of cleansing and a new beginning. At the end of *Havana Black*, as a hurricane approaches, Conde welcomes it warily as he starts writing, hoping that at least "the memory" of his generation will be salvaged (259).

And yet, for all his wish to start anew, there are some elements of the New Man that remain very much present in Conde's reflections. As the archetype of a Cuban man, even at a transitional stage, Conde and his universe are strongly masculine, as was the ideology that proclaimed the New Man. The novels of the series are a celebration of male bonding both professionally and privately. In addition, Conde is unable to distance himself from Che Guevara's ideals of love and sacrifice for humanity, perhaps because of their connection to the Christian tradition that was still so strong in Cuba. In Che Guevara's words: "At the risk of seeming ridiculous, let me say that the true revolutionary is guided by great feelings of love. . . . Our vanguard revolutionaries must make an ideal of this love of the people, of the most sacred causes, and make it one and indivisible" ("Socialism" 15). The difference between Che Guevara's and Conde's concepts of love is that Guevara's love has to do with collective sacrifice, while Conde's has to do with person-to-person solidarity. At the end of the series, Conde says to his bewildered boss that he wants to move his readers and "speak of love between men [*sic*]" (*Havana Black* 228). And indeed, beyond the general tone of pessimism and negativity, Conde holds on to the love that his friends and colleagues provide. Despite the hatred and disgust that Conde displays for mankind when it comes to corruption, he feels strong sympathy for the underdog, "people who spend the week eating rice and beans after working an eight or ten hour day, and sometimes without even having a wall on which to hang a calendar . . ." (*Havana Black* 55). The spirit of social justice of Socialism, in an abstract sense, is thus not lost in Padura's novels.

In many respects, Padura's novels are a tribute to the withering away of revolutionary ideology and the current search for alternate ideologies or narratives in Cuba. In *Vientos de cuaresma* this is shown in the representation of "friquis" or rebellious youth, while in *Havana Black* it is demonstrated in an impassioned defense of religion by a friend of Conde, Candito el Rojo, who becomes a Jehovah's Witness. Candito states that his church is the only place where one can hear about love, peace, and hope, and that practicing religion is better than "selling beer or buying stolen leather to make shoes" (*Havana Black* 79) as he was doing before. Conde replies that religion is taking the place of politics as an expression of the wish for a better society, which is arguably the case in present-day Havana, wherein people are seeking a way out of the current state of stagnation of the Revolution. In an effort to break with the yoke imposed on his generation, Conde does not adhere to any of these alternative beliefs, but remains questioning and observing, perhaps like Padura himself.

## A Retrospective Look at 1960s Cuba and Beyond

As one looks back at the first decade of the Revolution, up to the watershed of 1971, the New Man reveals itself as an empty construct, a hollow model of identity that was filled with different contents according to the needs of the moment. This model was invoked during campaigns and mobilizations, predominantly in the 1960s, as a means to harangue the masses to strenuous work and sacrifice. The New Man represented an ideal of perfection that in Cuba, a society with deep Catholic roots, bore resemblance to the idea of a higher being that believers needed to imitate. According to the Christian tradition, God becomes a man, which allegedly brings this model closer and more attainable to humankind. Despite his name, in Cuban revolutionary discourse the New Man remained an abstract ideal that was never specifically embodied by any living person. In the words of Che Guevara, who coined the term in his 1965 article, "In this period of the building of socialism we can see the new man being born. His image is not completely finished—it will never be, since the process goes forward hand in hand with the development of new economic reforms" (Guevara, "Socialism" 7). Since the revolutionary regime has continued to envisage more changes, and the Revolution itself is supposedly still ongoing, the New Man has never materialized.

The invaluable contribution of the novels examined here is that in contrast to the vague and ephemeral references to the New Man in political discourse, the novels feature a fleshed out New Man, as they trace the development of diverse forms of revolutionary identity. In addition, a look at the novels also reveals that the underlying characteristics of the New Man in every campaign not surprisingly form a rather limited and homogeneous picture of the identities that were approved by the state. In these fictions of identity of the early years it becomes clear that writers' enthusiasm and fervor for the Revolution were reined in at the prospect of a constrictive ideal of identity, and thus consciously or unconsciously the writers uncovered the inhibiting aspects of the presentation of the New Man in every campaign. Such writers' and intellectuals' critiques of revolutionary identity are worth revisiting, since from their vantage point on the early years they provide depth to issues with which historians and social scientists are still grappling. A cultural critique of the New Man in the 1960s can be highly prophetic of the pitfalls generated in revolutionary ideology.

Thus *Maestra voluntaria* (1962) is a fictional document that helps readers understand why the peasants were objectivized rather than liberated by literacy instruction, as teachers tended to take other teachers as models and their prejudices against the peasants became entrenched. In political speeches and teachers' memoirs, peasants were viewed as well-disposed individuals but lacking in judgment and agency. The early years of the Revolution contributed to the protagonist role of the city of Havana in administrative matters, despite the pretense that the Revolution was carried out by the peasants and geared toward their interests. While the regime cultivated an exalting attitude toward the rural and the simple, rather than the urban and the material, the planning of the Revolution was largely engineered from Havana or larger cities such as Santiago in the province of Oriente, and urban needs took precedence over the needs of other areas of the island.

Malabre, the protagonist of *Memorias del subdesarrollo* (1965), fails to embody the public persona of a committed writer that the Revolution encouraged, which hinders his ability to be a credible critic of the regime. The novel represents the character's confusion and the obstacles that got in the way of representing that committed public role for most writers: intellectual elitism and attachment to bourgeois notions of class; materialism; disengagement from other people, in particular the common folk; and an excessive regard for the importance of one's body. The last item refers metaphorically to the resistance harbored by many writers and intellectuals against certain characteristics of revolutionary identity. Malabre, as a representative of writers and intellectuals, rejects sacrifice and hardship, emphasizes what is individual and private rather than collective and shared, and, given the existential reading of the novel, maintains his own view and perception of others rather than accepting an official view on reality.

Malabre advocates an ideal of creativity and independence for the artist that clashed with the duty of commitment that official discourse demanded. Given these conflicts, the character reveals that many writers found it impossible to argue in favor of the Revolution, even as a merely public stance, and therefore had to resign themselves to silence or isolation as Malabre did. Thus the novel demonstrates that if some writers found the new form of culture liberating, given the wider access and diffusion of cultural products as well as the promotion of a nonelitist culture, many felt that the revolutionary culture stifled their creative potential. Malabre speaks out for José Lezama Lima, Virgilio Piñera, Severo Sarduy, Guillermo Cabrera Infante, Calvert

Casey, Antón Arrufat, José Rodríguez Feo, José Triana, César Leante, Gastón Baquero, and Reinaldo Arenas, to give but a few of the names of authors who suffered ostracism and persecution or were forced into exile. In addition, Malabre's focus on his own body and the threat that the Revolution poses to it becomes in hindsight a metaphor for the fact that some writers' open homosexuality was challenged by the regime, as I mentioned above.

*La última mujer y el próximo combate* (1971), which gives a visible body to the revolutionary woman, confirms the suspicion that the patriarchal concept of women of earlier times had not changed in essence during the Revolution, except that revolutionary duties were added to the usual demands of homemaking. What is more, women were expected to take care of their appearance and cultivate a stereotypically feminine image, and thus their role as objects of desire was strengthened. At the same time, in a work environment women were expected to divest themselves of their conventional femininity by displaying characteristics stereotypically associated with men, such as resistance, strength, and the unwavering commitment to the advancement of the country that supposedly only men could have. The novel also demonstrates that revolutionary discourse never resolved the paradox between the persisting high regard for the ideal of the mother and the belief that motherhood hindered women's progress in the Revolution. In fact, both the negative and positive images of women offered in the novel are evidence of the restrictive way in which official discourse defined female identity, and the highly disappointing role of Mercedes, the model of the New Woman, reveals that women were perhaps among the least served by the post-1959 Cuban regime. While it is true that the Revolution gave women reproductive rights and protected the legal status of single mothers, for instance, official discourse on women generated confusion and insecurity about their gender identity and downplayed the idea of unity among women unless such unity served the wider interests of the Revolution.

*Sacchario* (1970) pays tribute to the colossal task that the goal of Ten-Million-Ton Sugar Campaign entailed for Cuba, and to the spirit of nationalism the Sugar Campaign nurtured. The novel quotes the conventional founding fathers of Cuban tradition and aptly emphasizes the historical link between Cuba and sugar production. At the same time, the text also demonstrates the simplification that the concept of a Cuban revolutionary nation involved at the time, in which individuality became dissolved in the name of the collective, and where race and gender became subsumed to class, with white and heterosexual male being posited as the implicit norm. The figure of the New Man in *Sacchario* is somebody who, like the nation of Cuba, has to break with his past and start anew. And yet, the Revolution did not actively try to change the weight of tradition in Cuban culture, and the patriarchal prejudice and racial exclusion of previous eras persisted in people's minds. Darío attempts to become a hardened, committed revolutionary to whom pleasure is an unnecessary distraction, but he is unsuccessful when he is haunted by memories of a happy youth in Havana before 1959. In Darío the reader sees that the New Man is but the old man in a new Cuba, where government policies have changed, but people's attitudes and ways of thinking have largely remained the same.

*Los niños se despiden* (1968) is the most critical of all fictions of identity produced in Cuba in the 1960s, and yet it shares the enthusiasm and hope of the era. The novel emphasizes movement, heterogeneity, and process, rather than stillness, homogeneity, and stability when it comes to constructing identity, and it tackles issues of race, class, and gender that had largely been swept aside in discussions on the New Man. The novel's poetic vision outlines many of the problematic aspects of the new revolutionary identity and an increasingly institutionalized Revolution, but it still holds the belief that it is possible to draw the Revolution's path differently, in a way that will fulfill its promise of equality and freedom.

In contrast to the five other texts studied here, Padura's series of four detective novels set in the year of the fall of the Soviet bloc and written during the Special Period and its aftermath harbor hardly any belief in revolutionary ideology. In fact, the tetralogy is focused on finding out "what went wrong" with the regime's ideals and expressing the frustration of the people who feel that they gave their best years to the work of advancing the Revolution. With increasing force in every novel, these texts denounce the Revolution as a failed experiment on human beings, and no apologies or sympathetic explanations are provided. In the most recent novel by Padura, though not part of the tetralogy as it is technically not a detective story, Conde aptly observes that his generation is "tired of being historical and predestined" and "life has gone by them" (*Neblina* 200, 201).

Yet Padura's detective fiction offers more than bitter critique and despair, as he renews a popular genre that was born of political commitment and is now used to showcase the changing landscape of Cuban morals and identities. While Padura announces the death of the New Man, he and the writers of the 1960s examined here emphasize one aspect of revolutionary identity that has not been lost to the most critical mind, and that is the value of social solidarity and community. Beyond the enthusiasm, the doubts, the fear, and the reluctance of the early years, and the anger and the resentment of the recent time, the writers of these popular novels also revindicate individual creativity and imagination as powerful elements of social change. In Cuba, from the 1960s to the present day, it has become clear that identity is but a construct forged in official discourse and tailored to the needs of the moment. Narratives of identity of the Cuban Revolution have contributed to creating this construct, but they have also, perhaps inadvertently, exposed its limitations and tried to explore the liberating promise of the Revolution.

# Notes

### Introduction. The Culture That the Revolution Created

1. When relevant, I will provide a translation for the titles of works in Spanish. If an English translation of these works has been published, I will provide its title and publication date following those of the Spanish original. The publication date of the Spanish original and its English translation may not coincide with the date in the Works Cited if I have used a different edition. In the absence of a published translation, all translations from Spanish into English are mine. The page numbers of the quotations, unless I explicitly quote from a published translation, are from the original text in Spanish. After the first mention, the novels that are central to my study will be referred to by their Spanish titles, since all exist in Spanish editions. As explained below, there is an extant translation of *Memorias del subdesarrollo*, but I am not using it because it has substantial differences with the original.

2. Apart from these novels I have chosen, there are others that are devoted to representing the revolutionary years explicitly, but revolutionary identity is not their focus. These are Víctor Agostini's *Dos viajes* (1965); Juan Arcocha's *Los muertos andan solos* (1962); David Buzzi's *Los desnudos* (1982) and *La religión de los elefantes* (1968); Edmundo Desnoes's *El cataclismo* (1965); Samuel Feijóo's *Jira descomunal: Novela cubana, nativista, costumbrista, folklorista e ¡indigenista!* (1968); Raúl González de Cascorro's *Concentración pública* (1963); Manuel Granados's *Adire y el tiempo roto* (1967); Noel Navarro's *Los caminos de la noche* (1967); Loló Soldevilla's *El farol* (1964); José Soler Puig's *En el año de Enero* (1963); and Ezequiel Vieta's *Vivir en Candonga* (1966).

3. Clearly, there are writers who have been more critical than Leonardo Padura, such as Antonio José Ponte, whose UNEAC membership was suspended in 2003 (Whitfield 18). Because the focus of this study is institutional discourse, of which Padura is still a part despite his critical attitude, more critical writers such as Ponte are left out of my analysis.

4. Humberto Arenal's *El sol a plomo* (1959) and *Los animales sagrados* (1967), José Becerra Ortega's *La novena estación* (1959), José Soler Puig's *Bertillón 166* (1960), Hilda Perera Soto's *Mañana es 26* (1960), César Leante's *El perseguido* (1964), Edmundo Desnoes's *No hay problema* (1961), and Jaime Sarusky's *Rebelión en la octava casa* (1967) are some examples of novels that were published in Cuba during the first decade of the Revolution and were situated in the Batista years.

5. Virgilio Piñera had already been published as a playwright (*Electra Garrigó*, 1941), a novelist (*La carne de René*, Buenos Aires 1952 [*René's Flesh*, 1989]), a short-story writer (*Cuentos fríos*, Buenos Aires 1956 [*Cold Tales*, 1988]), and a poet (*La isla en peso*, 1943). José Mario was the founder of El Puente publishing house, which

lasted from 1960 to 1965. Ana María Simó was a member of the literary group El Puente and the author of the short story volume *Las fábulas* (1962).

6. These were not Zhadanov's exact words but, as Regine Robin tells us, this was the definition that was written in the statutes of the Soviet Writer's Union after the 1934 congress (Robin 11).

7. For an account of Sartre's comments on revolutionary Cuba during his several visits there, see Arcocha, "El viaje de Sartre" (Machover 231–39); de la Nuez.

8. Apart from the novels of my corpus, there are numerous novels that were written in the Revolution and present the characteristics of Socialist realist style, such as Manuel Feijóo's "Jira descomunal" (1968), Raúl González de Cascorro's *Concentración pública* (1963), Manuel Granados's *Adire y el tiempo roto* (1967), and Loló Soldevilla's *El farol* (1964), among others.

9. This statement is taken from an unofficial transcript of a debate that took place among Cuban writers in Havana, on July 15, 2004, as part of an exhibit on the 1960s in Cuban culture ("Mirar a los sesenta," July 9–August 31, 2004).

10. See, among others, Barradas, Duchesne, Leante, and Pogolotti for studies of Guevara's literary style; Geirola for a very detailed analysis of the influences of his writing; Lacqueur for the guerrilla context; Saldaña-Portillo for the reproduction of world development discourse; and I. Rodríguez for the influence of Guevara's writings in Central American revolutionary movements. In a different context but as a valuable contribution to the study of how ideology evolves, see Kapcia. For detailed interpretations of Fidel Castro's discourse, see Liss; and Rice.

11. See, for instance, Menton, or Rodríguez Coronel, who never questioned the term as a general period label and set the tone for most other studies. Bost and Zimmerman offer a different perspective, but they focus mostly on Reinaldo Arenas and Antonio Benítez Rojo.

12. Among the writers and intellectuals who contributed to the debate on committed literature one can cite the following: Ezequiel Martínez Estrada; Lisandro Otero; Roque Dalton et al.; Emir Rodríguez Monegal (*Paradiso*); Mario Vargas Llosa; José Mario; and Fausto Masó. Also significant were Leopoldo Ávila ("Sobre algunas corrientes") and later, Miguel Barnet et al.

13. For two such previous bibliographies, see Abella; and Casal, "Annotated."

14. For an excellent article on the subject of literature and politics in the "Revolution," see Méndez Ródenas, "Literature and Politics." On Edmundo Desnoes, see Méndez Ródenas, "Escritura"; Rodríguez Monegal, "Literatura: Cine"; and Santí, "Desnoes."

### Chapter 1. Speaking at Cross Purposes: The Failed Identification between Teachers and Students in the Literacy Campaign

1. An earlier version of this chapter was published as an article with the title "The Literacy Campaign and the Transformation of Identity in the Liminal Space of the Sierra" in *Journal of Latin American Cultural Studies* 10.1 (March 2001): 131–41. http://www.tandf.co.uk

2. Fidel's speeches are taken from a Web database, as shown in the works cited, where they are classified by date. Hence my mode of citation.

3. The campaign was by all accounts a successful one, as it countered the deplorable state of education in prerevolutionary Cuba: in 1953 9.2 percent of the people in Havana were illiterate, as were 33.2 percent of the people in the countryside (Pérez-Stable, *Origins* 30). When the rebel soldiers entered Havana in January 1959, 80 percent of them were illiterate. In 1959–60, the total enrollment of children in municipal schools was 512,198; in 1960–61, the total number of pupils had increased to 1,118,942 (Medin 67). By August 1961, no less than 985,000 people who did not know how to read and write had been identified in the countryside (Thomas 1340). According to Alejandro de la Fuente, in 1953 (the year of the Cuban population census closest to 1961), the total population in the island was 5,829,029 (de la Fuente, "Race" 135).

4. See, for instance, Fidel's speech on the closing of the Literacy Campaign: "Today, the Cuban youth has played an extraordinarily important role, as no other youth in the world has, in the education and defense of their country. . . . We see in young people the strength that develops and grows, that is called to play a big role in the Revolution, to support the Revolution with its great enthusiasm, and its joy" ("El pueblo cubano," Nuiry Sánchez 82).

5. The double role of the literacy worker as soldier was made clear by Fidel in a 1961 speech: "The patrols of worker militia are moving inside the fence. They carry a book for combating illiteracy. They are moving against counterrevolutionaries and illiteracy at the same time" (19610128).

6. Since the first major mobilizations for the Literary Campaign took place in June, Fidel linked volunteer participation to the defense against imperialism: "It will be proof of the strength of the Revolution. It will be proof of the energy of the Revolution. . . . Remember that there will be hundreds of thousands of people, more than a million people, who will be able to join the ranks of truth and light, and that this is going to strengthen the Revolution, that this is a blow to Imperialism" (Ares 73).

7. As Fidel predicted, "The world has its eyes on us. . . . What we will do will be an example to the world. . . . While imperialism wants to destroy us and our Revolution, we are going to destroy imperialism with our example, our success" (19610514).

8. The idealization of the peasants as "the people" with intrinsically revolutionary characteristics was already clear when Fidel was living in the Sierra as a guerrilla fighter. In a letter to Frank País from the Sierra, Fidel wrote: "Here the word 'people' which is so often utilized in a vague and confused sense, becomes a living wonderful and dazzling reality. *Now* I know who the people are: I see them in that invincible force that surrounds us everywhere. . . . Who has organized them so wonderfully? Where did they acquire so much ability, astuteness, courage, self-sacrifice? No one knows! it is almost a mystery. They organize themselves alone spontaneously" (quoted in Hennessy 49, emphasis in the original).

9. This is a reading of Paulo Freire against himself, as he includes some very commendatory passages to Fidel and Guevara in the same edition of *Pedagogy of the Oppressed*. Of Fidel, for instance, Freire says: "Fidel gradually polarized the adherence

of the Cuban people, who due to their historical experience had already begun to break their adhesion to the oppressor. This 'drawing away' from the oppressor led the people to objectify him [the oppressor] and to see themselves as his contradiction. So it was that Fidel never entered into contradiction with the people" (Freire 146). Nevertheless, it is significant that in a book on literacy written ten years after the Literacy Campaign in Cuba there is no mention of this campaign. As Robert Mackie puts it, there may be a certain degree of "idealization" and "romanticization" of revolutionary leaders on the part of Freire, but "the politics that Freire advocates would be better served by dissolving, rather than augmenting, the legends surrounding Mao, Fidel and Che" (Mackie 112–13).

10. This climactic moment is marked by the passage: "Ok, Nereyda, in that case, such a cause is called Socialism, as you have very well stated. And what does the name matter if the facts clearly show that everything that is being done in Cuba today—whatever we call the doctrine behind our acts—is, besides fair, also necessary?" (D. García 101).

11. This same conception of history is the one represented in Miguel Barnet's testimonial narrative *Biography of a Runaway Slave*. Montejo, the elderly man who provides the witness account, has experienced slavery, the struggle for independence against Spain, and the subjection to U.S. imperialism, but he sees a victory over these three systems of oppression with the onset of the Revolution. Montejo's life illustrates the theory of the cycles of struggle of Cuban history that culminate and succeed in the 1959 Revolution.

## Chapter 2. Body versus Mind: An Intellectual's Memoirs Expose His Negative Image

1. As I explained above, the English translation *Inconsolable Memories* in fact differs significantly from the original text in Spanish. Since my focus is the Spanish text, I will refer to the novel with its original title in Spanish. The translations of the original Spanish text are mine, and the page numbers refer to the 1975 Spanish edition listed in the works cited.

2. Gil Blas Sergio and Roberto Fernández Retamar dispute that the *Ciclón* group was apolitical, in this and other issues of *La Gaceta de Cuba*. However, Sergio failed to explain in what ways these writers were politically involved (Sergio 15). Fernández Retamar added to the names that Piñera had supplied, including "José Antonio Portuondo, Ángel Augier, Mirta Aguirre, Dora Alonso, Carlos Felipe, Onelio Jorge Cardoso, Samuel Feijóo, Ernesto García Alzola, Alcides Iznaga, Aldo Menéndez." Fernández Retamar hailed all of these writers as actively involved in politics, but he conceded that owing to this involvement "they missed cohesion and persistence in the literary" (Fernández Retamar, "Generaciones" 4).

3. See the early accounts in de la Torriente; Karol, 237–42; Menton, 125–30; or more recent ones in Luis ("Autopsia" and "Exhuming"); and Báez 20–27.

4. As Lisandro Otero describes it in his memoir of those years, "They accused it [the movie] of avoiding the presence of militiamen, workers and literacy instructors,

in the image of the people it offered; those who appeared in the scenes of the nightlife were marginal, *lumpen*. To show only part of the truth was a way of lying about the Cuban reality, they said" (Otero, *Llover* 80).

5. Juan Marinello wrote, "The UNEAC has supported the Second Declaration of Havana in a strict and timely document. It must . . . spearhead a contribution of the highest interest: to ask all of its members and those who write in Cuba to persist in their tireless effort to find a style that represents our revolution and contributes to its victory. Our Latin American colleagues must heed the Cuban example and note that it is urgent to offer their creative ability to serve a common purpose that . . . will open powerful outlets to poems, essays, novels, and plays" (Marinello 42).

6. In his memoirs, Lisandro Otero offers very poignant observations about his own experience with a similar feeling of distaste at the beginning of the Revolution: "The financial stability that my family enjoyed made me get used to the resplendent face of a system that had been eradicated. For me, the universe that was disappearing was positive and pleasant. The world of consumer goods, good taste and proper care, cleanliness and the profusion of lights, of beautiful objects, was my natural space. I could not stand the slovenliness, the tackiness, the carelessness, the inefficiency, the ugliness that the social change had added as a result of the coming to power of the least favored classes. I did not crave opulence, as I was always indifferent to it, but I needed the material living conditions that any intellectual of the first world could enjoy" (*Llover* 22).

7. See the reaction of Mercedes Antón in a review published by *Unión* in 1966, which represents the anger that the protagonist of *Memorias* provoked in some readers at the time.

8. There are some anecdotal references that do not have much impact in the plot, but may have nevertheless resounded in the cultural debate of the epoch. For instance, Elena is constantly interrupting conversations with Malabre with love songs that she characterizes as "feeling" (*filin*, in Spanish). This is a reference to the controversy on this genre that was taking place at the time, in 1963. The debate on *filin* took place in the National Library, after Ella O'Farril's song "Good-Bye Happiness" was forbidden on the grounds that it was not appropriate to talk about unhappiness at that stage in the Revolution. O'Farril reportedly talked to Fidel, arguing that the song described an individual problem, and he allowed her to record it once again. Years later *filin* would be forbidden as a genre (Jaime Sarusky's intervention in "Literatura en los 60").

9. "Backwardness, the lack of technicians, the duty to give direction to a people . . . all this has marked the character and quality of our mass media in the past nine years. The press has been perhaps the most affected. The press . . . has limited itself, conditioned by sectarism . . . to give only certain news, present problems in terms of set phrases and slogans to avoid confusion and give the people a clear political direction" (Desnoes, "Armas" 41).

10. In Sartre's words "the nihilated [constituted by consciousness] in-itself, engulfed in the absolute event which is the appearance of the foundation or the upsurge

of the for-itself, remains at the heart of the for-itself as its original contingency. Thus the for-itself is supported by a perpetual contingency for which it becomes responsible and which it assimilates without ever being able to suppress it. The for-itself forever surpasses this contingency toward its own possibilities, and it encounters in itself only the nothingness which it has to be. Yet facticity does not cease to haunt the for-itself, and it is facticity which causes me to apprehend myself simultaneously as totally responsible for my being and as totally unjustifiable" (308–9).

11. "The flesh is the pure contingency of presence. It is ordinarily hidden by clothes, make-up, the cut of the hair or beard, the expression, etc. But in the course of long acquaintance with a person there always comes an instant when all these disguises are thrown off and when I find myself in the presence of the pure *contingency of his presence*" (343, emphasis in the original).

12. The original Spanish calls the visitor from the United States "el Americano," hence my translation.

### Chapter 3. Harvesting the Nation: How Cuba Became Unified in the Historical *Zafra*

1. An earlier version of this chapter was published as an article titled "The Historical *Zafra* and Nation Building in Revolutionary Cuba: Miguel Cossío Woodward's *Sacchario* (1970)" in *Revista de Estudios Hispánicos* 37.3 (2003): 613–34.

2. Among them are, for instance, Francisco García Moreiras's *Tiempo Muerto: Memorias de un trabajador azucarero* (1969) and Ana Núñez Machín's *Memoria amarga del azúcar* (1981).

3. Readers may recall Ortiz's distinction in *Cuban Counterpoint*: sugar represents authoritarianism, discipline, and rule, whereas tobacco connotes rebellion, dreaminess, and relaxation. Alcohol is the synthesis of both, or "fire, force, spirit, intoxication, thought, and action" (*Counterpoint* 93).

4. This critique of the avoidance of the topic of race in official revolutionary discourse is a common theme among scholars. Of note, Bobes; Booth; Casal, "Race"; Castellanos; de la Fuente; de la Fuente and Gasco; Luis, "En busca"; Martínez Echazábal; McGarrity; Moore; and Pérez-Sarduy and Stubbs. See also "Nación, raza y cultura," a special issue of *La Gaceta de Cuba* (2005) that tries to make explicit and at the same time mitigate this avoidance in an official cultural journal.

5. Christmas was not celebrated in Cuba again until December 1997, in anticipation of Pope John Paul II's visit.

6. "He is bending on the furrow. *Wake up, my sweetheart, wake up.* Be quiet. One needs to breathe. *Look, the sun is up.* To breathe. Darío has nicknamed him el Cantante. His voice is soft, like that of a bolero singer. He spends the day cutting. He cuts little cane, but nobody minds it, as long as he sings. He cheers the atmosphere. He is entertaining" (55). The lines emphasized are parts of songs.

7. *Guajiro* is a somewhat derogatory term for peasants in Cuba; *décima* is a tenline verse; the *guayabera* is a light-weight shirt commonly worn in the Caribbean.

8. "Chambelona" was a popular song with which politicians would enliven their demonstrations and rallies (Ortiz, *Catauro* 189); "sonsonete" is a repetitive rhythm.

9. The criticism of prerevolutionary Havana is a constant in the revolutionary novels of the first decade, such as in David Buzzi's *Los desnudos* (1967) and *La religión de los elefantes* (1968), Edmundo Desnoes's *El cataclismo* (1965), Manuel Granados's *Adire y el tiempo roto* (1967), and José Soler Puig's *Bertillón 166* (1960) and *En el año de Enero* (1963), to name just a few.

10. In *Next Year in Cuba* (1995) (*El año que viene estamos en Cuba*, 1997) Gustavo Pérez Firmat tells of a radio program that was popular in the early years of postrevolution exile in Miami. It featured a mailman who had formerly worked in Havana and would guess the exact location of the addresses that callers provided (Pérez Firmat 51). This kind of game was a means to reconstruct the city that exiles had left behind.

11. In his remembrance of prerevolutionary Havana, Antonio José Ponte also refers to Sloppy Joe's and laments its demise ("La fiesta vigilada" 28–31).

## Chapter 4. Frustrated Mothers, Virgin Workers, and Masked Whores. The "New Woman" at Work

1. An earlier version of this chapter has been published as "The New Woman in Cuban Revolutionary Discourse: Manuel Cofiño's *The Last Woman and the Next Combat* (1971)" in *Journal of Gender Studies* 14.1 (2005): 33–43. http://www.tandf. co.uk/journals/titles/0958923.asp.

2. While generally indifferent toward lesbians, and despite the negative international publicity that the UMAP camps elicited in the 1960s, the regime did aim at suppressing lesbians in the 1980s. Though these years fall out of the scope of my study, this action is worth mentioning as another indication of the conventional images of women that the regime fostered. According to Smith and Padula, in the mid-1980s the FMC banned lesbians from its ranks and encouraged neighbors to denounce them at meetings (173).

3. In Spanish, as well as in English, the unmarked grammatical term is the masculine one. Fidel was acting as if the audience was partially or totally male.

4. For instance, when referring to a project where mainly women worked, and the leaders were also women, Fidel stated that the existence of these female workers did away with the prejudice "that women are only capable of washing dishes, doing laundry, ironing, cooking, cleaning the house, and bearing children" ("Revolution Within the Revolution," Stone 50).

5. In Fidel's words: "The worst job. The most humiliating. The most contemptible. Discrimination. Underrating. That was all a woman in our country could expect from capitalism and imperialism. . . . Now no worker, no *head of family, finds himself obliged to send his daughter to work for the rich in some bar or at a brothel*, because that past, that nightmare, that odious fate that society foisted on Cuban women has vanished forever" (19661210, emphasis mine).

6. See Domínguez; Casal, "Revolution and *Conciencia*"; Ramos; López-Vigil; Lutjens, among others. See Cámara for a different view on the subject, from the standpoint of recent events.

7. In his words, "In the marks, mutilations, and transformations of the human body there is a conceptualization of revolutionary history. . . . It is implied that the monuments of the Revolution are those men and women who are alive and have contributed to it with two fluids: blood and sweat, and the live memory, in the collectivity, of those who sacrificed their lives" (Vidal 48).

8. I use the 1989 reprint of this book, but it was originally published in 1975. Also by Mulvey on this topic is "Afterthoughts on 'Visual Pleasure and Narrative Cinema,'" in which she makes slight modifications to her theory after the controversy it inspired. There will be more on this below.

9. See, for instance, the special issue of *Camera Obscura*, edited by Janet Bergstrom and Mary Anne Doane, devoted to the figure of "the Spectatrix," which Bergstrom and Doane saw as missing in Mulvey's theory. For other critical reactions to Mulvey, see, for instance, Stacey; Silverman; de Lauretis; Fuss; Kuhn; Doane; Russo; and Lebeau.

### Chapter 5. Toward a Revolutionary Utopia: Fluid Identities in a Child's Account

1. See Celutti Guldberg for a critical reading and a contextualization of Martínez Estrada's thesis.

2. After Fernández, one of the most important contributors to this debate was Oscar Collazos. In an article published in *Marcha* (August-September 1969), he advocated a literature committed to the revolutionary cause and high standards of "realism," meaning "verisimilitude" and "intelligibility" (Collazos 7–37). Julio Cortázar and Mario Vargas Llosa responded to the article (in December 1969 and April 1970 respectively). All of these articles were compiled in Collazos, Cortázar, and Vargas Llosa (*Literatura*).

3. The story changes in Fernández's novel *El vientre del pez* (1989) (The belly of the fish), which the author presents as a rewriting of *Los niños* (with Ibieta 49). The novel recounts the story of an exiled Cuban mother who lives with her son in New York during the Revolution. The mother creates a little Cuba in her apartment and gradually loses touch with reality. The son goes back to Cuba in 1970 and deeply regrets that he ever left it, but he is unable to fit into Cuban society. In *El vientre* the experience of exile during the Revolution is faced more openly, but the novel sticks to the usual ending of these narratives. For instance, Cristina García's *Dreaming in Cuban* (1992), a novel about Cuban exile, also ends with three members of a family realizing the dream of returning to Cuba after the Revolution but being unable to adapt to their original country.

4. See, for instance, Loló Soldevilla's *El farol* (1964), Edmundo Desnoes's *El cataclismo* (1965), Raúl González del Cascorro's *Concentración pública* (1963), José Soler Puig's *En el año de Enero* (1963), and Ezequiel Vieta's *Vivir en Candonga* (1966).

5. "She starts singing in my heart and she tells me everything with her singing.

When I sing what she tells me I do not make a mistake either. When my eyes close I continue to see the things that she tells me about. The things that those who are on the porch tell me, and those things are never forgotten. She speaks, they speak, but it seems that it is I who speaks silently; but it is not me because my words do not get tangled, I say them all. . . . When I grow up I am going to sit under a bush and I am going to write everything she tells me now, in the same way she describes it to me, without fear of making a mistake" (94).

6. "I learned that all these years in his company I had fed myself through his mouth or from his mouth; I learned to my utmost dismay that not only had I worn his clothes on my body but also had felt and thought through him . . .; I learned that I had spied on him in his sleep, dreamed his dream, disclosed his life, living it. All of this in a play of affinities and opposites, similarities and differences" (336).

7. I refer to Che Guevara's evocation of Fidel's alleged exceptional communication skills when communicating with large numbers of people: "In this Fidel is a master. His own special way of fusing himself with the people can be appreciated only by seeing him in action. At the great public mass meetings one can observe something like the dialogue of two tuning forks whose vibrations interact, producing new sounds. Fidel and the mass begin to vibrate together in a dialogue of growing intensity until they reach the climax in an abrupt conclusion crowned by our cry of struggle and victory" (Guevara, "Socialism" 3–4).

8. See Arnaldo Cruz-Malavé for a complete account of this process in Lezama (70–116). For the following brief itinerary through Lezama's works I am relying on Cruz-Malavé for bibliographical pointers.

9. In a passage reminiscent of the Gospel, in its reference to the need to become a child to enter the kingdom of heaven, the narrator describes the people on the boat to Sabanas as follows: "They all look like children. They behave and play like children. Now they all can go into a park, that's it. It is like the Day of the Three Kings, like Mother's Day, like my birthday, like the day we go into Sabanas" (313).

10. Enrico Mario Santí has also characterized *Paradiso* as a parricide, because of Lezama's deliberate misquotation of sources and authorities (Santí, "Parridiso").

11. As explained by Louis Pérez, "The centennial commemoration of the Grito de Yara (1868) served to define a unifying historical construct that gave decisive shape to Cuban historiography in 1968: *cien años de lucha.* The national past was set in a contextual sweep of a century-long struggle. A struggle in which successive generations of Cubans were summoned by history to dramatic action and heroic sacrifice" (Pérez 4).

12. In Che Guevara's words: "The individual in our country knows that the glorious period in which he happens to live is one of sacrifice. . . . In a real revolution, to which one gives his all and from which one expects no material reward, the task of the vanguard revolutionary is at one and the same time magnificent and agonizing. . . . The true revolutionary is guided by great feelings of love" ("Socialism" 14–15).

13. Derrida refers of course to the beginning of the Manifesto: "A specter is haunting Europe—the specter of Communism" (Tucker 473).

14. In Derrida's words: "It would be a matter of linking an *affirmation* (in particular a political one), *if there is any*, to the experience of the impossible, which can only be a radical experience of the *perhaps*" (35, emphasis in the original).

**Epilogue. Identity and Its Discontents: Leonardo Padura Fuentes Looks Back at the New Man**

1. In this chapter I use the published translations of two of the novels for my quotations. Since there are no translations of the other two novels as yet, I use my own translations.

# Works Cited

**Primary Texts**

Agostini, Victor. *Dos viajes.* Havana: Ediciones Revolución, 1965.

Aguililla, Araceli. *Por llanos y montañas.* Havana: UNEAC, 1978.

Alonso, Dora. *El año 61.* Havana: Letras Cubanas, 1981.

Arcocha, Juan. *Los muertos andan solos.* Havana: Ediciones Revolución, 1962.

Arenal, Humberto. *El sol a plomo.* Havana: Cruzada latinoamericana de difusión cultural, 1959.

———. *Los animales sagrados.* Havana: Instituto del Libro, 1967.

Arenas, Reinaldo. *Celestino antes del alba.* Caracas: Monteávila, 1980.

———. *El mundo alucinante.* Caracas: Monteávila, 1982.

———. *Hallucinations: Being an Account of the Life and Adventures of Friar Servando Teresa de Mier.* Trans. Gordon Brotherston. New York: Harper and Row, 1971.

———. *Singing from the Well.* Trans. Andrew Hurley. New York: Penguin, 1987.

Arrufat, Antón. *Los siete contra Tebas.* Havana: Unión, 1968.

Barnet, Miguel. *Biografía de un cimarrón.* Havana: Letras Cubanas, 1980.

———. *Biography of a Runaway Slave.* Trans. W. Nick Hill. New York: Curbstone, 1995.

———. *Canción de Rachel.* Madrid: Alianza, 1967.

Becerra Ortega, José. *La novena estación.* Havana: Siglo XX, 1959.

Borges, Jorge Luis, and Adolfo Bioy Casares. *Seis Problemas para Don Isidro Parodi.* Buenos Aires: Sur, 1942.

———. *Six Problems for Don Isidro Parodi.* Trans. Norman Thomas de Giovanni. New York: Dutton, 1981.

Buzzi, David. *La religión de los elefantes.* Havana: Unión, 1968.

———. *Los desnudos.* Havana: Letras Cubanas, 1982.

Cabezas, Omar. *Fire from the Mountain. The Making of a Sandinista.* Trans. Kathleen Weaver. New York: Crown, 1985.

———. *La montaña es algo más que una inmensa estepa verde.* Mexico City: Siglo XXI, 1982.

Cabrera Infante, Guillermo. *Three Trapped Tigers.* Trans. Donald Gardner and Susan Jill Levine. New York: Harper and Row, 1971.

———. *Tres tristes tigres.* Barcelona: Seix Barral, 1991.

Camus, Albert. *L'etranger.* Paris: Gallimard, 1961.

Carpentier, Alejo. *El reino de este mundo.* Mexico City: Iberoamericana de publicaciones, 1949.

———. *El siglo de las luces.* Barcelona: Seix Barral, 1988.

———. *Explosion in the Cathedral*. Trans. John Sturrock. Boston: Little Brown, 1962.

———. *La consagración de la primavera*. Barcelona: Plaza and Janés, 1978.

———. *The Kingdom of This World*. Trans. Harriet de Onís. New York: Knopf, 1957.

Cofiño, Manuel. *Cuando la sangre se parece al fuego*. Havana: Unión, 1977.

———. *La última mujer y el próximo combate*. Havana: Casa de las Américas, 1971.

Collazo, Miguel. *El viaje*. Havana: Unión, 1968.

Cossío Woodward, Miguel. *Sacchario*. Havana: Casa de las Américas, 1970.

Desnoes, Edmundo. *El cataclismo*. Havana: Ediciones Revolución, 1965.

———. *Inconsolable Memories*. Trans. Edmundo Desnoes. London: Deutsch, 1967.

———. *Memorias del subdesarrollo*. Tabasco, Mexico: Joaquín Mortiz, 1975.

———. *No hay problema*. Havana: Ediciones Revolución, 1961.

Desnoes, Edmundo, and William Luis, eds. *Los dispositivos en la flor. Cuba: literatura desde la revolución*. Hanover, N.H.: Ediciones del Norte, 1981.

Díaz, Jesús. *Las iniciales de la tierra*. Madrid: Alfaguara, 1987.

———. *The Initials of the Earth*. Trans. Kathleen Ross. Durham, N.C.: Duke University Press, 2006.

*El brigadista*. Dir. Octavio Cortázar and Luis Rogelio Nogueras. ICAIC, 1977.

Feijóo, Samuel. "Jira descomunal: Novela cubana, nativista, costumbrista, folklorista e ¡indigenista!" *Islas* 29 (1968): 300–457.

Fernández, Pablo Armando. *El libro de los héroes*. Havana: Casa de las Américas, 1964.

———. *El vientre del pez*. Havana: Unión, 1989.

———. *Los niños se despiden*. Havana: Casa de las Américas, 1968.

García, Cristina. *Dreaming in Cuban*. New York: Ballantine, 1992.

García, Daura Olema. *Maestra voluntaria*. Havana: Casa de las Américas, 1962.

García Moreiras, Francisco. *Tiempo muerto: Memorias de una trabajador azucarero*. Havana: Huracán, 1969.

González del Cascorro, Raúl. *Concentración pública*. Havana: Unión, 1963.

Granados, Manuel. *Adire y el tiempo roto*. Havana: Casa de las Américas, 1967.

*Hiroshima Mon Amour*. Dir. Alain Resnais. Argos Films, 1959.

Indio Naborí [Jesús Orta Ruiz]. "Mujeres Federadas." *Mujeres* 15 October 1962: 59.

Leante, César. *El perseguido*. Havana: Ediciones Revolución, 1964.

Lezama Lima, José. 1993. *Paradiso*. Madrid: Cátedra, 1964.

———. *Paradiso*. Trans. Gregory Rabassa. Normal, Ill.: Dalkey Archive Press, 1993.

Manzano, Matilde. "Apuntes de una alfabetizadora." *Casa de las Américas* 19 (1963): 91–117.

*Memorias del subdesarrollo*. Dir. Tomás Gutiérrez Alea and Edmundo Desnoes. ICAIC, 1968.

More, Thomas. *Utopia*. London: Penguin, 1986.

Nabokov, Vladimir. *Pale Fire*. New York: Putnam, 1962.

Navarro, Noel. *Los caminos de la noche*. Havana: Granma, 1967.

Núñez Machín, Ana. *Memoria amarga del azúcar.* Havana: Editorial de Ciencias Sociales, 1981.

Otero, Lisandro. *La situación.* Havana: Casa de las Américas, 1963.

———. *Pasión de Urbino.* Buenos Aires: J. Álvarez, 1967.

Padilla, Heberto. *Fuera de juego.* Barcelona: El Bardo, 1970.

Padura Fuentes, Leonardo. *Havana Black.* Trans. Peter Bush. London: Bitter Lemon Press, 2006.

———. *Havana Red.* Trans. Peter Bush. London: Bitter Lemon Press, 2005.

———. *La neblina del ayer.* Barcelona: Tusquets, 2005.

———. *Máscaras.* Barcelona: Tusquets, 1997.

———. *Paisaje de otoño.* Barcelona: Tusquets, 1998.

———. *Pasado perfecto.* Barcelona: Tusquets, 2000.

———. *Vientos de cuaresma.* Barcelona: Tusquets, 2001.

Perera Soto, Hilda. *Mañana es 26.* Havana: Lázaro Hermanos, 1960.

Pérez Firmat, Gustavo. *El año que viene estamos en Cuba.* Houston: Arte Público, 1997.

———. *Next Year in Cuba: A Cubano's Coming of Age in America.* Trans. Gustavo Pérez Firmat. New York: Anchor, 1995.

Piñera, Virgilio. *Cold Tales.* Trans. Mark Shafer. Hygiene, Colo.: Eridanos Press, 1988.

———. *Cuentos fríos.* Buenos Aires: Losada, 1956.

———. *La carne de René.* Buenos Aires: Siglo XX, 1952.

———. *La isla en peso: Obra poética.* Havana: Unión, 1998.

———. *René's Flesh.* Trans. Mark Shafer. Boston: Eridanos Press, 1989.

*PM.* Dir. Sabá Cabrera Infante and Orlando Jiménez Leal, 1961.

Randall, Margaret, trans. and ed. *Breaking the Silences: 20th Century Poetry by Cuban Women.* Vancouver: Pulp, 1982.

*Retrato de Teresa.* Dir. Pastor Vega. New Yorker Video, 1980.

Rodríguez Feo, José. "Impresiones de un alfabetizador." *Casa de las Américas* 9 (1961): 50–57.

Sartre, Jean-Paul. *La Nausée.* Paris: Gallimard, 1978.

Sarusky, Jaime. *Rebelión en la octava casa.* Havana: Editorial Letras Cubanas, 1967.

Simó, Ana María. *Las fábulas.* Havana: Ediciones Revolución, 1962.

Soldevilla, Loló. *El farol.* Havana: Ediciones Revolución, 1964.

Soler Puig, José. *Bertillón 166.* Havana: Ministerio de Educación, 1960.

———. *El derrumbe.* Santiago de Cuba: Consejo Nacional de Universidades, 1964.

———. *En el año de enero.* Havana: Unión, 1963.

Vieta, Ezequiel. *Vivir en Candonga.* Havana: Unión, 1966.

## Speeches

Castro, Fidel. "19601011. At the First National Congress of Municipal Education." <http://www1.lanic.utexas.edu> 26 July 2006.

———. "19610128. Castro Scores Escambray Revolutionaries." <http://www1.lanic.utexas.edu> 26 July 2006.

———. "19610409. Education and Revolution." <http://www1.lanic.utexas.edu> 26 July 2006.

———. "19610514. Castro Pledges 100 Percent Literacy." <http://www1.lanic.utexas.edu> 26 July 2006.

———. "19610817. Castro Speaks on Literacy Campaign." <http://www1.lanic.utexas.edu> 26 July 2006.

———. "19610818. Plenary Session of Literacy Campaign Workers." <http://www1.lanic.utexas.edu> 26 July 2006.

———. "19620606. Castro Interview in Nouvelle Critique." <http://www1.lanic.utexas.edu> 26 July 2006.

———. "19621002. First National Congress of Federation of Cuban Women." <http://www1.lanic.utexas.edu> 26 July 2006.

———. "19630116. Closing of the Congress of Women of the Americas." <http://www1.lanic.utexas.edu> 26 July 2006.

———. "19650220. Castro Speaks to the Federation of Women." <http://www1.lanic.utexas.edu> 26 July 2006.

———. "19660502. May Day Celebration." <http://www1.lanic.utexas.edu> 26 July 2006.

———. "19660929. Speech to Sugar Cane Workers." <http://www1.lanic.utexas.edu> 26 July 2006.

———. "19661204. Castro Speaks to Teachers, Girl Graduates." <http://www1.lanic.utexas.edu> 26 July 2006.

———. "19661210. Speech at the Close of the FMC Congress." <http://www1.lanic.utexas.edu> 26 July 2006.

———. "19661219. Castro Speaks at Havana University Graduation." <http://www1.lanic.utexas.edu> 26 July 2006.

———. "19690105. Castro Addresses Mark School Dedication." <http://www1.lanic.utexas.edu> 26 July 2006.

———. "19690108. Castro Speech at Valle del Perú Polyclinic." <http://www1.lanic.utexas.edu> 26 July 2006.

———. "19690130. Castro Inaugurates Artificial Breeding Center." <http://www1.lanic.utexas.edu> 26 July 2006.

———. "19690314. Twelfth Anniversary of Attack of Presidential Palace." <http://www1.lanic.utexas.edu> 26 July 2006.

———. "19690515. Castro Addresses Animal Science Congress." <http://www1.lanic.utexas.edu> 26 July 2006.

———. "19690527. Castro Speaks at INRA-Dap Merger." <http://www1.lanic.utexas.edu> 26 July 2006.

———. "19690604. Visit of Tram Buu Kiem to Cuba." <http://www1.lanic.utexas.edu> 26 July 2006.

———. "19690714. Castro Addresses 1970 Sugar Harvest Rally." <http://www1.lanic.utexas.edu> 26 July 2006.

———. "19691019. Fidel Addresses Central University Graduates." <http://www1.lanic.utexas.edu> 26 July 2006.

———. "19691028. Castro Launches Ten-Million-Ton Sugar Harvest." <http://www1.lanic.utexas.edu> 26 July 2006.

———. "19691106. Castro Stresses FAR's Participation in Sugar Harvest." <http://www1.lanic.utexas.edu> 26 July 2006.

———. "19700421. Funeral for Five Men Killed in Action." <http://www1.lanic.utexas.edu> 26 July 2006.

———. "19700521. Premier Castro 20 May Report on Sugar Harvest." <http://www1.lanic.utexas.edu> 26 July 2006.

———. "19700824. Speech on the FMC Tenth Anniversary." <http://www1.lanic.utexas.edu> 26 July 2006.

———. "19700929. Castro Speech on Havana Domestic Radio." <http://www1.lanic.utexas.edu> 26 July 2006.

———. "19701208[a]. Castro Addresses Plenum of Basic Industry Workers." <http://www1.lanic.utexas.edu> 26 July 2006.

———. "19701208[b]. Castro Addresses Plenum of Basic Industry Workers. Part II." <http://www1.lanic.utexas.edu> 26 July 2006.

———. "Clausura del primer congreso de escritores y artistas de Cuba." Nuiry Sánchez 50–57.

———. "Discurso de Clausura del Primer Congreso Nacional de Educación y Cultura." Casal, *El caso*, 115–22.

———. "Discurso del 22 de Marzo, 1959." *Revolución*, 23 March 1959, 24–27.

———. "El pueblo cubano proclama ante el mundo que Cuba es territorio libre de analfabetismo." Nuiry Sánchez 80–89.

———. "History Will Absolve Me." *Revolutionary Struggle 1947–58*. Vol. 1 of *Selected Works of Fidel Castro*. Cambridge, Mass.: MIT Press, 1972. 165–221.

———. "Palabras a los intelectuales." Nuiry Sánchez 22–42.

———. "Revolution within the Revolution." Stone 48–54.

———. "Segunda declaración de La Habana." Nuiry Sánchez 90–107.

———. "The Struggle for Women's Equality." Stone 55–73.

———. "Words to the Intellectuals." *Radical Perspectives in the Arts*. Ed. Leopoldo Baxandall. London: Penguin, 1972. 267–98.

Communist Party of Cuba. Ministerio de Justicia of Cuba. *La mujer en Cuba socialista*. Havana: Orbe, 1977.

———. "Thesis: on the Full Exercise of Women's Equality." Stone 74–105.

Departamento de Investigación Bibliográfica de la Biblioteca Nacional José Martí. "Literatura cubana en la revolución." *Revista de literatura cubana* 2–3 (1984): 153–207.

Dorticós, Oswaldo. "Apertura del primer congreso de escritores y artistas de Cuba (Fragmentos)." Nuiry Sánchez 43–49.

Espín Guillois, Vilma. *Cuban Women Confront the Future.* Melbourne, Australia: Ocean, 1991.

———. "Discurso en el acto conmemorativo del Décimo Aniversario de la Federación de Mujeres Cubanas." *La mujer en Cuba* 13–27.

———. "Discurso en el acto de constitución de la Federación de Mujeres Cubanas." *La mujer en Cuba* 1–27.

———. "Informe Central del Congreso de la Federación de Mujeres Cubanas (1962)." *Informes centrales de los congresos de la FMC.* Havana: FAR, 1990. 5–39.

———, ed. *La mujer en Cuba.* Havana: Editora Política, 1990.

Guevara, Ernesto Che. "El socialismo y el hombre en Cuba." *El Socialismo y el hombre en Cuba.* New York: Pathfinder, 1992. 51–73.

———. *Episodes of the Revolutionary War.* New York: International Publishers, 1968.

———. *Escritos y discursos.* Havana: Ciencias Sociales, 1985.

———. "Notas para el estudio de la ideología de la revolución cubana." Nuiry Sánchez 14–21.

———. *Obras escogidas: 1957–67.* Havana: Ciencias Sociales, 1985.

———. *Pasajes de la guerra revolucionaria.* Havana: Unión, 1963.

———. "Que la universidad se pinte de negro, de mulato, de obrero, de campesino." Nuiry Sánchez 11–20.

———. "Socialism and Man in Cuba." *Socialism and Man in Cuba.* Trans. Anonymous. New York: Pathfinder, 1989. 1–17.

Nuiry Sánchez, Nuria, ed. *Pensamiento y política cultural cubanos: Antología.* Vol. 2. Havana: Pueblo y educación, 1987.

Stone, Elizabeth, ed. *Women and the Cuban Revolution.* New York: Pathfinder, 1981.

## Secondary Sources

Abella, Rosa. "Bibliografía de la novela publicada en Cuba, y en el extranjero por cubanos, desde 1959 hasta 1965." *Revista Iberoamericana* 62 (1966): 307–18.

Álvarez, Federico. "Perspectiva y ambigüedad en *Memorias del subdesarrollo.*" *Casa de las Américas* 39 (1966): 148–50.

Álvarez, Imeldo. *La novela cubana en el siglo XX.* Havana: Letras Cubanas, 1980.

Anderson, Benedict. *Imagined Communities: Reflections on the Origin and Spread of Nationalism.* London: Verso, 1995.

Anthias, Floya, and Nira Yuval-Davis. *Woman-Nation-State.* New York: St. Martins, 1989.

Antón, Mercedes. "*Memorias del subdesarrollo*: El cataclismo." *Unión* 1 (1966): 164–67.

Arcocha, Juan. "El viaje de Sartre." Machover 231–39.

Ares, Guillermina. *Alfabetización en Cuba: Momentos cumbres de la Revolución cubana.* Havana: Editora política, 2000.

Argüelles, Lourdes, and B. Ruby Rich. "Homosexuality, Homophobia and Revolution: Notes Toward an Understanding of the Cuban Lesbian and Gay Male Experience." *Signs* 9.4 (1982): 682–99.

Arias, Salvador. "Literatura cubana (1959–78)." In *La cultura en Cuba socialista*. Havana: Letras Cubanas, 1982.

Ávila, Leopoldo. "Sobre algunas corrientes de la crítica y la literatura en Cuba." *Verde Olivo* 9.47 (1968): 14–18.

Báez, Luis. *Junto a las voces del designio: Revelaciones del poeta Pablo Armando Fernández*. Havana: Ciencias Sociales, 2003.

Bakhtin, Mikhail. *The Dialogic Imagination: Four Essays by M. M. Bakhtin*. Ed. Michael Holquist. Austin: University of Texas Press, 1981.

Bakhtin, Mikhail, and P. N. Medvedev. "The Formal Method in Literary Scholarship." Morris 124–36.

Barnet et al. *Literatura y arte nuevo en Cuba*. Barcelona: Estela, 1971.

Barradas, Efraín. "El Che, narrador: Apuntes para un estudio de *Pasajes de la guerra revolucionaria*." *Literatures in Transition: The Many Voices of the Caribbean Area*. Ed. Rose Minc. Gaithersburg, Md.: Hispamérica and Montclair State College, 1982. 137–45.

Barthes, Roland. *The Pleasure of the Text*. New York: Hill and Wang, 1975.

Bejel, Emilio. *Gay Cuban Nation*. Chicago: University of Chicago Press, 2001.

"Belleza." *Mujeres* 15 August 1966: 26–27.

Benítez Rojo, Antonio. "La cultura caribeña en Cuba: Continuidad versus ruptura." *Cuban Studies* 14.1 (1984): 1–17.

———. "Power/Sugar/Literature: Toward a Reinterpretation of Cubanness." *Cuban Studies* 16 (1986): 9–31.

Bergstrom, Janet, and Mary Ann Doane, eds. *The Female Spectator: Contexts and Directions*. Special issue of *Camera Obscura* 20,21 (1990).

Bermúdez, José Ramón. *La imagen constante: El cartel cubano el siglo XX*. Havana: Letras Cubanas, 2000.

Bhabha, Homi K. *Nation and Narration*. London: Routledge, 1990.

———. *The Location of Culture*. London: Routledge, 1994.

Bobes, Velia Cecilia. "Cuba y la cuestión racial." *Perfiles latinoamericanos* 8 (1996): 115–37.

Booth, David. "Cuba, Color and Revolution." *Science and Society* 11.2 (1976): 129–72.

Bost, David H., and Lisa Zimmerman. "The Cuban Novel of the Revolution: A Postmodern Perspective." *South Eastern Latin Americanist* 35.3–4 (1991–92): 1–15.

Braham, Persephone. *Crimes against the State, Crimes against Persons: Detective Fiction in Cuba and Mexico*. Minneapolis: University of Minnesota Press, 2004.

Bunck, Julie Marie. *Fidel Castro and the Quest for a Revolutionary Culture in Cuba*. University Park: Pennsylvania State University Press, 1994.

———. "Women's Rights and the Cuban Revolution." *Cuban Communism 1959–1995*. Ed. Irving L. Horowitz. New York: Transaction, 1995. 427–49.

Butler, Judith. *Gender Trouble: Feminism and the Subversion of Identity*. New York: Routledge, 1990.

Cabrera Infante, Guillermo. "La Habana para los fieles difunta." *Mea Cuba*. Barcelona: Plaza & Janés, 1992. 120–25.

Cachán, Manuel. "*Los años duros*: La Revolución del discurso y el discurso de la Revolución cubana." *Explicación de textos literarios* 1 (1990–91): 84–94.

Cámara, Madeline. "Una promesa incumplida: la emancipación de la mujer cubana a finales del siglo XX." *Mujeres cubanas: Historia e Intrahistoria*. Ed. Instituto Jacques Maritain. Miami: Universal, 2000. 67–78.

Camayd Freixas, Erik. "Ambigüedad e ideología en *Memorias del subdesarrollo*." *Plaza* 10–11 (1985): 31–47.

Campuzano, Luisa. "Cuba 1961: Los textos narrativos de las alfabetizadoras; Conflictos de género, clase y canon." *Unión* 26 (January–March 1997): 52–57.

———. "La revista Casa de las Américas en la década de los sesenta." *Le discours culturel dans les revues latino-americaines (1940–70)*. Ed. Claude Fell et al. Paris: Presses de la Sorbonne Nouvelle, 1992. 55–64.

Carpentier, Alejo. "Apología de la novela policíaca." *Crónicas*. Vol. 2. Havana: Letras Cubanas, 1985.

———. "Papel social del novelista." *Literatura y arte nuevo en Cuba*. Eds. Mario Benedetti et al. Barcelona: Estela, 1971. 153–69.

Casal, Lourdes. *El caso Padilla: Literatura y revolución en Cuba*. Miami: Universal, 1971.

———. "Images of Women in Pre- and Postrevolutionary Cuban Novels." *Cuban Studies* 17 (1987): 25–50.

———. "Literature and Society." *Revolutionary Change in Cuba*. Ed. Carmelo Mesa-Lago. Pittsburgh: University of Pittsburgh Press, 1971. 447–71.

———. "Race Relations in Contemporary Cuba." *The Cuba Reader*. Eds. Philip Brenner et al. New York: Grove, 1990.

———. "Revolution and *Conciencia*: Women in Cuba." *Women, War and Revolution*. Eds. Carol Berkin and Clara M. Lovett. New York: Homes and Meier, 1980. 183–206.

———. "The Cuban Novel, 1959–1969: An Annotated Bibliography." *Abraxas* 1 (1970): 77–92.

Casañas, Inés, and Jorge Fornet. *Premio Casa de las Américas: Memoria*. Havana: Casa de las Américas, 1999.

Castellanos, Jorge, and Isabel Castellanos. "The Geographic, Ethnologic and Linguistic Roots of Cuban Blacks." *Cuban Studies* 17 (1995): 95–109.

Celutti Guldberg, Horacio. "Peripecias en la construcción de nuestra utopía." *De varia utopica*. Vol. 3. Bogotá: Publicaciones de la Universidad Central, 1989. 225–35.

"Círculo de estudios de la FMC." *Mujeres* 1 August 1963: 124–27.

Clark, Katerina. *The Soviet Novel: History as Ritual*. Chicago: University of Chicago Press, 1981.

Collazos, Oscar. "Encrucijada del lenguaje." *Literatura en la revolución y revolución en la literatura*. Eds. Oscar Collazos, Julio Cortázar, Mario Vargas Llosa. Mexico City: Siglo XXI, 1970. 7–37.

Conboy, Katie, Nadia Medina, and Sarah Stanbury, eds. *Writing on the Body: Female Embodiment and Feminist Theory*. New York: Columbia University Press, 1997.

Cossío Woodward, Miguel. E-mail interview with the author. January 2006.

Cruz-Malavé, Arnaldo. *El primitivo implorante: El sistema poético del mundo de José Lezama Lima*. Amsterdam: Rodopí, 1994.

Dalton, Roque, et al. "Diez años de la revolución: El intelectual y la sociedad." *Casa de las Américas* 56 (1969): 172–81.

de la Campa, Román. "*Memorias del subdesarrollo*: Novela/Texto/Discurso." *Revista Iberoamericana* 152–53 (1990): 1039–54.

de la Fuente, Alejandro. *A Nation for All: Race, Inequality and Politics in Twentieth-Century Cuba*. Chapel Hill: University of North Carolina Press, 2001. 53–71.

———. "Race and Inequality in Cuba (1899–1981)." *Journal of Contemporary History* 30 (1995): 131–68.

de la Fuente, Alejandro, and Laurence Gasco. "Are Blacks 'Getting Out of Control'? Racial Attitudes, Revolution and Political Transition in Cuba." *Toward a New Cuba? Legacies of a Revolution*. Eds. Miguel A. Centeno and Mauricio Font. London: Lynne Riener, 1997. 53–71.

de la Nuez, Iván. *Fantasía roja: Los intelectuales de izquierda y la Revolución cubana*. Barcelona: Debate, 2006.

de la Torriente, Loló. "La política cultural y los escritores y artistas cubanos." *Cuadernos americanos* 5.22 (1963): 47–56.

de Lauretis, Teresa. *Technologies of Gender: Essays of Theory, Film and Fiction*. Bloomington: Indiana University Press, 1989.

Derrida, Jacques. *Specters of Marx: The State of Debt, the Work of Mourning and the New International*. New York: Routledge, 1994.

Desnoes, Edmundo. "America Revisited: An Interview with Edmundo Desnoes." Interview with William Luis. *Latin American Literary Review* 21 (fall–winter 1982): 7–20.

———. "Cuba: caña y cultura." *Casa de las Américas* 11.62 (1970): 46–58.

———. "La educación del gusto popular." *Unión* 3–4 (1962): 78–82.

———. "Las armas secretas." *Casa de las Américas* 3 (1968): 32–43.

———. *Punto de vista*. Havana: Instituto del Libro, 1967.

Doane, Mary Ann. "Film and the Masquerade: Theorizing the Female Spectator." Eds. Conboy, Medina, Stanbury. 177–93.

Domínguez, Virginia. "Sex, Gender and Revolution: The Problem of Construction and the Construction of a Problem." *Cuban Studies* 17 (1987): 7–23.

Dopico Black, Georgina. "The Limits of Expression: Intellectual Freedom in Revolutionary Cuba." *Cuban Studies* 19 (1989): 107–42.

Duchesne, Juan. "Las narraciones guerrilleras. Configuración de un sujeto épico de nuevo tipo." *Testimonio y literatura*. Eds. René Jara and Hernán Vidal. Minneapolis: Institute for the Study of Ideologies and Literature, 1986. 85–137.

"Ella y él." *Mujeres* 1 November 1962: 16–17.

Engels, Friedrich, and Karl Marx, "Manifesto of the Communist Party." Tucker 469–501.

Equipo de la Editorial Ciencias Sociales. *Territorio libre de analfabetismo.* Havana: Ciencias Sociales, 1981.

Fagen, Richard. *The Transformation of Political Culture in Cuba.* Stanford, Calif.: Stanford University Press, 1969.

Fernández, Henry, David Grossvogel, and Emir Rodríguez Monegal. "3 on 2: Desnoes, Gutiérrez Alea." *Diacritics* 4.4 (1974): 51–64.

Fernández, Pablo Armando. "Autopsia de *Lunes de Revolución.*" Interview with William Luis. *Plural* 11.126 (1982).

——. Interview with Emilio Bejel. *Escribir en Cuba: Entrevistas con escritores cubanos.* Ed. Emilio Bejel. Río Piedras: Editorial de la Universidad de Puerto Rico, 1991. 79–91.

——. Interview with Gabriella Ibieta. *Hispamérica* 17–18.51 (1988): 47–61.

——. Interview with Mauricio Font. *Areíto* 5.19–20 (1979): 42–45.

Fernández Moreno, César, ed. *América Latina en su literatura.* Mexico City: Siglo XXI, 1977.

Fernández Retamar, Roberto. *Calibán y otros ensayos: Nuestra América y el mundo.* Havana: Arte y Literatura, 1979.

——. "Generaciones van, generaciones vienen." *La Gaceta de Cuba* 2 (1962): 4.

——. "Hacia una intelectualidad revolucionaria." *Casa de las Américas* 7.4 (1967): 4–20.

Fernández-Vázquez, Antonio. *La novelística cubana de la revolución.* Miami: Universal, 1980.

Fornet, Ambrosio. "A propósito de *Sacchario.*" *Casa de las Américas* 11.64 (1971): 183–85.

——. "*Casa de las Américas*: Entre la revolución y la utopía." *La cultura de un siglo: América latina en sus revistas.* Ed. Saúl Sosnowski. Madrid: Alianza editorial, 1999. 421–37.

——. Introduction. *Bridging the Enigma: Cubans on Cuba.* Ed. Ambrosio Fornet. Special issue of *South Atlantic Quarterly* 96.1 (1997): 1–16.

——. "Las ideas estéticas de Marx." *Casa de las Américas* 34 (1966): 124–28.

Foucault, Michel. "What Is an Author?" *The Foucault Reader.* Ed. Paul Rabinow. New York: Pantheon, 1984. 101–21.

Freire, Paulo. *Pedagogy of the Oppressed.* New York: Continuum, 1995.

Fuentes, Carlos. *La nueva novela hispanoamericana.* Mexico City: Joaquín Mortiz, 1972.

Fuss, Diana. "Fashion and the Homospectatorial Look." *Critical Inquiry* 18 (summer 1992): 713–37.

García Alzola, Ernesto. "El realismo poético de Manuel Cofiño." *Texto crítico* 29 (1984): 100–19.

Geirola, Gustavo. *Teatralidad y experiencia política en América Latina 1957–77.* Irvine, Calif.: Gestos, 2000.

González, Flora. "De lo invisible a lo espectacular en la creación de la mulata en la cultura cubana: Cecilia Valdés y María Antonia." *Revista Iberoamericana* 184–85.64 (1998): 543–57.

González Echevarría, Roberto. "*Biografía de un cimarrón* and the Novel of the Cuban Revolution." *The Voice of the Masters: Writing and Authority in Modern Latin American Literature.* Austin: University of Texas Press, 1985. 110–23.

———. "Criticism and Literature in Revolutionary Cuba." *Cuban Studies* 11.1 (1981): 1–19.

———. *Myth and Archive: A Theory of Latin American Narrative.* Cambridge: Cambridge University Press, 1990.

Hall, Stuart. "Encoding, Decoding." *The Cultural Studies Reader.* Ed. Simon During. London: Routledge, 1993. 90–103.

Hennesy, Alistair. "Latin America." Ionescu and Gellner 28–62.

Hill Collins, Patricia. *Black Feminist Thought: Knowledge, Consciousness and the Politics of Empowerment.* New York: Routledge, 1990.

Hobsbawm, E. J. "Revolution." *Revolution in History.* Eds. Roy Porter and Mikulas Teich. Cambridge: Cambridge University Press, 1986. 5–46.

Hodges, Donald. *Intellectual Foundations of the Nicaraguan Revolution.* Austin: University of Texas Press, 1986.

Hosking, Geoffrey. *Beyond Socialist Realism: Soviet Literature since Ivan Denisovich.* New York: Holmes and Meier, 1980.

Howe, Linda. *Transgression and Conformity: Cuban Writers after the Revolution.* Madison: University of Wisconsin Press, 2004.

Ionescu, Ghita, and Ernest Gellner, eds. *Populism: Its Meaning and National Characteristics.* New York: Macmillan, 1969.

Jameson, Fredric. "Periodizing the 60s." *The Ideologies of Theory: Essays 1971–86.* Vol 2. Minneapolis: University of Minnesota Press, 1988. 178–208.

Kapcia, Antoni. "Martí, Marxism and Morality: The Evolution of an Ideology of Revolution." *Cuba After Thirty Years. Rectification and Revolution.* Ed. Richard Gillespie. London: Frank Cass, 1990. 161–83.

Karol, K. S. *Guerrillas in Power: The Course of the Cuban Revolution.* Trans. Arnold Pomerans. New York: Hill and Wang, 1970.

Keeble, Alexandra, ed. *In the Spirit of Wandering Teachers: Cuban Literacy Campaign, 1961/Con el espíritu de los maestros ambulantes: La campaña de alfabetización cubana, 1961.* Melbourne, Australia: Ocean Press, 2001.

Kirk, John. *José Martí: Mentor of the Cuban Nation.* Tampa: University of South Florida Press, 1983.

———. "Leonardo Padura Fuentes: Symbol of the New Cuban Literature. Comments on *Pasado perfecto.*" Unpublished manuscript. n.d.

Kirk, John, and Leonardo Padura, eds. *Culture and the Cuban Revolution: Conversations in Havana.* Gainesville: University Press of Florida, 2001.

Kuhn, Annette. "The Body and Cinema: Some Problems for Feminism." Eds. Conboy, Medina, Stanbury. 195–207.

Kutzinski, Vera. *Sugar's Secrets: Race and the Erotics of Cuban Nationalism.* Charlottesville: University of Virginia Press, 1993.

Lacan, Jacques. *The Four Fundamental Concepts of Psychoanalysis.* New York: Norton, 1981.

Lacqueur, Walter. *Guerrilla: A Historical and Critical Study.* Boston: Little, Brown and Co., 1976.

Leante, César. "Los pasajes del Che." *El espacio real.* Havana: UNEAC, 1975. 89–98.

Lebeau, Vicky. *Short Cuts: Psychoanalysis and Cinema; The Play of Shadows.* London: Wallflower, 2001.

Leiner, Marvin. *Sexual Politics in Cuba: Machismo, Homosexuality and AIDS.* Boulder, Colo.: Westview, 1994.

Le Riverend, Julio. "Martí: Ética y acción revolucionaria." *Casa de las Américas* 57 (1969): 38–54.

Lezama Lima, José. "Coloquio con Juan Ramón Jiménez." *Obras completas.* Vol. 2. 1975. 44–65.

———. "Imágenes posibles." *Obras completas.* Vol. 2. 1975. 152–67.

———. "La cantidad hechizada." *Obras completas.* Vol. 2. 1975. 797–890.

———. "La expresión americana." *Obras completas.* Vol. 2. 1975. 279–369.

———. *Obras completas.* Vol. 2. Mexico City: Aguilar, 1975.

———. "Ritmo y destino de una pequeña ciudad." Machover 61–65.

Lie, Nadia. *Transición y transacción: La revista cubana Casa de las Américas (1960–1976).* Gaithersburg, Md.: Hispamérica, 1996.

Liss, Sheldon. *Fidel! Castro's Political and Social Thought.* Latin American Perspectives Series 13. Boulder, Colo.: Westview, 1994.

"Literatura en los 60." Unofficial transcript of a meeting at the Museo de Bellas Artes in Havana. July 2005.

López Valdizón, José María. "*Maestra voluntaria* de Daura Olema." *Casa de las Américas* 13–14 (1962): 55–56.

López-Vigil, María. "Cubanas: Trazos para un perfil, voces para una historia." *Ni paraíso ni infierno: Cuba.* Managua, Nicaragua: Envío, 1999. 115–43.

Luis, William. "En busca de la cubanidad: El negro en la literatura y cultura cubana." *Heterotopías: Narrativas de identidad y alteridad latinoamericana.* Eds. Carlos Jáuregui and Juan Pablo Dabobe. Pittsburgh: Instituto Nacional de Literatura Latinoamericana, 2003. 391–419.

———. "Exhuming *Lunes de Revolución.*" *The New Centennial Review* 2.2 (2002): 253–83.

Lumsden, Ian. *Machos, Maricones and Gays: Cuba and Homosexuality.* Philadelphia: Temple University Press, 1996.

Lutjens, Sheryl. "Reading Between the Lines." *Latin American Perspectives* 22.2 (1995): 100–124.

Machover, Jacobo, ed. *La Habana 1952–1961.* Madrid: Alianza, 1995.

Mackie, Robert, ed. *Literacy and Revolution: The Pedagogy of Paulo Freire.* New York: Continuum, 1981.

Marinello, Juan. "Una literatura al nivel de nuestra revolución." *Unión* 1.1 (1962): 40–42.

Mario, José. "La narrativa cubana de la Revolución." *Mundo nuevo* 41 (1969): 48–54.

Martínez Echazábal, Lourdes. "The Politics of Afro-Cuban Religion in Contemporary Cuban Cinema." *Afro-Hispanic Review* 13.1 (1994): 16–22.

Martínez Estrada, Ezequiel. "El nuevo mundo, la isla de la utopía y la isla de Cuba." *Casa de las Américas* 33 (1965): 87–110.

———. "Por una alta cultura popular y socialista cubana." *Unión* 1 (1962): 40–42.

Masó, Fausto. "Literatura y Revolución en Cuba." *Mundo nuevo* 32 (1969): 50–54.

McGarrity, Gayle L. "Race, Culture and Social Change in Contemporary Cuba." *Cuba in Transition: Crisis and Tranformation.* Eds. Sandor Halebsky and John Kirk. Latin American Perspectives Series 9. Boulder, Colo.: Westview, 1992. 193–205.

Medin, Tzvi. *Cuba: The Shaping of the Revolutionary Consciousness.* Boulder, Colo., and London: Lynne Riener, 1990.

Méndez Ródenas, Adriana. "Escritura, identidad, espejismo en *Memorias del subdesarrollo* de Edmundo Desnoes." *Identidad cultural de Iberoamérica en su literatura.* Ed. Saúl Yurkievich. Madrid: Alhambra, 1986. 333–40.

———. "Literature and Politics in the Cuban Revolution: The Historical Image." *A History of Literature in the Caribbean.* Ed. A. James Arnold. Vol. 1. Amsterdam: John Benjamin's, 1994. 283–94.

Méndez y Soto, Ernesto. "Panorama de la novela cubana de la revolución (1959–79)." Diss. Northwestern University, 1975.

Menton, Seymour. *Prose Fiction of the Cuban Revolution.* Austin: University of Texas Press, 1975.

Ministerio de Cultura of Cuba. *Alfabeticemos.* Havana: Imprenta Nacional, 1961.

Molyneux, Maxine. "State, Gender and Institutional Change: The Federación de Mujeres Cubanas." *Hidden Histories of Gender and the State in Latin America.* Eds. Elizabeth Dore and Maxine Molyneux. Durham, N.C.: Duke University Press, 2000. 291–319.

Moore, Carlos. *Castro, the Blacks and Africa.* Los Angeles: University of California, Center for AfroAmerican Studies, 1988.

———. "Cuban Communism, Ethnicity and Perestroika: The Unmaking of the Castro Regime." *Caribbean Quarterly* 42.1 (1996): 14–30.

Moreno Fraginals, Manuel. "Desgarramiento azucarero e integración nacional." *Casa de las Américas* 11 (1970): 6–22.

Morris, Pam, ed. *The Bakhtin Reader.* London: Edward Arnold, 1994.

Mraz, John. "*Memories of Underdevelopment*: Bourgeois Consciousness/Revolutionary Context." *Revisioning History. Film and the Construction of a New Past.* Ed. Robert E. Rosenstone. Princeton, N.J.: Princeton University Press, 1995. 102–14.

"Muchachas de hoy." Editorial. *Mujeres* 1 January 1969: 19.

"Muestre una rodilla perfecta." *Mujeres* 1 August 1966: 24–25.

Mulvey, Laura. "Afterthoughts on 'Visual and Narrative Cinema' inspired by *Duel in the Sun."* *Popular Fiction: Technology, Ideology, Production, Reading.* Ed. Tony Bennett. London: Routledge, 1990. 138–51.

———. *Visual and Other Pleasures.* Bloomington: Indiana University Press, 1989.

"Nación, raza y cultura." Special issue of *La Gaceta de Cuba* 1 (2005): 1–80.

Navarro, Desiderio. "In Medias Res públicas: Sobre los intelectuales y la crítica social en la esfera política cubana." *Ensayo cubano del siglo XX.* Eds. Rafael Hernández and Rafael Rojas. Mexico City: Fondo de cultura económica, 2002. 689–707.

Nora, Pierre. *Realms of Memory: Rethinking the French Past.* New York: Columbia University Press, 1996.

Ortega, Julio. *Relato de la utopía: Notas sobre la narrativa cubana de la revolución.* Barcelona: La Gaya Ciencia, 1973.

Ortiz, Fernando. *Contrapunteo cubano del tabaco y el azúcar.* Caracas: Biblioteca Ayacucho, 1987.

———. *Cuban Counterpoint: Tobacco and Sugar.* Trans. Harriet de Onís. New York: Knopf, 1947.

———."Los factores humanos de la cubanidad." *Revista Bimestre Cubana* 45 (1940): 161–87.

———. *Nuevo catauro de cubanismos.* Havana: Ciencias Sociales, 1985.

Otero, Lisandro. *Llover sobre mojado: Memorias de un intelectual cubano (1957–1997).* Mexico City: Planeta, 1999.

———. "Notas sobre la funcionalidad de la cultura." *Casa de las Américas* 12.68 (1971): 94–107.

Oviedo, José Miguel. "Un personaje de Camus en La Habana." *Plural* 55 (1976): 58–71.

Padilla, Heberto. "Intervención en la Unión de Escritores y Artistas Cubanos." *Poesía y política. Poemas escogidos de Heberto Padilla.* Madrid: Playor, 1974. 105–19.

Padura Fuentes, Leonardo. "Epilogue: Living and Creating in Cuba. Risks and Challenges." Kirk and Padura 177–87.

———. Interview with Juan Armando Epple. *Hispamérica* 24.71 (1995): 49–66.

Pereira, Armando. *Novela de la Revolución Cubana (1960–1990).* Mexico City: UNAM, 1995.

Pérez, Louis. "Toward a New Future, from a New Past: The Enterprise of History in Socialist Cuba." *Cuban Studies* 15.1 (1985): 1–14.

Pérez-Sarduy, Pedro, and Jean Stubbs. *AfroCuban Voices: On Race and Identity in Contemporary Cuba.* Gainesville: University Press of Florida, 2000.

———. "¿Y qué tienen los negros en Cuba?" *Encuentros de la cultura cubana* 2 (1996): 37–58.

Pérez-Stable, Marifeli. "Cuban Women and the Struggle for *Conciencia.*" *Cuban Studies* 17 (1987): 51–72.

———. *The Cuban Revolution: Origins, Course and Legacy.* New York: Oxford University Press, 1993.

Phaf, Ineke. *Novelando La Habana.* Madrid: Orígenes, 1990.

Piñera, Virgilio. "Notas sobre la vieja y la nueva generación." *La Gaceta de Cuba* 2 (1962): 4.

Piñera, Virgilio, et al. "*No hay problema.*" *La Gaceta de Cuba* 4 (1962): 5–6.

Pogolotti, Graziella. "Apuntes para el Che escritor." *Casa de las Américas* 46 (1968): 152–55.

Ponte, Antonio José. "La fiesta vigilada." *Cuba y el día después. Doce ensayistas nacidos con la revolución imaginan el futuro.* Ed. Iván de la Nuez. Barcelona: Mondadori, 2001. 23–33.

Portuondo, José Antonio. *Astrolabio.* Havana: Editorial de Arte y Literatura, 1973.

———. *Itinerario estético de la revolución cubana.* Havana: Letras Cubanas, 1979.

"Primer aniversario de *Mujeres.*" Editorial. *Mujeres* 15 November 1962: 1.

Quintero Herencia, Juan Carlos. "El espacio de la maldición. Escenografías del *Calibán* de Roberto Fernández Retamar." Eds. Sklodowska and Heller 55–89.

———. *Fulguración del espacio: Letras e imaginario institucional de la Revolución Cubana (1960–1971).* Buenos Aires: Beatriz Viterbo, 2002.

Quirk, Robert E. *Fidel Castro.* New York: Norton, 1993.

Quiroga, José. *Cuban Palimpsests.* Minneapolis: University of Minnesota Press, 2005.

Rama, Angel. "Norberto Fuentes: El narrador en la tormenta revolucionaria." *Literatura y clase social.* Mexico City: Folios, 1983.

Ramos, Ana. "La mujer y la revolución en Cuba." *Casa de las Américas* 65–66 (1971): 56–72.

Randall, Margaret. *Gathering Rage: The Failure of 20th Century Revolutions to Develop a Feminist Agenda.* New York: Monthly Review, 1992.

Rangel, Carlos. *Del buen salvaje al buen revolucionario.* Caracas: Monteávila, 1972.

Renan, Ernest. "What Is a Nation?" Bhabha, *Nation.* 11–20.

Rice, Donald E. *The Rhetorical Uses of the Authorizing Figure: Fidel Castro and José Martí.* New York: Praeger, 1992.

Rinascita. "Rinascita entrevista a Sartre." *Unión* 1 (1964): 149–57.

Robin, Regine. *Socialist Realism: An Impossible Aesthetic.* Stanford, Calif.: Stanford University Press, 1992.

Rodríguez, Iliana. *House/Garden/Nation: Space, Gender and Ethnicity in Post-Colonial Latin American Literatures by Women.* Durham, N.C.: Duke University Press, 1994.

Rodríguez Coronel, Rogelio. *La novela de la Revolución cubana, 1959–79.* Havana: Letras Cubanas, 1986.

Rodríguez Monegal, Emir. *El Boom de la novela latinoamericana.* Caracas: Tiempo Nuevo, 1972.

———. "Literatura: Cine: Revolución." *Revista Iberoamericana* 41 (1975): 579–91.

———. "*Paradiso* en su contexto." *Mundo nuevo* 24 (1968): 40–44.

Rojas, Rafael. "El intelectual y la revolución: Contrapunteo cubano del nihilismo y el civismo." *Encuentro de la cultura cubana* 16–17 (2000): 81–87.

Ruppert, Peter. *Reader in a Strange Land: The Activity of Reading Literary Utopias.* Athens: University of Georgia Press, 1987.

Russo, Mary. "Female Grotesques: Carnival and Theory." Eds. Conboy, Medina, Stanbury 319–36.

Said, Edward W. *Beginnings: Intention and Method.* New York: Columbia University Press, 1985.

———. *Orientalism.* New York: Vintage, 1994.

Saldaña-Portillo, Josefina. *The Revolutionary Imagination in the Americas and the Age of Development.* Durham, N.C.: Duke University Press, 2003.

Salper, Roberta L. "Ideología y visión de la mujer en los cuentos de Manuel Cofiño." *Hispamérica* 46–47 (1987): 57–70.

Santí, Enrico Mario. "Edmundo Desnoes: La sub-novela." *Estudios cubanos* 11.1 (1981): 49–64.

———. "Parridiso." *José Lezama Lima: Textos críticos.* Ed. Justo C. Ulloa. Miami: Universal, 1979. 91–104.

Sarmiento, Domingo F. *Facundo: Civilización y barbarie. Vida de Juan Facundo Quiroga.* Mexico City: Porrúa, 1991.

Sartre, Jean-Paul. *Being and Nothingness.* New York: Philosophical Library, 1956.

Séjourné, Laurette. *La mujer cubana en el quehacer de la historia.* Mexico City: Siglo XXI, 1980.

Sergio, Gil Blas. "Una generación no es un grupo." *La Gaceta de Cuba* 3 (1962): 15–16.

Serrano, Pío. "La Habana era una fiesta." Machover 244–70.

Silverman, Kaja. *Male Subjectivity at the Margins.* New York: Routledge, 1992.

Sklodowska, Elzbieta. *Testimonio hispanoamericano: Historia, teoría, poética.* New York: Peter Lang, 1992.

Sklodowska, Elzbieta, and Ben Heller, eds. *Roberto Fernández Retamar y los estudios latinoamericanos.* Pittsburgh: Instituto Internacional de Literatura Hispanoamericana, 2000.

Smith, Lois M., and Alfred Padula. *Sex and Revolution: Women in Socialist Cuba.* New York: Oxford University Press, 1996.

Smith, Verity. "What Are Little Girls Made of Under Socialism?: Cuba's *Mujeres* (Women) and *Muchacha* (Girl) in the Period 1980–1991." Special Issue of *Studies in Latin American Popular Culture.* Eds. Harold E. Hinds and Charles M. Tatum. Vol. 14 (1995): 1–15.

Smorkaloff, Pamela María. *Literatura y edición de libros: La cultura literaria y el proceso social en Cuba.* Havana: Letras Cubanas, 1987.

Sommer, Doris. *One Master for Another: Populism as Patriarchal Rhetoric in Dominican Novels.* Boston: Amherst College, 1983.

Soto, Francisco. "*Celestino antes del alba*: Escritura subversiva [*sic*]/Sexualidad transgresiva." *Revista Iberoamericana* 57.154 (January–March 1991): 345–55.

Soto Cobián, A. "Retrospectiva de la mujer cubana." *Mujeres* 15 March 1969: 4–5.

Stacey, Jackie. "Desperately Seeking Difference." *The Sexual Subject: A* Screen *Reader in Sexuality*. Eds. John Coughie and Annette Kuhn. New York: Routledge, 1992. 244–57.

Stuckey, J. Elspeth. *The Violence of Literacy*. Portsmouth, N.H.: Boynton/Cook, 1991.

Thomas, Hugh. *Cuba: The Pursuit of Freedom*. New York: Da Capo, 1998.

Torrents, Nissa. "Women Characters and Male Writers: A Cuban Approach." *Feminist Readings on Spanish and Latin American Literature*. Eds. L. P. Condé and S. M. Hart. Lewiston, N.Y.: Edwin Meller, 1991. 173–93.

Tucker, Robert C. *The Marx-Engels Reader*. New York: Norton, 1978.

UNESCO. *Métodos y medios utilizados en Cuba para la supresión del analfabetismo: Informe de la Unesco*. Havana: Pedagógica, 1965.

"Un millón de mujeres en la producción." Editorial. *Mujeres* 1 August 1966: 7.

Valbuena Prat, Manuel. *Diccionario Latino-Español*. Paris: Librería de Garnier Hermanos, 1865.

Vargas Llosa, Mario. "Sobre el *Paradiso* de Lezama." *Mundo nuevo* 16 (1967): 89–95.

Vera-León, Antonio. "Jesús Díaz: Politics of Self-Narration in Revolutionary Cuba." *Latin American Literary Review* 41 (1993): 65–79.

Vidal, Hernán. *Para llegar a Manuel Cofiño: Estudio de una narrativa revolucionaria cubana*. Minneapolis: University of Minnesota Press, 1984.

Vitier, Cintio. *Lo cubano en la poesía*. Havana: Instituto del Libro, 1970.

Waugh, Patricia. *Metafiction: The Theory and Practice of Self-Conscious Fiction*. London: Methuen, 1984.

Weiss, Judith. *Casa de las Américas: An Intellectual Review of the Cuban Revolution*. Chapel Hill, N.C.: Estudios de hispanófila, 1977.

White, Hayden. *Metahistory: The Historical Imagination in Nineteenth-Century Europe*. Baltimore: Johns Hopkins University Press, 1973.

Whitfield, Esther, ed. Prologue. *Un arte de hacer ruinas y otros cuentos*. By Antonio José Ponte. Mexico City: Fondo de cultura económica, 2005. 9–31.

Zizek, Slavoj. *The Sublime Object of Ideology*. London: Verso, 1994.

# Index

Ana Serra was born and raised in Seville, Spain. She is currently an assistant professor of Spanish and Latin American studies at American University. She has published articles on Cuban literature and film and Latin American cultural studies. Her latest research is on Cuban culture in the 1990s in Cuba.